Confessions of a Data Scientist... or Warrior-Priest?

Lessons From 25 Years of Data Science, Performance Measurement and Decision Support

To Rich —
In honor of your
favorite question —
"what's the SO WHAT?"

Ron Schack

Ron Schack, Ph.D.

ISBN: 978-1-6847-0071-4 (sc)
ISBN: 978-1-6847-0070-7 (e)

Because of the dynamic nature of the Internet, any web addresses or links contained in this book may have changed since publication and may no longer be valid. The views expressed in this work are solely those of the author and do not necessarily reflect the views of the publisher, and the publisher hereby disclaims any responsibility for them.

This book is a work of non-fiction. Unless otherwise noted, the author and the publisher make no explicit guarantees as to the accuracy of the information contained in this book and in some cases, names of people and places have been altered to protect their privacy.

Any people depicted in stock imagery provided by Getty Images are models, and such images are being used for illustrative purposes only.
Certain stock imagery © Getty Images.

Lulu Publishing Services rev. date: 04/10/2019

For Lisa

INTRODUCTION

Due to the prevalence of the application of algorithms to data on internet and social media, there is a constant stream of information regarding data science being generated and delivered to us. Once someone has taken any action which might flag them as interested in data science, the cascade begins. This book is part of that cascade, but I think it has some important content that is a bit different, because it reflects my 25 years of working on data science, performance measurement, and decision support issues.

I have worked as a data analyst for a state agency, and, for the past 18 years, as a consultant to federal, state, local government and non-profit organizations. I have (for the most part) enjoyed this experience and have few regrets related to this work.

I have learned a whole lot too… 25 years of learning related to doing data and performance work in public sector and non-profit organizations. This book is rather eclectic…part memoir, part thought-piece, part case-stud(ies), part primer/manual…but I think it works.

My intent is to provide insight into many challenging areas of data science, performance measurement and decision support work. Since my experience is primarily in the public sector, most of my examples and many of the issues I discuss are related to public-sector projects; however, many of the lessons could be applied to similar problems in the private sector.

This book does not offer a "comprehensive performance management framework" nor is it a "data science for dummies" book.

It is targeted to people who are interested in data science/analytics/performance measurement work, or who are already working in the field. Hopefully this book will provide insight into many of the challenges and problems that they will (or have already) encountered, and provide some guidance as to their next steps in their development as data scientists. *I have tried to provide plain language explanations of some concepts that I believe are often misunderstood and/or misused, or that many data scientists may not have encountered (but that I think may be helpful to them).*

One of the devices I happened upon while writing this book is categorizing some of my essential lessons as **"Schackzioms™."** [1] I couldn't resist this, so if you are troubled by this, just think of them as "tips." I do believe that, taken together, they constitute some critically important advice for anyone doing data science.

Along the way, the reader will encounter this writer's love of music, history, philosophy, puns, irony, and sarcasm. Being who I am, I could not have written this book any other way. Think of it as the price of admission ☺.

I would love to hear from you about what you liked, disliked, and found useful about this book. Feel free to contact me at ron_schack@yahoo.com. Readers please note: Because of the number of charts and other figures in this book, layout was a challenge. I intentionally left some space between sections in some cases to present the figures in the most useful manner possible.

I hope everyone enjoys this book as much as I enjoyed writing it; and I especially hope that it will help some readers on their personal data science trajectory.

Sincerely,

Dr. Ron Schack
The Data Grotto
Manchester, Connecticut
October 2018

---

[1] The ™ symbol is part of the fun. I do not believe I am going to have to fight a trade war over this term ☺.

TABLE OF CONTENTS

1

"ALL THE SCARS ARE ON THE INSIDE"

"All the scars are on the inside." Blue Oyster Cult, *"Veteran of the Psychic Wars"*

A Data Parable

The situations, names and positions of people have been changed out of respect and fear of retribution (not really ☺).

Ten data people sat around a conference table, discussing an upcoming data presentation. They had worked for a year thinking through the kind of data that would be presented, gathering data from various agencies and systematically working to overcome the barriers to reporting the data that a legislative committee asked for. As they reviewed the draft presentation, several questions arose.

One of the data people, George, who had been working diligently on a longitudinal study, said that he was ready to share the results of the study, but that *he was afraid that the information that was asked for was not what was really wanted, or really of interest...*

Another, Tabitha, looking at the presentation, which included comparisons of outcome data against the goals set by the committee, pointed out that the LARGE graphic arrow symbols, intended to show the positive or negative progress toward the goals, were a bit *ambiguous and confusing*...an observation that several others agreed with...

George also pointed out that the *data on several of the charts in the presentation did not agree with data from the longitudinal study*. Arthur, the leader of the workgroup, indicated that this was probably due to "administrative adjustments" made after the data were sent to George...

The group then moved to a discussion of some program data that the group hoped would be available for the presentation, but that were not yet available, because the individual program sites had not yet

1

provided the data to the agency in charge of the program. Dean, a representative of the individual program sites, indicated that this was partly because the data were only **due** to the agency a few weeks prior, and because repeated requests to the individual sites that had not yet provided the data had gone unanswered. Also, these data were reported in ***individual excel data sheets*** that were subsequently aggregated as the data were received. However, no representative of the agency in charge of the data was at the meeting…

Given that you can't really do much with data you don't have, the group continued with their review of the presentation. As they reviewed additional tables and charts, they realized that the label on an important chart was not clear, and that this might cause confusion when the data were presented. However, clarifying the label required significant technical description, which the workgroup wanted to avoid…further discussion revealed that the chart did not include all the participants that everyone at the table thought it did…this made the labeling issue easier to resolve, but ***the data people (being data people) smiled (or grimaced) at each other knowingly, understanding that the chart no longer meant what they thought it did…***

Moving along with their review of the presentation, George and Arthur agreed that the small numbers in one of the tables made it inappropriate to report percentages, and considered eliminating the table. However, Christoph, a high-level director but also a member of the workgroup, pointed out that the small numbers represented a target population that was very important to members of the legislative committee…and that ***not reporting on the target population at all would be a mistake and might derail the presentation.*** Arthur and George proposed creating a small narrative instead of reporting the numbers or percentages…the workgroup embraced this as a workable alternative.

Finally, as the "next steps" portion of the presentation was reviewed, the group talked about the future beyond the current set of reports and studies, and the need for an underlying measurement infrastructure that could support their work. They decided to better articulate that need. After this intense session, the group wrapped up the review, feeling ready for the presentation but wishing it could be better……

I attended this meeting as I was writing this book. I have attended many such meetings over the course of my career. This kind of meeting is both familiar and unusual. It is unusual to get this many data people in a room at the same time, and that the discussion generally yielded workable solutions to most of the issues raised. It is familiar in that even after a year of preparation, such issues persisted, and may have gone unnoticed until "called out" during the presentation itself. Just consider the kinds of challenges that were discussed and (in some cases) addressed at the meeting [we will discuss these in the book in the chapters indicated]:

- A study was initiated where the initial study questions were either no longer of interest, or had been in some ways superseded by other more immediately relevant questions [discussed in chapter 2];

- A data display device, intended to clarify the numbers being presented, ended- up causing more confusion [chapter 6];

- The same information from the same data source for the same time periods, extracted at different times, yielded different numbers [chapter 3];

- Key data were not available at the time the data were needed for analysis; this was due to on-going administrative and policy issues, as well as the use of a relatively archaic data collection method [chapters 1 and 10];

- Data as operationalized in an analysis was not operationalized in the manner generally understood [chapter 10];

- The tension between the need to report on key target populations and small cell sizes was revealed [chapter 6];

- The distinction between one-shot studies/evaluations and a continuous measurement infrastructure, and the need for both was discussed [chapter 14].

Again, what is notable is that all of these issues came up while discussing **one** data presentation to **one** legislative committee. They are emblematic of a wide array of issues faced by data scientists on a daily basis. While none of them were transcendent problems that threatened to render the data presentation a disaster, if not addressed they could have created a seriously bad data day. As I mentioned above, the workgroup in question, consisting of worthy data people, came up with workable solutions to most of these issues. However, often this is not the case. Data analyses are not always reviewed with such vigor by such a competent group. Sometimes it is up to the data scientist herself to ensure that issues such as these are dealt with before an analysis is presented. Much of this book is an attempt to provide guidance to data scientists in the hopes of avoiding (or managing) these, and many other issues. Just think, if one meeting can uncover such an array of issues (after a long development effort), think of all the potential issues that go unnoticed until a data presentation occurs, or not at all.....

What is a data scientist?

A data scientist is someone who understands how to collect, compile, restructure, analyze, visualize and present/report data from various sources.

This is a pretty broad definition, I know. It may not correspond with the picture of "data scientist" you have in your head. Depending on the needs of the organization the data scientist works for, the tasks can be very different. Some data scientists spend most of their time doing the front-end parts of the process (the new term for these people is data engineer), creating and managing databases (which can be quite challenging depending on the size and nature of the databases in question). Others do that, as well as generate reports out of the databases but don't do much analysis. Others do all of that, and do interpretive analysis. Sometimes this can include integration of "big data" into predictive models, or using machine learning and/or artificial intelligence approaches. Some do other kinds of performance analysis, statistical analysis, or evaluation. Some do all the above. Some do just certain pieces, such as working with "big data" and dealing with the specific challenges related to vast data sets.

Not all data scientists are the same…

The background of data scientists can vary considerably. Many have a substantial programming/application development background. Many have a substantial statistical background. Some have a background in business administration, public administration, or public policy. Others come from a math or geography background. Or other hard science background, like biology, chemistry or physics. Whatever their initial training, most data scientists will come to acquire some expertise in many of these areas. Like most things, there is a continuum of competency and expertise with data science. Lots of people "do (some aspect of) data science" as part of their job (like preparation of a spreadsheet on a regular basis). Some people have done one or more "data oriented projects." While most would agree that this alone doth not a data scientist make, I would like to emphasize that data science requires a sustained commitment to understanding data, its analysis and its use to solve real world problems. Involvement in a single data project, or doing a few excel spreadsheets now and then probably isn't enough. But, these activities are a gateway to a larger dataverse, and could lead to doing more and more work in these areas. Rather than trying to precisely define what makes a data scientist a data scientist, I will just say that multiple elements need to be in place—1) working with data is your first and primary function; 2) you have the technical expertise and training to understand theoretical and practical challenges of the work; and 3) you are committed to using data to improve decisions.

An Interdisciplinary approach works best….

As suggested above, data scientists are asked to conduct many kinds of data compilation, integration and analytic tasks. This means that data scientists need to learn how to understand the context of the activities or programs about which they are gathering data. The process and outcome variables of interest need to be operationalized, and this needs to be grounded in an understanding of the activities, organization, program or policy arena under-study. Most successful data scientists do not apply a "black box" solution to the data problems they are trying to solve. They develop a comprehensive understanding of the problem and apply the interdisciplinary skills and methods needed to solve these problems.

I do have to say here that what some describe as "analysis" stretches the term a bit. Simply charting a variable over of time is not "analysis" …although it could support one. **Generating a screen-full of colorful data displays, and saying "voila" …is not analysis; nor is it data science**. I might sound like a curmudgeon about this, but I think it is an important distinction. I am not saying generating the "analytics" is not important…and a lot of analysis could not occur without them…but I am saying that we should not equate these things. We will explore this further in the next chapter. I do get a bit nervous, however, when so much that is published and discussed regarding data science emphasizes the technology associated with data science rather than underlying analytic concepts.

Data Scientist as Warrior Priest

The term "Data Scientist" is relatively new, *but the occupation has evolved from prior iterations of data people doing data stuff.* The enormous growth in the need for "big data" analysis, especially analytics focused on the internet or data gathered from sources "resident" on the internet, has fostered the growth in this field. Before that, the clarion-call for outcome measurement in the public sector since the 1980's and 1990's, and the renewed focus on data-driven decision making also generated a lot of growth. In addition, the innovative application of artificial intelligence (AI) approaches to supporting decision making has created a groundswell of interest in data science.

I consider myself a data scientist. Not just because it is the in- vogue term for what I do, but because I like the appropriate specificity of it. When other terms are used--- analyst, program evaluator, performance management consultant…they usually don't capture the centrality of data, or suggest the myriad ways data can manifest themselves in this analytic work. It also suggests that there is *real science* behind these data activities, and this is something that has not been emphasized enough over the years, especially when the work is considered an "IT" function, or even worse, and accounting function. Done correctly, this work does use the scientific method when appropriate, and should be acknowledged as an interdisciplinary branch of statistics, computer science, geography, math, psychology, public policy, and business and public administration, among others.

Now, aside from being a data scientist, I also feel that over the years I have acted as a data evangelist. ***A warrior-priest for data-driven performance analysis.*** I say "warrior"-priest because not only have I been a data evangelist, but I have also fought (sometimes bloody) battles for the use of data throughout my career. Ever since my early days as a staff analyst at the Connecticut Department of Labor, I have pushed for better use of data to make decisions, constantly trying to convince people that "measurement is worth it" and that "collecting these data add value." I consistently fight for sharing performance data, and for pursuing the opportunities for improvement that are shown in the data analyses.

In 2006, The Co-chairs of the CT General Assembly Appropriations Committee asked my consulting firm to help them apply Results-Based Accountability™ to their budget process. My business partners and I held information sessions with staff from 44 state agencies, explaining how Results-Based Accountability worked, and how they could analyze and report their program performance measures to the Appropriation committee prior to and during the budget process. ***Believe me, I felt like a performance measurement evangelist then!*** Just like any congregation, there were some agency staff that were listening rapturously to every word of the sermon; others were scowling and saying they were already providing all the data that might be required, still others were sitting in the back of the church hoping not to be noticed. Nor was this the first time that I was put in this position as a performance management consultant.

At various times during my career, I have done "magical mystery performance measurement tours""— conducting training across a city, state or the country on data collection, analysis, and problem solving. While many people were appreciative and felt the that information I provided was useful, many were skeptical. They felt that this was just a "flavor of the month," or, worse, the data really wouldn't be used to improve anything. To them, such efforts seemed like exercises in futility.

When this happened early on in my career, I was surprised, imagining that if executive-level staff hired me, they were surely in a position to champion data-driven performance...only to find out that I was expected to do the convincing. Over the years, I have had to convince many audiences... from executives themselves, to sometimes resistant (or skeptical, fearful or jealous) upper and middle management, to front-line staff and even customers of the programs being measured.

While I was working at the CT Department of Labor, I was asked to train staff at each of the department's 18 job centers in how to use the new job center performance reports my unit created.

Since I knew the material so well, I thought this would be easy. **Nope!** Some staff resented that their performance was being scrutinized, and/or felt like the measures left out too many factors that may affect the performance outcomes we were seeking. Also, it was clear that some resented me (a young whipper-snapper of 27, with four years at the Labor Department, trying to tell them how to manage their performance)! A lot of staff were receptive to the new reports (and me), but there was enough resistance to make the training challenging.

I felt this resistance again when I was selected for a special team that conducted several activity-based costing (ABC) studies. ABC required staff to do "work distribution forms," reporting how much time they spent on each activity they did that day/week/month. Most staff sounded off about having to complete the work distribution form. Some worried that reporting the amount of time they spent on various activities was a prelude to lay-off recommendations. It was hard for them to see that making processes more efficient could help them in the long run.

The way to combat this resistance is by being prepared. Anticipate the questions regarding the value of data collection, data measurement, and data analysis. *Acknowledge* the possible risks associated with these activities. *Demonstrate that you understand* that data are not the only inputs into the decision process... that many decisions have legal or political components that cannot be superseded by data. *Tell a little story* about the time the data said one thing but the decision leaned in another direction. But THEN ask them, despite these issues:

- Wouldn't you rather know what the data have to say, and start from a position of fact?
- Wouldn't you rather be able to point to a stream of evidence when you make a decision? [And now, with data more accessible, analyzable, and displayable (is that a word?) than ever before, can you really contend that data will not be useful in operating your program or running your organization?]
- Do you want your organization to be LEFT BEHIND by others that do use data?

My Path to Data Science

After working on this book for a while I realized that readers might want to know how I came to do the work that I do. It wasn't a straight-line path, by any means, but once I discovered the joys of data science, more and more of my efforts were focused on data. ***If you don't really care about my path to data science, that is okay too…feel free to skip to the next chapter—I won't mind, really*** ☺ However, I do believe reading a bit about the path I took might be instructive, and may help readers think about their next steps on the data science path. So here it is….

I enjoyed science classes in high school. I was decent in math, but certainly no math wizard. However, that was due more to a lack of focus rather than a lack of ability. I did take a very interesting philosophy class as a senior, however, and I was hooked. I enjoyed all kinds of philosophy, but I particularly enjoyed logic and epistemology. I was so interested in philosophy, in fact, that I decided to major in philosophy in college, even though many of my friends and relatives said, "what are you going to do with that?" or "how are you going to get a job with a philosophy degree?" Throughout my undergraduate days, I continued to take philosophy classes, including a fascinating class in symbolic logic, and interesting classes in epistemology, metaphysics, and even medieval philosophy. I also took some interesting classes in political science (I ended up double majoring in philosophy and political science), economics, and statistics. My last semester as an undergraduate I did an internship at the Connecticut Department of Environmental Protection. As part of the requirements for getting credit for the internship, I wrote a paper on the department's efforts to clean up Long Island Sound, for which I actually won an unexpected prize (that even had money attached to it!). Working at DEP gave me a direction I did not have up to that point …I decided I wanted to work for the government, and try to make a difference. Even then, I realized I wasn't really interested in working for the private sector and constantly focusing on the bottom line, although I had nothing against other people doing that. In fact, I did take a fascinating course in Entrepreneurship my senior year (that included as guest speakers the people who created Subway and the inventor of Smartfood and Annie's Shells and Cheddar), and I had and have a great deal of respect for people who take a business concept and make it real in a viable, sustainable way. My continued interest in innovation and entrepreneurship turns up later, both at the CT Department of Labor and as I moved into consulting.

Upon graduation, I worked as a temporary employee at DEP for a while, but the budget was very tight for DEP at that time, and eventually I needed to look for other work. I was not a happy camper, because I liked the work I was doing at DEP. I was working as an assistant to one of DEP's legislative liaisons, and she really let me see how the sausage was made, as they say, at the legislature. I knew then I wanted to work for state government, but probably not as an elected official or staff to one. I took the Connecticut Career Trainee (CCT) Exam, which was a "qualifying exam" for people interested in gaining entry-level employment with the state. I scored well and I was offered at job at the Connecticut Department of Labor (CTDOL) as an unemployment insurance fact-finding examiner. This was a job adjudicating unemployment insurance claims...deciding whether someone who was separated from their job for some reason other than lack of work could receive unemployment compensation. It was the best of the state jobs I was offered, so I took it. I HATED this job, but it paid well, had good benefits, and was a government job, so it was at least consistent with my desire to work for the public. After about a year in this position I felt that in order to get to something better I had to get a Master's degree, so I went back to UCONN and began taking courses in their Masters of Public Affairs program[2]. I took these courses at night, while I continued to work full time at CTDOL. At this point in my career, I was a member of a public employee union. One of the benefits the union negotiated was tuition reimbursement, which I took full advantage of. I feel tuition reimbursement is an important benefit that many employers should offer. It is a way to encourage professional development of their staff, and a way to provide employees with eventual upward mobility that they otherwise might not have.

The MPA program was another important step in my development as a data scientist. There were some great courses in that program, including managerial statistics, program evaluation, public budgeting and program and policy development. While I was taking those courses, CTDOL was undergoing a reorganization. The new deputy commissioner, Lawrence Fox, and the executive director, Bennett Pudlin both felt the department needed to change. This involved making the organizational chart flatter (fewer layers of management)[3], cross training unemployment insurance and employment service staff, and [critical for my development], implementing many aspects of Total Quality Management (TQM) and Continuous Improvement (CI). One of the ways they did this was to conduct a series of pilot projects, including measuring the effectiveness of the changes embodied in those projects. They developed an ad-hoc group of volunteers to implement, administer, and measure these pilots. By this time (1992) I had taken a lateral transfer to the unemployment insurance technical unit, and this put me in position to participate in these ad-hoc pilots. CTDOL had hired a consultant,

---

[2]   The MPA program at the University of Connecticut was one of the first MPA programs in the country, founded in 1977. At the time I started in the program several of the faculty from the very early days of the program remained. **David Walker**, who had been a member of the Johnson Administration, was on the faculty, as was my eventual doctoral dissertation advisor, **Carol Lewis** and another of my dissertation committee members, **David Gilmour**. They taught intergovernmental administration, public budgeting, and administrative law, respectively...some of the best courses I have ever taken at any time during my long college career.

[3]   This was truly a massive and unheard of reorganizational effort at the Connecticut Department of Labor, which was traditionally a less-than innovative department, partly because most of its funding was federal, with many long-standing and rather archaic policy, procedural, and organizational approaches...some dating back to the federal enabling legislation for the unemployment insurance and employment service programs in the 1930's and 40's.

Dr. Barry Goff, then a professor at the UCONN School of Education, to provide some training in research methods to the ad-hoc pilot groups. This is when I first met Barry. Little did I know that I would start a consulting firm with him 8 years later. I consider my participation in these pilots the unofficial start of my career as a data scientist.

At the same time I was working on the CTDOL pilots (my pilot was related to conducting customer focus groups), I was getting more and more interested in performance measurement. Performance measurement was coming up more and more often in my classes, especially with the release of the book *Reinventing Government* by Osbourne and Gaebler[4]. Vice President Al Gore had cited this book in his work with the National Performance Review[5]. Around the same time, Congress passed the Government Performance and Results Act (GPRA), which required all federal agencies to create performance measures and performance goals for their programs. The parallel efforts of those performance pilots and my growing interest in performance measurement led me to write a paper about performance measurement in my program evaluation class, taught by Dr. Robert Kravchuk. Dr. Kravchuk and I later expanded this paper and submitted it for publication in *Public Administration Review*. This paper[6] was a big deal to me, being my first published article. It has since turned up in "classics of public administration" volumes and continues to be cited regularly. The paper was an early effort at creating principles of performance measurement, and was a pretty good attempt…although I would substantially modify it now if I could re-write it (some of the modifications will be shared in this book, but not labeled as such).

Following those pilots, publishing that paper, and completing my Master's degree, I was ready to do data science/performance measurement work full time. One of the newly organized units at CTDOL was the performance measurement unit. ***I really wanted to be in that unit.*** I pestered Alice Carrier, the Director of Operational Support at CTDOL (and someone who became one of my key mentors), constantly until the unit was established and the analyst position posted. I applied and got it! This is another lesson I have used throughout my career…if you want something, you need to go out and GET IT….if you just sit and watch the opportunity will pass you by.

Working in the performance measurement unit was the perfect position for a nascent data scientist. The unit was small…just a manager, two analysts (one of which was a former manager who didn't really analyze data, but did other important work for the unit), and a secretary. The unit

---

4   Osbourne and Gaebler, (1992). Reinventing Government. Lexington, MA, Addison-Wesley.

5   Gore, Albert. (1993). From Red Tape to Results: Creating a Government That Works Better and Costs Less: Report of the National Performance Review. Washington, DC, Random House.

6   Kravchuk, Robert S. and Schack, Ronald W., "*Designing Performance Measurement Systems Under The Government Performance and Results Act of 1993*," Public Administration Review, May/June, 1996.

was initially responsible for developing approaches to measuring the performance of all employment service and unemployment insurance programs. The data for these programs resided on mainframe computers, but we took the huge reports that were generated from the mainframes and created user-friendly reports (usually using Microsoft Excel) from them. We also collected, compiled and analyzed customer survey data. We analyzed these survey data using the Statistical Program for the Social Sciences (SPSS).

Learning SPSS was another milestone for me. I had some exposure to SPSS in my Master's degree program[7], and working in the performance measurement unit gave me the opportunity to really learn how to use it (with some help from Barry Goff, who had been hired by CTDOL to provide technical assistance to the unit). Learning SPSS was critical for two reasons: 1) I started to apply statistics to real world problems, and 2) I began to learn the inherent limitations and challenges of the analysis of transactional and individual record level data. Over several years, I was also sent to USDOL sponsored statistics training at Arizona State University. These courses taught me a lot about methods I had not yet been exposed to, like time-series analysis and logistic regression. While at CTDOL I also took other computer courses, such as SQL, that enhanced my understanding of database structure and how to generate reports using database queries.

I had been in the unit for two years when the manager of the unit, Rick Batt, retired. This gave me the opportunity to move into the manager position. For the next five years, I developed the unit from a four-person to a ten-person operation, with expanded responsibilities and capabilities. ***I "cut my teeth" in this position and enjoyed almost every minute of it.***

By the end of my Master's degree program in 1993 I was seriously considering doing a doctoral degree. My family and work obligations made the University of Connecticut the best choice. At the time, UCONN did not have a public policy doctoral program, so I pursued a doctoral degree in political science with concentrations in public policy, public administration and American government.

People often ask me why I got my doctoral degree. They insist I didn't "need" one for the work I was doing. I wasn't interested in being a college professor (full time), so why would I expend so much time and effort in getting one? My first answer, I think, is that I genuinely love learning and there was (and is) so much out there to learn. I think, too, that I wanted my doctorate to establish that my

---

[7]   Actually, my first exposure to SPSS was in an undergraduate statistics class…SPSS was on the university mainframe, and we had to create SPSS syntax using punch cards. That was in 1986. Seven years later, I was using SPSS on a PC at my desk at work…this was only a few years after PC's with internal hard drives were readily available. I was in graduate school around that time, and learned LISREL (a program for doing structural equation modeling) using a PC version…but one where you still had to hand-specify co-variate matrices….let's just say no fun at all ☺).

opinion was worthy of attention. I know now that people can value your opinion without a credential attached to it, but at the time I was acutely aware whenever I was in the room with other data experts and one or more had PHDs and I didn't. I just didn't like the disparity. Finally, and this was purely personal, I really wanted to prove to myself that I could do it.

Part of the requirements for a doctoral degree were either fluency in a language other than English, or concentrations in a technical methodology. For me, at this stage of my development, I went with the technical track. I took several advanced courses in statistics, including statistics for behavioral sciences and structural equation modeling (SEM). These courses, taught by a very highly regarded psychology professor (Dr. David Kenny)[8], solidified my understanding of statistics and gave me a good foundation for predictive modeling. Dr. Kenny also provided me with a link to one of the fathers of social science research, Donald Campbell[9] I also worked with another professor, Dr. Carmen Cirincione, who got me interested in decision sciences, especially group decision making. I did an independent study in decision making with Dr. Cirincione that formed the basis of my further independent exploration of the science of decision making and decision support.

---

[8] Professor Kenny was involved in the first evaluation of Sesame Street, and wrote several important methodological works, including "Correlation and Causality" and, with Donald Campbell, "A Primer on Regression Artifacts."

[9] Donald Campbell contributed two milestone books in the field of social science research: Campbell and Stanley's 1963 classic, "Experimental and Quasi-Experimental Designs For Research," and Cook and Campbell's "Quasi-Experimentation: Designs and Analysis For Field Settings" (1977). Having a link to Donald Campbell, for a social scientist, is kind of like a current pope having a link back to St. Peter ☺).

While doing this course work in the doctoral program and subsequently working on my dissertation, which concerned the accuracy of local government revenue forecasts, I continued to manage the CTDOL Performance Measurement Unit. We were doing a great deal of innovative work in the unit, and I began traveling a lot, sharing what we were doing at national conferences, and being asked to participate on federal workgroups on the newly passed Workforce Investment Act of 1998 and other measurement issues. We were doing ground breaking work in linking process and outcome measures, and using GIS to support and enhance our performance work. We were setting up new data collection systems, matching service record data with data from the unemployment insurance wage file, and creating innovative performance dashboards, both on paper and on the web.

However, by 1999 the administration at CTDOL had changed (twice), and the new administration[s] didn't seem as interested in or supportive of my work. The

> Some Clients of The Charter Oak Group, LLC:
>
> - USDOL Senior Community Employment Program
> - San Diego Workforce Partnership
> - Philadelphia Career Link Consortium
> - Commonwealth of Kentucky Workforce Investment Board
> - District of Columbia Employment Service
> - Connecticut General Assembly
> - CT Juvenile Justice Oversight Committee
> - CT Early Childhood Cabinet
> - CT Department of Education
> - CT Department of Children and Families
> - CT Judicial Branch
> - Capital Workforce Partners
> - The Justice Education Center, Inc.
> - The William Caspar Graustein Memorial Fund
> - The Connecticut Data Collaborative

unit was still doing excellent work, but things were feeling different. As I was finishing up my doctoral degree, Barry Goff asked if I would like to join him in forming a new consulting company. After some soul searching, I decided to leave state government employment and go into business with Barry as a performance consultant. This was a HUGE step for me; I had a secure job in state government, I had advanced very quickly and was well-respected. Just as I was feeling truly comfortable with the work and my role as the manager of the unit, I decided to abandon that and go into work for myself... Why? Other than the diminished support I was receiving from the administration, I wanted to apply my data science abilities to other areas...other levels of government, and other policy arenas. Also, I had advanced almost as far as I was going to go as a (non-appointed) state employee...and I couldn't see myself in the same or similar position working with the same subject matter for the next 20 or 30 years...so I made the leap.

A few years before, Barry Goff had left UCONN and started to do consulting on his own. Occasionally, he would sub-contract with other researchers on projects, but found he really needed a partner to go after larger, more involved projects. So in 2000 we created The Charter Oak Group, LLC, and began our consulting journey together. Barry and I had gotten to know each other while Barry was consulting with CTDOL, and we got along well. Barry has a doctoral degree in social psychology, so his background is a bit different from mine[10], but our backgrounds are complementary and we work well together.

I am not going to narrate the history of the Charter Oak Group here or go on about all the different projects we have been involved in. Some of the things I learned from these projects will be shared in later chapters. Suffice it to say that we have been able to sustain the Charter Oak Group for the past 17 years, maintaining many clients for long stretches (5 or more years). In 2003, we added another partner, Bennett Pudlin (the retired former executive director of the CT Department of Labor who helped initiate the CTDOL reorganization). Bennett's background as a Yale-educated attorney and his years as an executive in state government gave COG more capacity and allowed us to grow. My experiences with the Charter Oak Group form the basis of this book.

Recently my two business partners, being 20+ years older than I, began scaling back their consulting efforts. We decided to keep COG going as long as the three of us are doing some work together. However, we also wanted to be able to do other things.[11] For me, it that meant doing some teaching and considering creating a non-profit think-tank called Data Grotto. As I was thinking about moving forward with Data Grotto (which is still under development), and my experiences over the past 25 years, I began writing little "thought pieces" about my experiences. Some of these became blog posts for my website, while others helped me think through the structure and strategic focus of Data Grotto. This book emerged from those efforts.

---

[10] Barry also had a non-traditional path to data science, beginning his adult life as an English teacher, later studying to be a family therapist before settling in on data science (especially program evaluation and performance measurement).

[11] Bennett helped create an organization to help undocumented immigrants stay in this country and with the process of becoming legal residents, while Barry continues to work on his stunning garden with his wife, Mary...and is rumored to be working on a cookbook....

2

"THERE IS MADNESS IN THESE METHODS"

"Some civil servants are just like our loved ones, they work so hard, and try to be strong..." Talking Heads, "Don't Worry About The Government"

Above all, I want this book to be useful to practitioners...I hope it will get them to consider some of the challenges I note and the issues I raise. I would like it to act as a catalyst for those interested in data science, particularly as it applies to performance measurement...a catalyst to continue pursuing these areas, and to do so with a wider and deeper appreciation of the issues involved. For those new to data science, or those coming from a different data science arena, I hope my plain language explanations will help them get acclimated to the areas in which I have a great deal of experience. At the same time, this is not tutorial in SPSS, R, GIS, HADOOP or machine learning. There are plenty of those out there. Rather, this is an "advanced foundational" primer, and a series of lessons distilled from my 25 years fighting the good data fight.

We begin by considering how analysis tasks are initiated, and the potential resistance an analyst may encounter when they begin to kick-off an analysis project, especially a performance measurement analysis.

Why measure? Why Bother Collecting Data?

When asked this question "why measure?" I wish I could respond with **"42"** -- as the great computer in "Hitchhikers Guide To The Galaxy" responded when asked the ultimate question of life, the universe and everything. However, I do not have the benefit of being a plot device in a humorous science fiction novel. From the first time I was assigned a performance measurement-related task, I was confronted with the question, "why are we doing this?" "What good are these measures for anyway?" Some asking that question were just trying to get out of doing the work associated with collecting the data; others had worked hard to help support the collection, compilation, and analysis of data...

only to have the report promptly find a place on a shelf never to be referred to again. Still others firmly believed that most decisions are made using little or no actual data. Whether the question is "why measure?" or "why do data matter?" or some variant of "we know what we need to do without data—so why bother?" you need to be prepared to respond.

The first task of any data scientist is to demonstrate how their work adds value. Sometimes it is obvious—the work has been requested from the highest levels of the organization; or it is required in order to comply with a policy, regulation, or statute. Other times, the product of the data activity is inherently desirable—like information on customer preferences coming out of a "big data" data mining analysis. Often, however, even when your work has executive sponsorship and some important reasons why it is being done have been communicated, the data scientist is still asked to demonstrate why data collection, compilation, and analysis are being done. This is likely, for example, if the data scientist holds a conference call or a series of meetings with different departments or agencies to get the "data-ball" rolling. The sponsor of the data project may have said something about the need for data and the importance of the project in the email or phone call that prompted the data scientist to meet with the new department or organization....but when the data scientist gets there they are confronted with blank stares. ***What is this about? Why are we doing this? Don't we already do something like this? Hasn't this been done before?***

Over the years, I have learned to always be ready to demonstrate the value of the data collection, compilation, or analysis task I am undertaking. If the project has been outlined already, bring that, and any references to statutes or regulations or policies that require the work you are undertaking. It may mean that you should bring a sample report, a critical comparison, or information regarding how the method has been used in other

> **Schackziom Number 1:** Always be ready to demonstrate the value of the data collection, compilation, or analysis task you are undertaking. You cannot expect others to intuitively understand the importance of your work.

units, departments, or jurisdictions. Do not expect people to just take your word for it. **The worst part is that once you do this, you cannot expect the question not to arise again.** New people might become involved, or staff that seemed "satisfied" with your explanation will ask the question again as the project enters a new phase. This means that you should always have this material available, and always be ready to respond to such questions. ***Unanswered, these questions can linger, fester, and spoil the positive energy around a data project.***

A legitimate concern that people raise regarding data collection activities generally, and performance measurement in particular, is that the emphasis on data diverts time and other resources from the "actually work" of service provision. Sometimes, this extends to ANY required data collection or reporting, especially in the human services field. The feeling is that staff should be working with clients, not spending time doing data collection. The complaint is heard in many areas, including the medical field. This is not a concern to be lightly dismissed. You need to show that you are sensitive to these concerns, and emphasize that the data being collected are necessary and not just "nice to have." The problem of double (or even treble) data entry is also a concern…when you begin asking staff to enter data into two or more data systems (because one doesn't have the needed data elements, but is required for federal reporting, for example) you need to be very cognizant of this and the extra burden this puts on staff. This is where talking to the staff doing the work is very important, or your data collection strategy may fail and you will not get the needed data for the analysis.

The "Lone Cowboy-Analyst" Temptation

Sometimes, encountering this kind of resistance can send the data scientist scurrying back to his or her cubicle, thinking "I don't need them, I will just get the data myself." If you listen with your imagination enough, you can almost hear the "pout." The temptation is to become the isolated, but cool, "Lone Cowboy-Analyst," doing everything yourself and unilaterally issuing your analysis. This is usually a mistake. Most of the time, you can't generate data yourself…the data comes from those doing the work. It is usually better to have the people doing the work, or generating the data, buying into the data project and supporting your analysis. Also, doing your analysis in a team context enriches the analysis and helps avoid stupid mistakes or tunnel vision. It also helps to avoid misinterpreting data that you are using for your analysis. This last one is very important to avoid, and happens a lot. If you get new data (data that you have not worked with previously), even data with an elaborate data dictionary, the data fields may not mean what you think they mean, or they may not be used the way the original database creator intended. If you proceed with your analysis without checking on the actual meaning of the variable(s), or the actual way a data field is being utilized, your analysis will be wrong. This tends to happen more often when an analyst tries to do everything themselves. It also tends to happen when the data analyst does not check with the people doing the work…the ones entering data into the system. So, please…involve others with your work…and not just remotely either…where possible, get in the same room with people. Of course, at some point you do have to be alone, at your computer, doing the analysis…and for that you need the proper set of tools.

The Data Scientist Software Toolkit

Throughout this book I will be referring to the various software tools I use to in my work. In almost every case, I could have used something other than what I decided to use to do what I did. There are a lot of options out there. But I do use specific software for specific tasks, so I thought I would take a minute to talk about them.

We data scientists have a vast array of tools to choose from. Our choice of tools depends upon many factors, such as:

- What tasks we are performing
- What tools we have been exposed to
- What tools our organization makes available
- If working with others, what tools are available to them

Basic tools

I have several basic tools that I have used since I began my data science journey. They have been around for 30 years or more. Of course, they have been updated many times and are still viable tools today.

The first of these tools is **Microsoft Excel**. This tool is easy to use, available in nearly every organization, and is very flexible and robust. Of course, it is "just a spreadsheet" tool, so it is not the best tool for multivariate statistical analysis or predictive modeling, although it can support these activities. Some people insist you can do almost anything using Excel. I think that is pushing it. With so many great statistical and analytical packages out there, with very good user interfaces, even doing something like multiple regression using Excel seems a little silly. On the other hand, sometimes you may not have access to those packages, and Excel might just save you.[12]

Excel is also the first and only data collection tool that many small programs have...they simply set up a spreadsheet and start collecting data for each service transaction and every individual they serve. For many small programs, this may be sufficient, if done carefully and consistently. On the other hand, I have some excel nightmare data collection stories as well (we will defer those until later).

My next foundational tool is **SPSS**, the **S**tatistical **P**rogram for The **S**ocial **S**ciences. SPSS is incredibly powerful. I do most of my statistical analysis, hypothesis testing, and predictive modeling using SPSS. I use SPSS because I come out of a social science tradition; many coming out of economics and related disciplines use **SAS** instead. These two packages are very similar and have similar long-term development histories.

---

[12] For a demonstration of just how flexible Excel is, check out "Statistical Analysis: Microsoft Excel" and "Predictive Analytics: Microsoft Excel" by Conrad Karlberg.

Much of what can be done in Excel and SPSS can now be done in **R**, which is an open source data structuring, analysis, and reporting tool. A companion program, **R St**udio, has a nice user interface and makes R a bit easier to use. **R** is very flexible, and has a vast library of code for different analytic and statistical tasks. I use R when SPSS doesn't contain a particular function or test or when SPSS requires a specialized module that I do not want to pay for! My daughter, a PHD student at Victoria University in New Zealand, does EVERYTHING in R…and she is doing sophisticated clustering analyses of marine organisms called Bryozoans. For those of you recently out of university, who have never really worked with SPSS or SAS, you may be likely to skip SPSS or SAS altogether and just go with R. That is a fine alternative, although I find SPSS very user friendly and quick for many basic statistical functions. I find I can do a lot of stuff faster in SPSS than in R. It is not that you can't use R to do them, it is just easier for me to do it in SPSS, and the output more readily usable, than if I did the same thing in R. It is a personal choice, one driven by my previously developed expertise with SPSS. There are other programming languages that compete with R, such as Python. I have not used Python but it clearly has a very large code library available as well. As with many things, your choice of tool will be driven by what you have been exposed to along the way; people tend to get comfortable with the tools they use a lot. ***However, part of the new data scientist paradigm is to be able to switch between tools with alacrity. Learn as many of them as you can, when you can.***

There are several tools related to data display and presentation, including **Microsoft Powerpoint**, **Adobe Illustrator**, **Tableau**, and **Prezi** which I use depending upon on the task and how quickly I need to get something together. I will defer discussion of these until Chapter 7, when I discuss data visualization and presentation at length.

Specialized Tools

Now we are moving beyond the basics. There are some more specialized tools that I use as well. The primary difficulty with most of these is their cost, but they are very good and worth it if you do enough of the kind of analysis they support. I use a software called **Forecast Pro** for time series analysis. It has excellent features and will select a recommended forecast approach based upon the time series you upload. It is a bit expensive, but well worth if you do a lot of time-series analysis.

Since I have a particular interest in structural equation modeling (SEM), I am partial to a SEM tool that easily interfaces with SPSS, called **AMOS** (which stands for **A**nalysis **O**f **M**oment **S**tructures). AMOS has a great user interface. You can draw your SEM model, and if you add the right variables names to the model it will write the code directly from the model. A very useful feature.

Another specialize software that I use is **ArcGIS**, both the desktop and the on-line versions. ArcGIS is the industry standard for geographic information software, and is very flexible and robust. ArcGIS on-line keeps most of the code and data on the web, and allows you to do a lot of stuff without the need for purchasing the desktop version. However, you can do a lot of mapping now using open-source tools like R. In fact, all but one of the maps in Chapter 15 of this book were produced using R.

There is also a great open source machine learning tool called **WEKA**. WEKA stands for ***Waikato Environment for Knowledge Analysis***. It provides a uniform interface to many different learning algorithms, along with methods for pre-and post-processing and for evaluating the results of learning schemes on any given data set. I like WEKA because it not only lets you apply an array of important algorithms, but it also has some great visualization tools.

Beyond these tools, there are many database interrogation and reporting tools, like Microsoft Access, SQL, Oracle BI and SAP Business Intelligence that may be available or in use in your organization. If you are working with truly large datasets, you may need to work with **HADOOP**, **APACHE** or other distributive database applications. More and more often, non-SQL database structures are being utilized because they may be quicker to access and utilize, or reduce storage requirements. It is important for data scientists to keep up with these new database approaches.

Of course, these tools are subject to GI-GO (garbage in—garbage out) and are only as good as the data that are uploaded to them. And none of them, no matter how snazzy, no matter how great the user interface, how great the AI front end is, will do an analysis without you. You hold the power, and the responsibility, to do great analytical work. I recently saw a prediction that AI will put data scientists out of work by 2025. I don't agree. Our jobs will change, and AI will be a big part of that, but there will always be a place for people who understand data and data analysis, and can look behind the curtain of AI to understand what actually is being done.

Data-Analysis-Information Sequence

So now you have heard about all the different kinds software that I typically use for analysis. This is probably a good time to talk about just what I mean by analysis.

Analysis is a process that transforms data into information. The process is really an iterative one, somewhat but not completely linear. See Figure 1 below.

FIGURE 1 TURNING DATA INTO INFORMATION

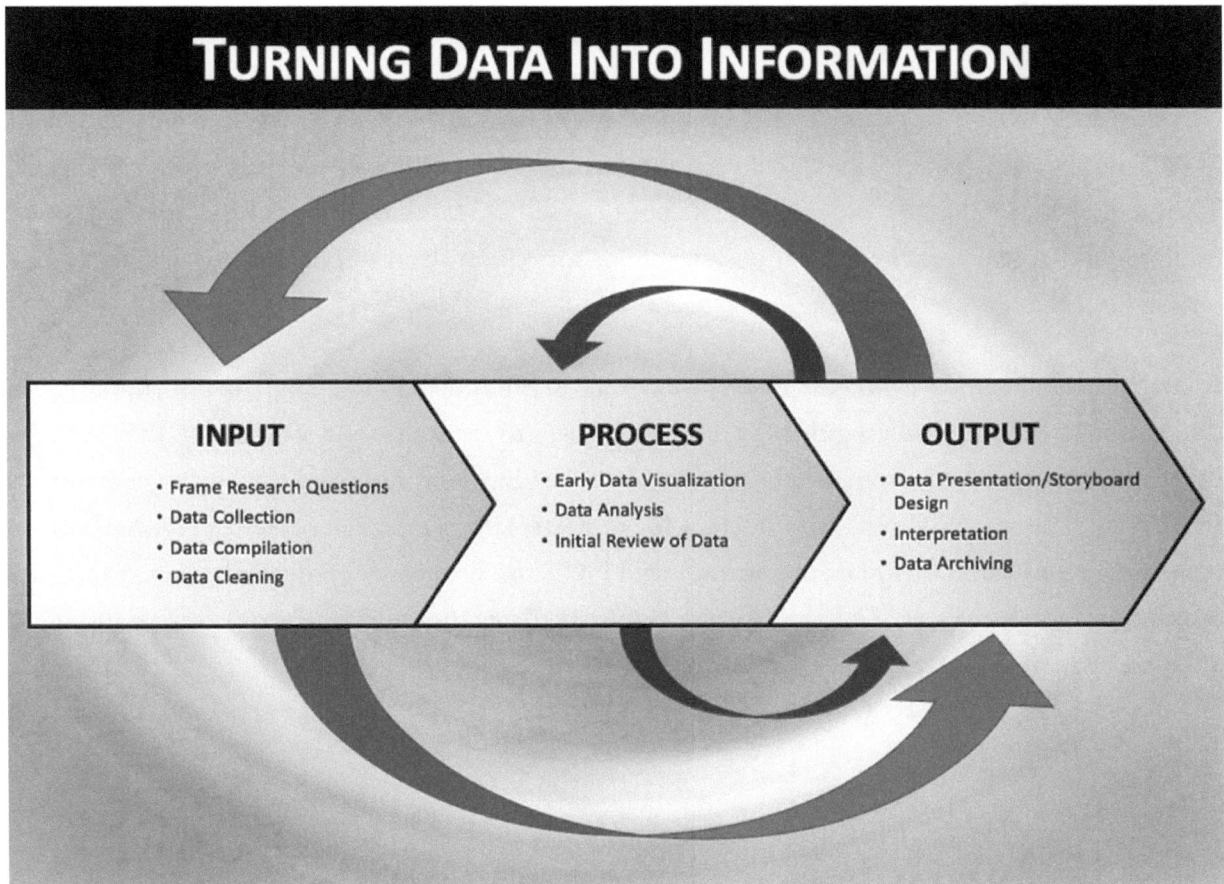

I could have added more steps to this diagram, such as "operationalize measures," etc., but I wanted to emphasize the transformational steps. The next chapter will fully detail the data analysis cycle. I also want to emphasize here that there is an "iterative analytic refinement" process that occurs. After the initial analysis of data, there will be some output and some visualizations generated. The analyst will examine this output and make a "first approximation" judgment as to the implications of that output. That initial judgment may then be presented to key informants—people who through experience and expertise are best positioned to determine whether the "first approximation analysis" is correct or on the right track. They may also suggest alternate or additional interpretations of the analysis. The analyst may then go back and check the data, conduct more analysis, and re-present the data. After additional confirmation, a fully realized analysis is provided to the client or other sponsor of the work.

As I mentioned in Chapter 1, often someone (non-data scientists, usually) will take some data and "whip up" some charts...and claim that they "just cranked out" this analysis. Well, in my view generating a few tables or charts, by itself, is not analysis. It may be a foundation for an analysis that follows, but it is not analysis. I think a lot of people (again, often non-data scientists) get caught up in the mission of generating the output (wow! Look at the pretty chart I can produce!), and when that is accomplished they feel the job is done. Even experienced data scientists can fall into this trap.

Creating some charts in excel, or generating reams of output by pushing some menu options in SPSS is **not** doing analysis. This is like a monkey pushing the buttons in the Mercury space capsule. The monkey may be taught the proper sequence to make the capsule move, but the monkey doesn't understand that sequence...why he is pushing those buttons, or the relationship between pushing the buttons and the spacecraft moving, is beyond him.

Analysis comes from an *__informed examination__* of that output. Do the comparisons supported by the output reveal practically significant differences? Are they meaningful in some way? Discerning the implications of the output is the mission of the analyst, and does not end with generation of the output. The reason I emphasize this is **a lot of material I see on data science emphasizes the technology and the creation of the output, and NOT the necessary analysis that must follow if the output is to be of use.** The next chapter fully articulates the analysis process, from framing the question to sharing the results.

3

WHAT KEY IS THIS ANALYSIS IN?

"Who am I? Why am I here?" Vice Admiral James Stockdale, USN (Retired), during vice-presidential debate (1992).

This chapter is intended to provide some foundational guidance regarding data analysis. This is elemental stuff, and I am not pretending that I am saying anything new or groundbreaking here. However, as with several other sections of this book, I am including my thoughts on these topics because I so often see analysis go off the rails because some of these basic principles have not been considered or adhered to.

Framing The Question

Sometimes the most challenging aspect of an analysis project is determining what exactly the client (or your boss) wants. This can be particularly difficult in data science because there are so many possible questions to be answered, and levels of analysis utilized in trying to answer those questions.

The issue of "framing the question" is critical because it is **so easy to not quite get it right**, and spend a lot of time on analysis that will ultimately not answer the question that needs answering. One of the best ways is to talk to your sponsor (your boss or your client) and have them articulate the question in regular language. Some questions they may pose include:

1. We need to know whether our program costs are competitive?
2. We need to know why we are not achieving our performance targets?
3. We need to know if whether this program will work if we try it in New Haven (or Singapore).
4. We need to know what will our workload look like over the next year?
5. We need to know how our customer demographics have changed since we started, and what they will be like five years from now.

6. We need to know how many youth are served by our system?

7. We need to know how many people this agency serves, across all of our programs, and what their characteristics are?

8. We need to know whether our community is achieving the results we want for our elderly?

9. We need to know what mix of services is most successful in achieving positive outcomes for [name subgroup of customers].

You may have noticed the level of analysis for many of these questions differs substantially. The first five questions relate to a program, although the focus of each question differs significantly. The seventh question relates to an agency as-a-whole. The sixth relates to a service system. The eighth question relates to an entire community.

These differing levels of analysis suggest that you may use very different approaches when attempting to answer these questions. ***You need to understand just what kind of question(s) you are trying to answer.*** Sometimes, when the original question has been answered, new questions are raised. The analyst should be ready for this. Or, once getting the answer they expected from the analysis, the data consumers immediately move on to the next question. It can almost feel like the original analysis was unnecessary. Analysts should try to anticipate this, so that the data collected can be utilized to answer the follow-up questions as well.

As the above set of questions suggests, questions to be answered truly come in all flavors. But, there are some ways to deconstruct questions so you can get to the "essential nugget.":

1) Is the question about individuals? Teams? Programs? Organizations? Systems? Municipalities? States? Nations? Activities? Processes? (this speaks to level of analysis).

2) Is the question about everyone in a jurisdiction, or some sub population (like the elderly, those justice-involved, or youth 16-24?).

3) Is the question about a policy? If so, as implemented by whom? A number of different national state, or local agencies? A specific agency? A service system?

4) Is the question about whether a program or service is effective? Or is it about how a program or service is being operated?

5) Is the question descriptive, exploratory, or confirmatory? (see discussion regarding the difference between exploratory and confirmatory analysis later in this chapter).

6) What is the purpose of the question? To demonstrate success? To inform a new program design? To identify opportunities for improvement? To inform the planning and/or budget process? To build theory or otherwise add to the knowledge base?

These questions can help narrow things down a lot. Once you fully articulate the question or set of questions, then you can move onto to identifying the elements of the analysis.

As my path to data science suggests, I have always had a keen interest in performance measurement and program evaluation, and as such many of my examples in this book are drawn from these analytic arenas. However, data scientists conduct all kinds of other analytic tasks, from revenue and expenditure forecasting, to workload forecasting, to market analysis, determining customer preferences, pricing analysis, budget and fiscal analysis, predictive modeling...decision analysis of all kinds...the list is never ending. The principles shared in this book regarding data operationalization, collection, integration, analysis, and presentation can be applied to all of these analytic tasks, not just those associated with performance measurement. ***All of these tasks start with a question that needs to be framed.***

Once the question is framed you can go on to identify the elements of the analysis and develop the analytic design:

1. What is the unit of analysis for this question? That is, what are you comparing? Individuals? Grantees within a program? Different Programs? Cities, States, or Countries? What is the lowest level of data you will be working with? Can you get down to individual record data (whatever the individual unit of analysis may be)?
2. Develop the analytic design...is it a hypothesis test, a time series analysis, explanatory model, a predictive model?
3. What data source(s) will be necessary?
    a. Are the data sources internal or external?
    b. If internal, do you have direct access to them or do you need to get access or data extracts from someone else in the organization?
    c. If external, do you have direct access to them or do you need to get access? Are the data open source or will you have to purchase the data?
    d. If multiple data sources are used, do you anticipate data integration problems? [See Chapter 10].
4. What data elements and/or performance metrics will be needed? How will they be operationalized? [See Chapter 10].
5. What is the time frame of the analysis?
6. What are the threats to the validity and reliability of the analysis?
7. Who is the audience for the analysis? [This will guide you as to the language you use in the presentation of the results, the type and amount of technical detail, including references, and the overall length of the presentation (in written form or in actual "presentation" form].

8. And, of critical importance: a) when are the analysis results expected ☺ and b) Is there a prior expectation regarding the results of the analysis? This is important not because it would cause you to alter your findings, but because if your findings are different from those that are expected you need to be prepared to have a very different kind of conversation with the sponsors of the work.

Threats to Validity

Threats to validity are often discussed in terms of preparing for and review a formal study, but some or all of them may apply to almost any analysis you might perform.

There are two primary categories of validity: internal and external. External validity concerns generalizability of results, and will be discussed at various other times in this book. Internal validity concerns potential biases that may be introduced into the study design, and/or the measurement constructs used in the study. There are three types of internal validity that we need to worry about:

- Content validity (do items measure the content they are intended to measure)
- Predictive or concurrent validity (do results correlate with other results?)
- Construct validity (do items measure hypothetical constructs or concepts?)

As you operationalize each variable in your analysis, you need to ask yourself if the variable is measuring what you are intending to measure with the variable. Sometimes it is best to use more than one variable as different, alternative ways to measure what you are intending.

You also need to check whether your variables have predictive or concurrent validity…are the variable(s) you are using to measure something consistent with other, similar variables?

Finally, if you are measuring a latent variable (a hypothetical construct that cannot be measured directly). We will talk more about these in later chapters. You need to make sure that the variables you are using to measure these constructs make sense, measure different possible dimensions of the construct, and that these cohere appropriately as an index.

Below, I have tried to provide plain language descriptions of some of the classic threats to validity[13]:

- History

This threat to validity deals with what happened to participants prior to receiving the treatment. If something happened that has an amplifying or attenuating effect on the treatment, results could then be biased.

- Maturation

Maturation deals with the simple fact that participants continue to develop: it can be difficult to separate normal developmental advances from treatment effects.

- Regression

Regression to the mean is one of those inexplicable but true phenomena. Over time, extreme values tend to migrate (or regress) to the mean. As such, cases of extreme treatment effects will tend not to persist.

- Selection

One of the most common and manipulated threats to validity. If those provided a treatment are selected because they are most likely to succeed, or most likely to be affected positively by the treatment, then the results will be biased in the direction of a positive treatment effect.

- Mortality

This one is easy. Participants drop out studies, for many reasons. These dropouts may tend to bias the study, often toward positive treatment effects.

- Diffusion of Treatment

Sometimes the nature of the treatment makes it difficult to prevent those not in the treatment group from receiving the treatment, thus reducing the size of detected treatment effects.

- Compensatory/Resentful demoralization

---

[13] These threats to validity were originally articulated in the work of Campbell and Stanley (1963), <u>Experimental and Quasi-Experimental Designs For Research</u>.

If those that do not receive the treatment are demoralized, or develop resentful uncooperative attitudes, then they become less likely to succeed and bias the study toward positive treatment effects.

- Compensatory rivalry

This is just the opposite compensatory demoralization…those that do not receive treatment develop a "rivalrous" attitude, where they are motivated to do better than they otherwise would…strangely biasing toward smaller treatment effects.

- Testing

Sometimes the timing or sequencing of testing (such as giving tests too close together), can be a threat to a valid assessment of the treatment effect.

- Instrumentation

Sometime the instrumentation is flawed or changes in a way that makes it difficult to accurately assess the treatment effect.

Exploratory and Confirmatory Analysis

A key distinction should be made between exploratory and confirmatory analysis. As the label suggests, *exploratory analysis* is the examination of data for trends, patterns, and relationships, without having a pre-conceived idea of what those trends, patterns, or relationships may be. "Data mining," is an example of an exploratory analytic approach [See Chapter 12 for more on exploratory analysis in the context of big data]. *Confirmatory analysis,* on the other hand, is examination of data in an attempt to confirm a suspected relationship between variables, or a dynamic that would create a particular kind of trend or pattern. Hypothesis testing is a kind of confirmatory analysis.

Confirmatory analysis is a key component of the scientific method. Without waxing philosophic on the scientific method in general, I do want to point out that hypothesis testing, with its emphasis on disconfirmation, still begins with a **declared notion, or proposition,** of the relationship between variables. A testable proposition could be something like, "There will be differences in reading outcomes by gender." When reading outcomes are collected, the average reading outcome for males can be compared with the average reading outcome for females. If there is a substantial, statistically significant difference [see Chapter 12 for more on effect size and significance testing], then you can claim the data are consistent with your proposition. [Of course, the *null hypothesis* is that there is no difference, and if you find one you are said to have *disconfirmed the null,* but enough of that].

Take a minute to consider the difference between this process, that of starting off with a declared notion or testable proposition, and a process where you just take a data set and start looking for relationships and differences among variables. You might still find that there are differences in reading outcomes for males and females, but without the prior declared notion this difference may be just a random, chance, difference. This is called "capitalizing on chance" and it can be a real problem with exploratory analysis.

A related problem is *spuriousness*, where two variables appear to be related to one another when they are actual related to one or more unidentified variables. Since exploratory analysis can be like feeding random variables into the hopper, turning the crank, and checking to see what comes out, it is easy to unknowingly discover correlations that may be (but are not obviously) spurious. Confirmatory analysis tends to avoid this problem, because thoughtful testable propositions (usually) do not include variables that would be likely to be spurious.

I want to emphasize here that the above discussion does not mean exploratory analysis is not appropriate or not useful. Sometimes, looking for unexpected relationships between variables in a data set can yield surprising results. The key, however, is to then develop a possible reason or reasons for that unexpected relationship, create a testable proposition, and ***use a different data set (or a held-back portion of the original data set)*** to conduct a confirmatory analysis to, um, confirm your results. This avoids capitalization on chance. And, if you can't come up with a reasonable reason why two variables are related, it could be that the relationship you have identified is spurious and you need to think further about the involvement of another variable, either measured or unmeasured. It still may make sense to use the information you have discovered in your exploration without confirmation, but you would have to be comfortable doing so without knowing the "why" of the relationship. I have always been leery of acting on information when I don't know "why" something might be occurring, but I sometimes do…especially if the risk/reward balance heavily favors the reward side ☺.

Three Tools To Help Conceptualize Your Analysis

This is a good time to delve a bit deeper into the "mechanics" of analysis. Throughout the analysis process, it is often useful to visualize the relationships between data sets, customer groups, concepts, and variables in different ways. The following three tools (and another better described in Chapter 9) have helped me enormously over the years, to deconstruct problems into their component parts, to understand different elements of a problem or to model possible relationships among variables in an analysis. There are many such tools; these are the ones I happen to use frequently. What should be remembered is that problems can be systematically deconstructed and examined prior to any quantitative analysis. Before you dive into a dark, deep, data pool, you should spend some time learning the water temperature, the chemical composition of the water, the topography of the pool's floor, and even the weather forecast! These tools can be used both to break down problems, or describe conditions or states of being, or inform the development of more elaborate descriptive or predictive models.

Venn Diagrams

The first approach, believe it or not, is VENN diagramming. While this may seem like it takes you back to 3rd or 4th grade math, VENN diagrams can be very helpful in understanding just what it is you are trying to analyze, and the different populations and levels of analysis you may be exploring. As you probably recall, Venn diagrams allow you to indicate how sets of things relate to one another. When you are trying to establish a sampling strategy, or visualize the relationship between target populations, systems, and programs, doing simple diagrams like this can be very helpful. I want to stop here and emphasize I am not trying to insult anyone's intelligence…I am not saying this is rocket science…but I am saying that sometimes we don't think of some simple ways of representing such relationships to clarify them. They are also particularly helpful when you are trying to communicate your understanding of these relationships to others.

FIGURE 2 SAMPLE VENN DIAGRAM

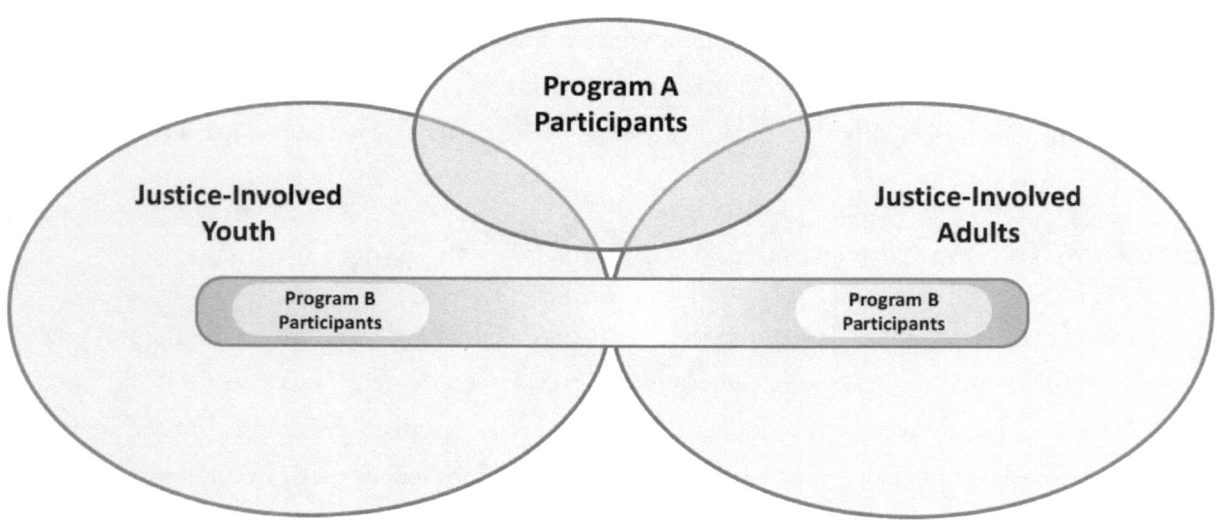

In Figure 2 above, the diagram shows two populations: justice involved youth and justice involved adults. The diagram shows that Program B draws clients from both populations, and only those populations, while Program A draws clients from both but also the non- justice-involved population. This may have implications as you frame questions for your analysis, as well as informing potential variable selection and sampling approaches.

The Matrix

The second tool, which may also make you smile (especially if you are a Keanu Reeves fan), is the matrix. When you think of the rows of a table as one axis of investigation (like different programs, different sites, different cities, different individuals), and the columns as dimensions (different core elements of the analysis, like customer characteristics, services, environmental factors, outcomes), and put them down on digital paper, they can help you to understand the scale of the problem, and help you to refine the different dimensions of the problem. Matrices can be particularly helpful in identifying patterns in qualitative data (pre-or -post coding). I often use them to do informal cross-case analysis, looking at what elements programs have in common, or common themes heard in multiple group interviews.[14] You can use a similar matrix if you are doing meta-analytic comparisons. In figure 3 below, the matrix represents the different program elements contained by different programs under study.

FIGURE 3 SAMPLE MATRIX

Program	Program Element			
	Limited Eligibility	Development of Individual Plan	Case Manager	Post Participation Follow-Up
A	Yes	No	Yes	Yes
B	No	Yes	Yes	No
C	Yes	No	No	Yes

Decision Trees

The third is using a decision tree process. This can be a precursor to doing a decision tree analysis using a machine learning approach, but I also use a "looser" version of decision trees to help me better understand the problem I am trying to solve. This can take the form of representing alternative

---

[14] For more on cross-case analysis, See Yin, Robert. (1994). Case Study Research: Design and Methods. Sage Publications, Thousand Oaks, CA.

possibilities in your analysis; prior to assigning any values to your model. It can also take the form of the "probability trees" of classic decision theory.[15] But I have found they can be very helpful in understanding any choice problem you are attacking, and to help you identify alternatives you may not have identified. In Figure 4 below, potential decisions regarding implementation of process choices are modeled, including the potential cost of those choices.

Figure 4 Sample Decision Tree

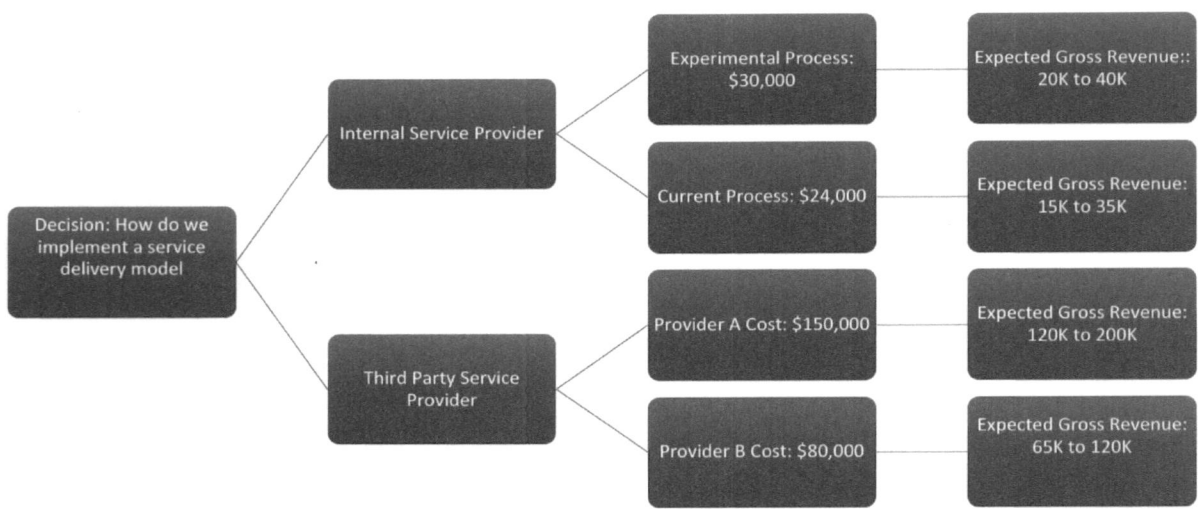

Another favorite tool of mine, process mapping (see Chapter 9), can also be used to help understand an activity stream or relationships between parts of a process. The next time you approach a problem, give these tools a try... You may find they help you to structure your analysis a bit differently; or develop a better sense of what the key dimensions of the analysis are, or help others to understand the elusive model that is in your head ☺

Sample Analysis Protocol

It is folly to believe that there is ONE WAY to do data analysis, or model building, or almost anything else in this glorious field of ours. I have encountered, however, data scientists that have begun their careers working on a narrow set of analytic tasks; the analytic training they receive is also sometimes limited, or tightly focused, as a result. While they were very good at those analytic tasks, some of them were never exposed to a general analytic protocol that could be applied to almost any analytic task. So, I am offering one here... Please note that this is a generic example of one basic kind of

---

[15]   See Baird, Bruce. (1989). <u>Managerial Decisions Under Uncertainty: An Introduction to the Analysis of Decision Making</u>. Wiley and Sons: New York.

analysis (analytic tasks vary dramatically), but I think is has the important elements that should be considered most analysis. I mostly provide directions and use examples from SPSS, but there usually is an analog in any statistical software (including open source software like R).

1. **Frame The Question (see above)**
2. **Determine The Elements of The Analysis/Develop Analytic Design (see page 33 above)**
3. **Import/Integrate Data. Make sure there are no duplicate records in individual record files.**

In **SPSS**, variable view, you can change the names of variables, add variable labels, add value labels, specify missing values, and designate the variable as nominal, ordinal or scale. *It is important to take the time to do this early on. It is tempting to rush to analysis, but your analysis output will be much better if you take the time to label and designate things correctly.*

If you believe there are duplicates in your file, you can use the IDENTIFY DUPLICATES function. If there are duplicates, you hopefully have some variable that serves as a unique ID for each record (such as people—SS#, CaseID, Last name and DOB, etc) and you can use that to ID the duplicates.

When you run ID duplicates, you get output that looks like this, that tells you how many duplicates you have.

FIGURE 5 DUPLICATES TABLE

Indicator of each last matching case as Primary

		Frequency	Percent	Valid Percent	Cumulative Percent
Valid	Duplicate Case	12	14.8	14.8	14.8
	Primary Case	69	85.2	85.2	100.0
	Total	81	100.0	100.0	

Sometimes you want to eliminate duplicates and have just one record per person or other unit of analysis. You can use the AGGEGRATE function for this.

You can tell SPSS to match the records on some key variable, and then COLLAPSE the duplicate records into one record. You can tell SPSS what to do with each variable (take the first, last, min or max value from the multiple records you are collapsing into one record).

The best way to direct the output of the aggregation is into a new file, so that if you do it wrong you can simply replace the file, and your raw data are untouched.

These de-duplication and aggregation steps are part of the data cleaning and compilation process. Sometimes these steps are not needed, if you have developed a data file yourself or get one that has been aggregated and cleansed already. These are basic steps, but they are often required in the real world.

4. **Once the data are in place, and integrated, be sure the data are not corrupt and that they are clean.**

- Are the values what you expect? Do the data "look" right?
- Be careful of "data shifts" where, as data are converted or imported into a new file, that data do not end up shifting or appearing under the wrong variable names. Sometimes this can be subtle and difficult to immediately diagnose.
- Are there erroneous values?
- Are there missing values? Decide what to do with them.[16]

You should then run some basic descriptive and frequencies to see what you have for your variables:

The DESCRIPTIVES function is a good place to start.

You can designate the variables you want to see, and ask for the minimum, maximum, standard deviation, and mean and sum for each variable.

---

[16] Be careful with missing values. Some kinds of analysis require NO missing values. There is a whole literature on different DATA IMPUTATION techniques to deal with those issues. Keep in mind that imputed values are NOT the same as actual values, and are used as a device to enable analysis, not to create "pretend" data.

FIGURE 6 DESCRIPTIVES TABLE

Descriptive Statistics

	N	Minimum	Maximum	Mean	Std. Deviation
EOY 2013attn	29	38%	100%	71.69%	17.982%
Q1 2014attn	29	73.00%	100.00%	86.4138%	9.41700%
Q2 2014attn	29	70.00%	100.00%	84.8621%	10.59219%
2013NumDs or Fs	29	0	11	5.34	2.649
M2_2014_NumDsFs	29	0	4	1.79	1.373
2013_eoy_DISCIPLINE	29	0	5	2.17	1.391
Q1_2014eoy_DISCIpLINE	29	0	3	.69	.891
Q2_eoy_DISCIPLINE	29	0	3	.62	.903
Gender	29	1	2	1.38	.494
Age	29	17	20	17.90	.724
Ethnicity	29	1	2	1.45	.506
Race	29	1	6	2.34	1.758
School Grade	29	11	12	11.79	.412
GPA 2013	29	.2	3.2	.862	.8364
GPA 2014	29	1.2	3.4	2.597	.5641
Valid N (listwise)	29				

You get output like this. You can check for any weird values (some max or min value that is way outside your expected range for the variable) as well as the "N" for each variable (if any record does not contain a value for the variable).

From there, you can use the FREQUENCIES function to show you the distribution for each variable. You can also generate histogram charts with the normal curve overlaid. The output that you get from the frequencies function looks like this:

FIGURE 7 FREQUENCY TABLE

Age

		Frequency	Percent	Valid Percent	Cumulative Percent
Valid	17	8	5.8	27.6	27.6
	18	17	12.3	58.6	86.2
	19	3	2.2	10.3	96.6
	20	1	.7	3.4	100.0
	Total	29	21.0	100.0	
Missing	System	109	79.0		
Total		138	100.0		

You should take a look at the distribution of each important variable in your analysis. Is it basically normally distributed? Is it REALLY non-normal (bimodal or extremely skewed?). Sometimes running a histogram (see Figure 8) can help you to readily visualize the distribution. You can also "go retro" and use stem-and-leaf plots (which are really cool when you learn how read them).

FIGURE 8 HISTOGRAM

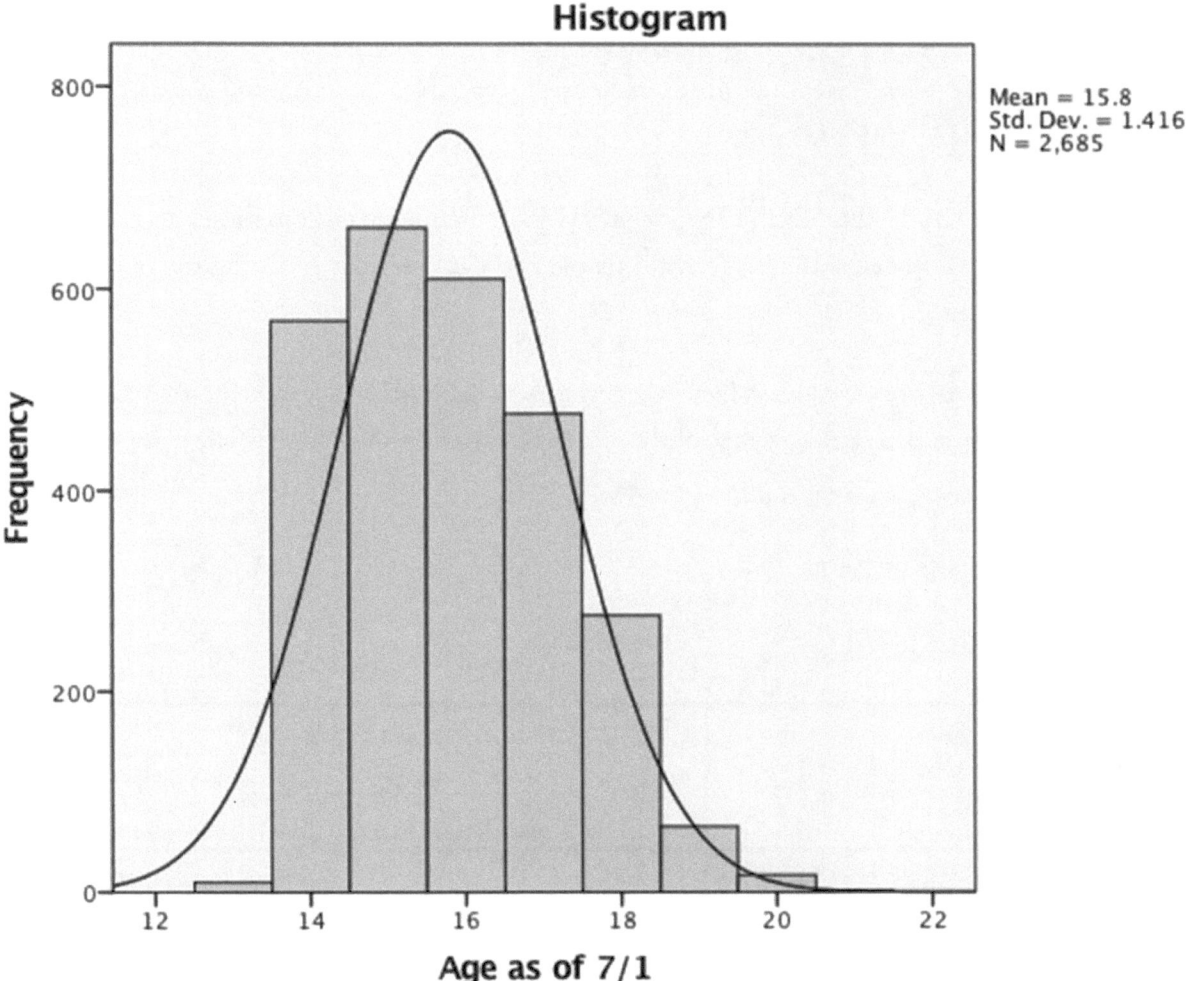

This is a good way to see the distribution of the data, which can be an important assumption to certain statistical tests. It is also another way to identify extreme or erroneous values.

However, these displays can also be used as a tool in final reporting…because they show the basic distribution of the variable—for survey data, they can show the array of responses for a survey question.

Computing New Variables

Sometimes you need to combine variables to make the data more analyzable. For example, computing a new variable by summing two other variables:

You can use the compute variable function to take values from other variables, perform mathematical operations on them, and put them in a new variable. The operations can be pretty complex, if necessary...watch parentheses!

You might want to create categories from an existing variable. You can use RECODE INTO DIFFERENT VARIABLBES for this.

You can also RECODE INTO EXISTING VARIABLES. While this is sometimes appropriate, you should stay away from that, because it transforms the raw data without retaining the raw data prior to the transformation.

You can also COMPUTE variables. Here we create a variable which represents the difference in attendance rates from 2013 to the average of the 1st and 2nd quarters in 2014. Use the compute variable function.

FIGURE 9 DESCRIPTIVES OUTPUT

Descriptives

	N	Mean	Std. Deviation	Std. Error	95% Confidence Interval for Mean		Minimum	Maximum
					Lower Bound	Upper Bound		
male	18	15.8333	19.87165	4.68379	5.9514	25.7153	-18.50	59.50
female	11	10.8636	15.78938	4.76068	.2562	21.4711	-12.00	40.00
Total	29	13.9483	18.29781	3.39782	6.9882	20.9084	-18.50	59.50

Then, you can compare such variables (attendance rates for males and females in this case): using 1 way analysis of variance.

FIGURE 10 ONE WAY ANOVA OUTPUT

ANOVA

	Sum of Squares	df	Mean Square	F	Sig.
Between Groups	168.627	ʾ1	168.627	.495	.488
Within Groups	9206.045	27	340.965		
Total	9374.672	28			

Notice while the mean difference in the first table appears to be significant (5 percentage points), the wide variation in both male and female scores and the relatively small cell size (things that figure into significance) renders this difference not significant.

5. **Look for relationships between dependent and independent variables (use correlation function, or again, something like one-way ANOVA:**

FIGURE 11 ONE WAY ANOVA TABLE, MULTIPLE DEPENDENT VARIABLES

ANOVA		Sum of Squares	df	Mean Square	F	Sig.
1. I felt safe during the summer league.	Between Groups	.259	1	.259	1.320	.252
	Within Groups	35.882	183	.196		
	Total	36.141	184			
4. I feel good about myself after the summer league.	Between Groups	.612	1	.612	5.031	.026
	Within Groups	22.274	183	.122		
	Total	22.886	184			
5. The coaches were nice to me.	Between Groups	.009	1	.009	.108	.743
	Within Groups	15.768	182	.087		
	Total	15.777	183			
6. Other kids were nice to me.	Between Groups	.080	1	.080	.232	.631
	Within Groups	63.045	182	.346		
	Total	63.125	183			
7. Other kids were nice to me, even during games.	Between Groups	.000	1	.000	.000	.983
	Within Groups	64.038	182	.352		
	Total	64.038	183			

The One-Way ANOVA function is great when examining a continuous dependent variable and one or more categorical predictor variables. It generates a table that shows, for each dependent variable of interest, whether there are significant differences on the dependent variable between the categories of the predictor variable. You can also apply a range of other tests designed to be more or less conservative regarding significant differences, such as Scheffe or Tukey's Honestly Significant Difference. I always smile when I read the name of that test…it reminds me of the movie Romancing The Stone, where Michael Douglas's character says that the "T" in his middle name stands for "Trustworthy" ☺

Another way of doing certain comparisons is using the CROSS TABULATION function. This is especially good when you want to answer questions like, "how many respondents were males AND Hispanic? Or, in this case, "how did employment outcomes vary by the type of worksite the client was placed at for their summer employment experience?"

FIGURE 12 SAMPLE CROSS-TABULATION

Sector * Employed at End Crosstabulation

		Employed at End		
		Employed	Not Employed	Total
Sector	Count	1	171	172
	% within Sector	0.6%	99.4%	100.0%
	% within Employed at End	0.5%	11.4%	10.0%
	% of Total	0.1%	10.0%	10.0%
For-Profit Company (Private)	Count	73	342	415
	% within Sector	17.6%	82.4%	100.0%
	% within Employed at End	35.4%	22.7%	24.2%
	% of Total	4.3%	20.0%	24.2%
Government Agency (Public)	Count	7	264	271
	% within Sector	2.6%	97.4%	100.0%
	% within Employed at End	3.4%	17.5%	15.8%
	% of Total	0.4%	15.4%	15.8%
Non-Profit Organization (Voluntary)	Count	125	729	854
	% within Sector	14.6%	85.4%	100.0%
	% within Employed at End	60.7%	48.4%	49.9%
	% of Total	7.3%	42.6%	49.9%
Total	Count	206	1506	1712
	% within Sector	12.0%	88.0%	100.0%
	% within Employed at End	100.0%	100.0%	100.0%
	% of Total	12.0%	88.0%	100.0%

This is the output that is produced. You can tell SPSS to add row, column and total percentages as well using the "cells" function. You can test for significant differences, when appropriate, using the chi-square function.

FIGURE 13 USING CROSS-TABULATION AS A DATA CLEANING TOOL

			Race			Total
		Missing	American Indian	black	White	
Gender	Missing	0	0	2	0	2
	Female	8	0	33	1	42
	Male	52	1	89	6	148
Total		60	1	124	7	192

You can also use cross-tabs to assist in data cleaning. Take a look at this cross tabulation. It is readily apparent that the data for race in this data set are not, shall we say, "fully realized." The analyst would have to decide what to do with this (the 60 cases without a race designation), especially if race was an important variable in the analysis

6. **Disaggregate dependent variable(s) on basic characteristic or process variables**

Depending on the nature of these variables, this may be done using the cross- tab function in SPSS or R, or using functions like one-way ANOVA. I find the pyramid chart function in SPSS very helpful for looking at two-way distributions.

FIGURE 14 PYRAMID CHART

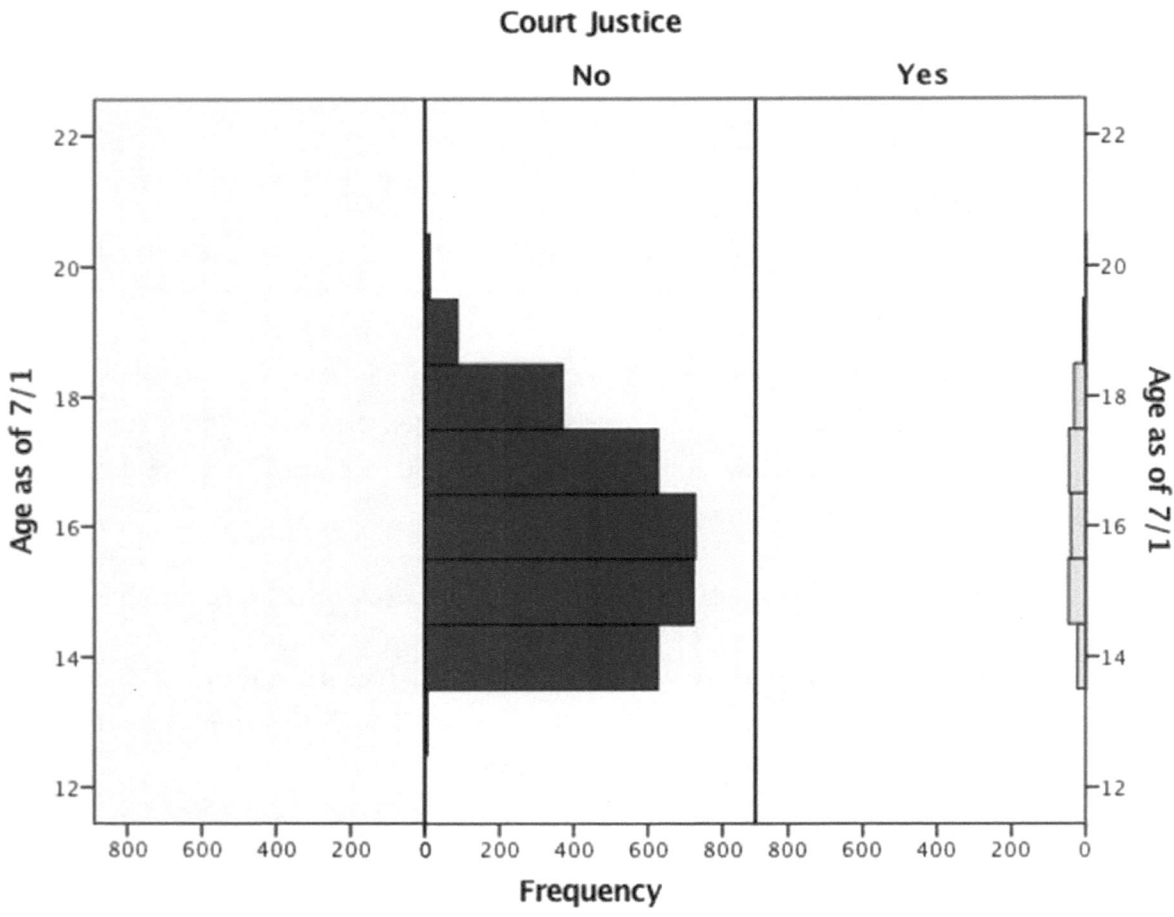

FIGURE 15 PYRAMID CHART OF DISTRIBUTION OF NUMBER OF SERVICE TYPES BY AGE

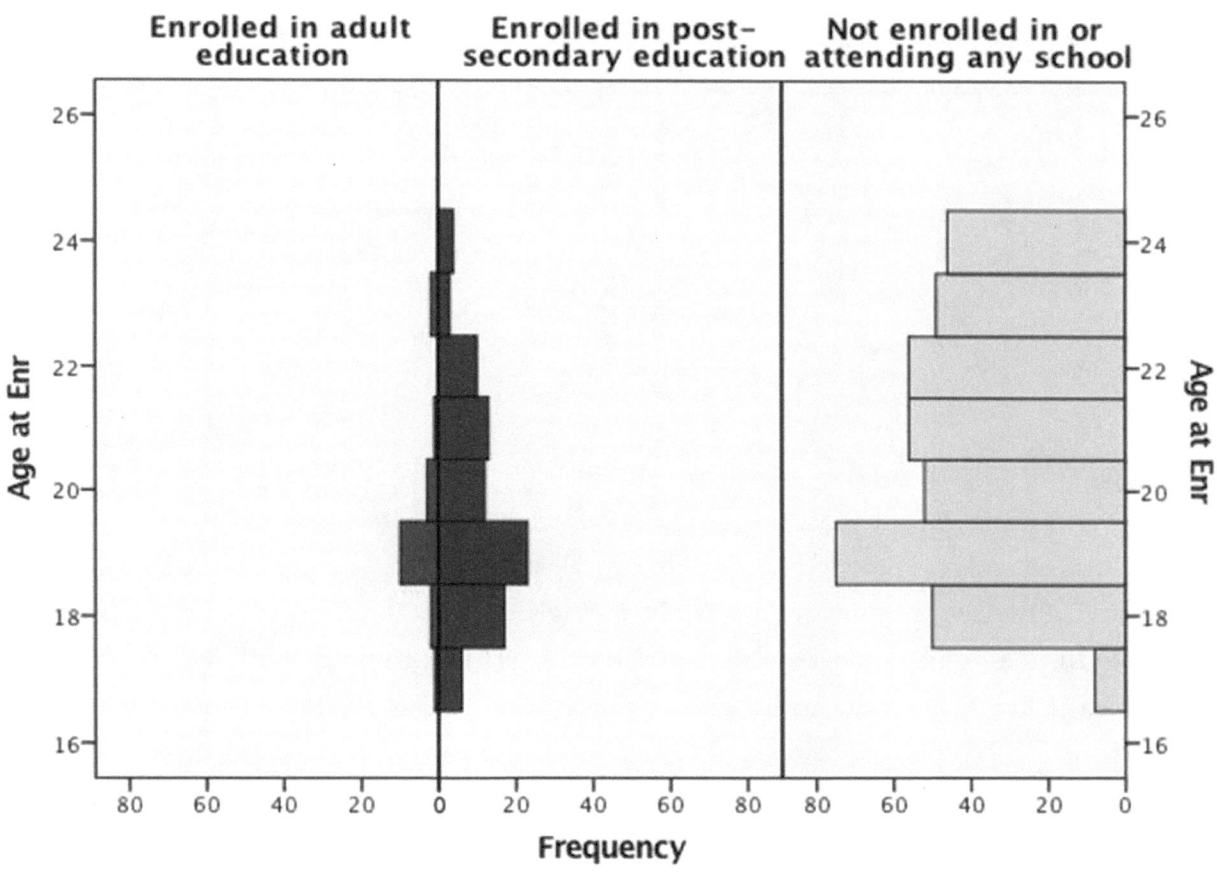

I sometimes use the WEKA visualizer to quickly review the scatterplots of multiple variables. SPSS also has a facility like this.

FIGURE 16 SAMPLE OF WETA SCATTER PLOT VISUALIZER

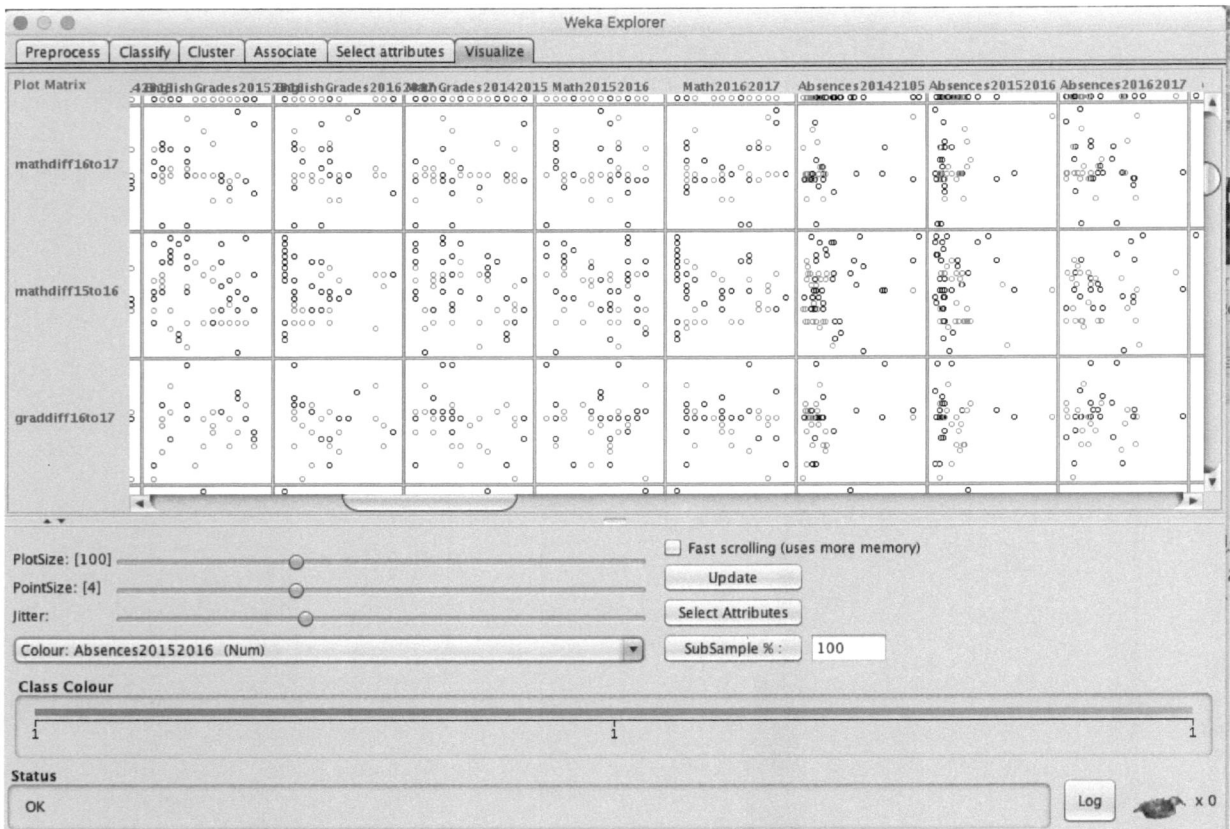

Relationships between two or more continuous or scale variables can be explored using a correlation matrix (see Figure 17). You can ask the software to flag significant differences at different threshold levels (like .01 or .05). The strength of the correlation increases as it approaches 1. Small correlations are between .2 and .4; moderate are between .4 and .6, and strong correlations are .6 or higher. The table will provide Pearson's correlation coefficient as well as the number of observations.

FIGURE 17 CORRELATION MATRIX

Correlations

		1. I felt safe during the summer league.	4. I feel good about myself after the summer league.	5. The coaches were nice to me.	6. Other kids were nice to me.	7. Other kids were nice to me, even during games.	8. The ECHO Core Values will help me in my life.
1. I felt safe during the summer league.	Pearson Correlation	1	.232**	.316**	.120	.085	.028
	Sig. (2-tailed)		.001	.000	.075	.209	.678
	N	223	222	222	222	222	221
4. I feel good about myself after the summer league.	Pearson Correlation	.232**	1	.357**	.241**	.179**	.287**
	Sig. (2-tailed)	.001		.000	.000	.008	.000
	N	222	222	221	221	221	220
5. The coaches were nice to me.	Pearson Correlation	.316**	.357**	1	.250**	.301**	.162*
	Sig. (2-tailed)	.000	.000		.000	.000	.016
	N	222	221	222	222	222	220
6. Other kids were nice to me.	Pearson Correlation	.120	.241**	.250**	1	.678**	.119
	Sig. (2-tailed)	.075	.000	.000		.000	.079
	N	222	221	222	222	222	220
7. Other kids were nice to me, even during games.	Pearson Correlation	.085	.179**	.301**	.678**	1	.188**
	Sig. (2-tailed)	.209	.008	.000	.000		.005
	N	222	221	222	222	222	220
8. The ECHO Core Values will help me in my life.	Pearson Correlation	.028	.287**	.162*	.119	.188**	1
	Sig. (2-tailed)	.678	.000	.016	.079	.005	
	N	221	220	220	220	220	221

**. Correlation is significant at the 0.01 level (2-tailed).
*. Correlation is significant at the 0.05 level (2-tailed).

Pearson's correlation measures the strength of association between two scale/interval measures. SPSS flags significant correlations.

Measuring Attitudes or Behavioral States Using Latent Variables

In my earlier discussion of validity, I mentioned the concept of a latent variable...a hypothetical construct, unmeasurable directly, that can be measured by linking multiple variables that point to different dimensions of that unmeasured variable. In my work, I use this a lot, to get at constructs like customer satisfaction, happiness, self-esteem, or resiliency.

FIGURE 18 EXAMPLE OF A LATENT VARIABLE

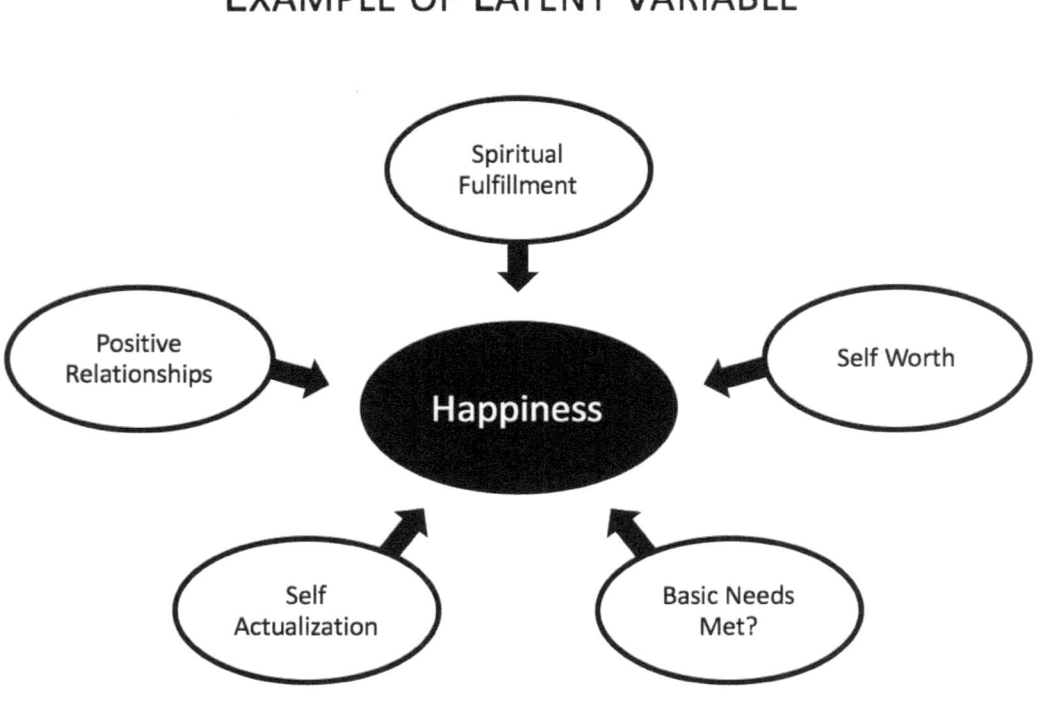

Check out Figure 18 above. Happiness is unmeasured, hypothetical construct, or latent variable. Notice that each of the variables representing a dimension of happiness may themselves be a latent variable. Working with variables like these may require the use of a method like factor analysis to choose the best variables to represent each of the latent variables in your analysis.

7. **If appropriate, conduct factor analysis on attitude or behavior, or other variables supporting latent variable analysis**

   ▪ This will tell you whether your questions for each dimension of the attitude "cohere" into appropriate clusters

The mechanics of factor analysis are too involved to cover here, but essentially factor analysis groups variables by looking at their correlational patterns. If you put 10 continuous variables into the "hopper," it will group them into clusters by similar patterns of covariation. Of course, those clusters should be theory driven as well. Those questions that cohere into a component or cluster can then be aggregated into an index. This index can be tested for reliability, using Cronbach's Alpha (see step 8).

FIGURE 19 ROTATED COMPONENT MATRIX FROM FACTOR ANALYSIS

Rotated Component Matrix[a]

	Component 1	Component 2
1. I felt safe during the summer league.	-.094	.692
4. I feel good about myself after the summer league.	.152	.719
5. The coaches were nice to me.	.219	.717
6. Other kids were nice to me.	.885	.140
7. Other kids were nice to me, even during games.	.903	.130
8. The ECHO Core Values will help me in my life.	.206	.398

Extraction Method: Principal Component Analysis.
Rotation Method: Varimax with Kaiser Normalization.

a. Rotation converged in 3 iterations.

Figure 19 above shows how factor analysis groups questions that are highly correlated together into factors or components. In this example, the two questions that are solidly in the first component are questions 6 and 7, both questions related to other kids treated the participants. The second component included questions 1, 4, and 5, (and possibly 8). Note that question 5 is related to how the coaches treated the participants. From a theory perspective, it ostensibly belongs with questions 6 and 7, but is actually correlated more strongly with questions 1 and 4. This may be because, for whatever reason, respondents have the same mind set when they answer question 5 as when they answer questions 1 and 4; but they are drawing on other experiences when they answer questions 6 and 7. The researcher would have to decide what to do with question 5 (which component it belongs in) as well as question 8. It is always preferable to have a theory driven reason to include a question in an index, so that should be a primary consideration. Once those decisions are made, indices can be created and tested using Cronbach's Alpha.

8. **If appropriate, create indices based on factors identified**

- Conduct reliability analysis using Cronbach's Alpha...this will tell you give you and indication of whether the indices actually "work" (that is, cohere as an index).

Unlike many of such tests, you ae not hoping to maximize or minimize Cronbach's alpha. Instead, you are looking for a "sweetspot" between, perhaps .5 and .8. Much under .5 and the items do not cohere enough to be reliable; much over .8 and they are probably too much alike...almost like multiple items are asking almost the same thing. All the items of an index should contribute something somewhat different to the index and not be repetitive.

When I teach research methods, students often get that "deer in headlights" look when they are asked to go ahead and test their hypotheses. *For some reason, when asked to **use** the data to test their propositions, what was clear to them before suddenly* becomes opaque. This condition is not restricted to students, either. I have seen data scientists who have not dealt with examining "testable propositions" since college, develop that same look. Worse, some, not wanting to admit this gap in training or recent experience, will just pretend. The likelihood of a valid and usable analysis diminishes greatly as the degree of pretending increases ☺

I emphasize to my students that what we are doing with hypothesis testing is COMPARING—we are comparing the scores on the dependent variable for one condition of one or more predictor variables to another condition on those predictor variables. This seems to help clarify things and gets students over the hypothesis hump.

9. **TEST your hypotheses**

- Use t-tests, z-tests for proportions,[17] bi-variate correlations, or One or Two-Way Analysis of Variance, or other tests as appropriate, to test your hypotheses.

There is, of course, a dizzying array of statistical tests that one can employ. Each analytic task may suggest a slightly different mix of tests, but generally I have a go-to set of tests I tend use often. The

---

[17] Sometimes it is easier to conduct z-tests outside of Excel, SPSS or other statistical package. There are several on-line z-test calculators that work well, including.....http://www.socscistatistics.com/tests/ztest/zscorecalculator.aspx.

procedures and tests in the table below have served me well; however, your analytic task may have features that require a different or supplemental set of procedures and tests. There are many kinds of analysis I am not covering here, such as complex time series analysis, Bayesian analysis, or econometric modeling (although many of the steps apply to these analysis tasks as well).

FIGURE 20 GUIDE TO STATISTICAL TESTS AND PROCEDURES

Situation	Procedure, Test
Does the mean of a continuous dependent variable significantly differ for dichotomous values of a categorical dependent variable	T-test
Continuous dependent variable and categorical independent variable with more than two categories	One-Way Analysis of Variance (means-comparison), Scheffe
Strength of relationship between two scale variables	Bi-variate correlation, Pearson's r
Comparison of Two Proportions	Z-score, Fisher's Exact Test
Do the values of a categorical variable differ significantly from each other	Cross Tabulation, Chi-Square
Do independent variables explain a significant proportion of the variation in a continuous dependent variable?	Multiple Regression, R^2
Extracting components from multiple continuous variables	Factor Analysis, Principle components
Determining whether multiple variables (such as Likert scale variables) cohere as an index	Reliability Analysis, Cronbach's Alpha

Of course, there are alternative tests, or additional tests that I could have selected for each of the above, but those listed in the table have served me well in many situations. Remember to always check the assumptions[18] of any test you might apply, some of them fail miserably if the data are not normally distributed, or at least close to being normally distributed. There is an entire array of different tests that should be used for non-parametric distributions[19], and the choice of measures of model fit for predictive models is endless, and far outside the scope of this book.

- **Remember to examine both statistical significance AND effect size (see Chapter 14).**

---

[18] The extent to which your data conform to the assumptions of these tests, and what you do about it if there are problems, is a very tricky balance. Most of the time there are at least what I would term "minor" violations of the assumptions; if they are in fact minor you can usually proceed. I knew a professor who did not get tenure because he was so concerned about these assumptions that he couldn't bring himself to publish any data analysis. While laudable, this approach slowed his career considerably.

[19] See Conover, W. J., (1999) Practical Non-Parametric Statistics. 3rd Edition. Wiley and Sons. New York.

Setting a target and interpreting p-values for significance tests can seem complex. The important thing to remember is that p-values are on a continuum, and the cut point for significance is set based on the nature of the analysis. If you are trying to locate some sub atomic particle, you probably want an extremely low p-value, maybe 0.00001, ….But if you're testing for whether your new resident awareness campaign is better than the old one or the new police response procedure is better, then you're probably willing to take a higher value, maybe even as high as 0.25. A standard practice for most social science is to set the p-value at .05.

Determine the size of the effect. The table below presents benchmarks based upon small, medium, and large effect sizes, based upon Cohen' recommendations[20].

10. **Closely assess the size of the effect.**

Figure 21 below shows benchmarks for small, medium, and large effect sizes, for different comparisons and different measures of effect size. Of course, these thresholds are somewhat arbitrary but can be useful in characterizing the size of an observed effect.

Please remember that ***even small effects*** may be important. Identifying small effects still add to our knowledge base. They could suggest future research (using larger samples or different methods), or they could accumulate over time into a larger effect.

FIGURE 21 BENCHMARKS FOR SMALL, MEDIUM AND LARGE EFFECT SIZES

	Relevant Measure of Effect	Effect Size Class		
		Small	Medium	Large
Comparison of Independent Means	cohen's d, hedges's g	0.2	0.5	0.8
Comparison of two correlations	q	0.1	0.3	0.5
Difference between proportions	cohen's g	0.05	0.15	0.25
Correlation	r	0.1	0.3	0.5
Cross tabution	w	0.1	0.3	0.5
ANOVA	f	0.1	0.25	0.4
Multiple Regression	R Squared	0.02	0.13	0.26

11. **BUILD predictive models if needed**

   ▪ Use regression, logistic regression, econometric modeling, time-series analysis, structural equation modeling (SEM), Bayesian approaches, or machine learning approaches as appropriate to develop predictive models, if this is part of your analysis task.

---

[20]   See http://core.ecu.edu/psyc/wuenschk/docs30/EffectSizeConventions.pdf

There are too many possible model building approaches to go into here. Notice, however, the model building starts relatively late in the process (although your analysis design should **anticipate** that you will be doing some model building). I say this because one should always be FULLY familiar with your data sets before you start doing complex modeling. These prior steps (1-10) build that familiarity, and can provide interim findings that are of interest. Be careful, too, that the model building approach you anticipate using will work given the nature of your data. For example, if the dependent variable is dichotomous, linear regression will not work…you probably need to use logistic regression or some other approach, which will be somewhat more complex and somewhat more difficult to interpret. Structural Equation Modeling (SEM) can also be useful when one or more outcome variables are dichotomous.

Re-check results; conduct sensitivity analysis; review threats to validity

Sensitivity Analysis is a method where you review your results by asking the question, "what would the results be like if I changed one or more of the variables? Or if I excluded one or more of the variables? You should examine your results be deliberately "tweaking" different aspects of your model. Models that contain latent variables are often described in terms of the **measurement model** and the **structural model.** The measurement model refers to the variables used to measure the latent variables in the model, and any other variables contained in the model. The structural model refers to the relationships between the latent variables (and their constellation of measurable variables) and the other non-latent variables in the model. Most software for employing modeling techniques, including regression analysis, have functions that allow you to review the model with different variables excluded. Beyond sensitivity analysis, you should review the threats to validity that I articulated earlier in the chapter. Did you forget something? Some potential source of bias? Do the results suggest that one or more of these threats may exist?

12. **Share Results**

Sharing results usually involves presenting your results visually, in table, chart, and diagram form. Please see Chapter 6 for a discussion the "Optics" of data presentation…

As I eluded to earlier, seasoned analysts (I would never label myself as seasoned, I am afraid I would be eaten) will have their own set of preferred tests and their own analytic sequences (which may vary depending upon the kind of analysis being conducted). I am not implying that the approach outlined above is the only way to do an analysis, or that these steps must be done in this order, no matter what. I have not covered the techniques for checking the underlying assumptions of some of these approaches, which again is outside of the scope of this book, but something that shouldn't be overlooked. The intent of this section was to help readers "visualize" the steps of an analysis, so they can see *there is a logical, coherent sequence* that *can* be followed, and that many analytic situations that involve hypothesis testing follow a relatively straightforward path.

I want to take the opportunity here to talk a little about the dynamics of defending your analysis. This can be tricky business, and it took me a while to become comfortable with this process. Of course, the first principle is to be honest. If someone points out a mistake or flaw in your analysis, own it. However, in practice the dynamic of this happening in public can be disconcerting. As a young data analyst I became defensive and my first instinct was to attack back. Try not to do that. Also, sometimes what is being pointed out isn't really a mistake or flaw, but a conscious choice. You need to make it clear why certain assumptions or decisions were made. Sometimes, however, it is best not to try to do that in a pubic or group setting. Other times, if data inconsistencies are found or the questions are sufficiently technical that you are not sure of the answer, it is best to say that the observation is interesting and you will look into it. Don't get caught in the trap of feeling like you have to answer all possible challenges to your analysis in the moment. Buy yourself some time to really think about the issue(s) being raised. Arrange to have an off-line discussion with the challenger(s) and de-escalate the situation.

4

"MY MONKEY-STYLE MEASUREMENT IS BETTER THAN YOUR DRAGON-STYLE MEASUREMENT!"

"Be Like Water," Enter the Dragon, Bruce Lee
"I will bend like a reed in the wind," Duke Paul Atreides, **Dune**, by Frank Herbert

Throughout my career, there has been a lot of debate about the "best" performance framework to use to guide measurement decisions and to inform the creation of performance reports. Some are not performance frameworks per se, but have been represented as such by consultants over time, or expanded from their initial intent, and have become de facto performance frameworks as a result. They all have some merit, and, if used with some common sense, an organization can use any of them to create a successful system of data driven decision making and continuous improvement. At the same time, *I wouldn't go so far as to say all of the approaches are created equal….some are more equal than others*. And, overtime, if you think an organization should consider another framework or adopt elements of another framework then phase those in as appropriate.

> **Schackziom Number 2:**
>
> **Worry less about what performance framework an organization is using, and more about fully utilizing the whichever framework is in use.**

I have seen performance measurement efforts go badly awry because the organization gets too caught up with whether or not they should "switch" the performance framework they are using. Because a great deal of effort may have been expended on the current framework, there can be considerable resistance to switching. It is my view that unless the organization is ready for it, trying to radically change the framework being utilized is a bad idea, and most of the time unnecessary. I recommend being like Bruce Lee or Duke Paul Atreides…*flexibly adapt the approaches as necessary to support the use of the data you are producing.*

Logic models

One of the most prevalent approaches to the systematic application of measurement is the creation of "logic models," which came out of the program evaluation literature. Harry Hatry of the Urban Institute[21] was one of the early proponents of the creation of such models, which outline the inputs, outputs, process, and expected outcomes and impacts of an intervention. Logic models can be helpful in understanding the intent of a program intervention, and the relationship between the resources utilized, the processes used, the outputs of those processes and the expected outcomes for participants. However, as Mark Friedman points out, they are not the holy grail and generally do not adequately depict the distinction between population level accountability and performance accountability, and can lead to the (inappropriate) assignment of responsibility to a program or agency for a population level result.[22]

However, when used appropriately, with those caveats in mind, logic models can, as their name suggests, help people understand the "logic" of the program. They can clearly show what "theory of change" is embedded in the intervention…in other words, how are the activities undertaken expected to produce change?

Figure 22 below shows the typical categories of a program logic model, including inputs, process, outputs, and outcomes. Sometimes another category, impacts, is also including. I think this category can lead to confusion regarding the distinction between population and performance accountability (it can be very difficult to attribute changes at the population level to a single program). Also, sometimes those building logic models can get confused by the term "impacts" and begin to try and differentiate shorter and longer term outcomes (or "proximate" and "distal" outcomes for performance measurement secret society members ☺), calling shorter term outcomes "outcomes" and longer term outcomes "impacts," which is not quite right and can create more confusion and false distinctions. All that being said, it is easily seen how such a model can be helpful in understanding the intent of a program and the expected outcomes.

---

[21] Wholey, Joseph, Hatry, Harry, and Newcomber, Katherine, (1994). Handbook of Practical Program Evaluation. San Francisco: Josey-Bass

[22] Friedman, Mark (2006). Trying Hard Isn't Good Enough. Santa Fe, NM. Tafford Press.

FIGURE 22 SAMPLE PROGRAM LOGIC MODEL

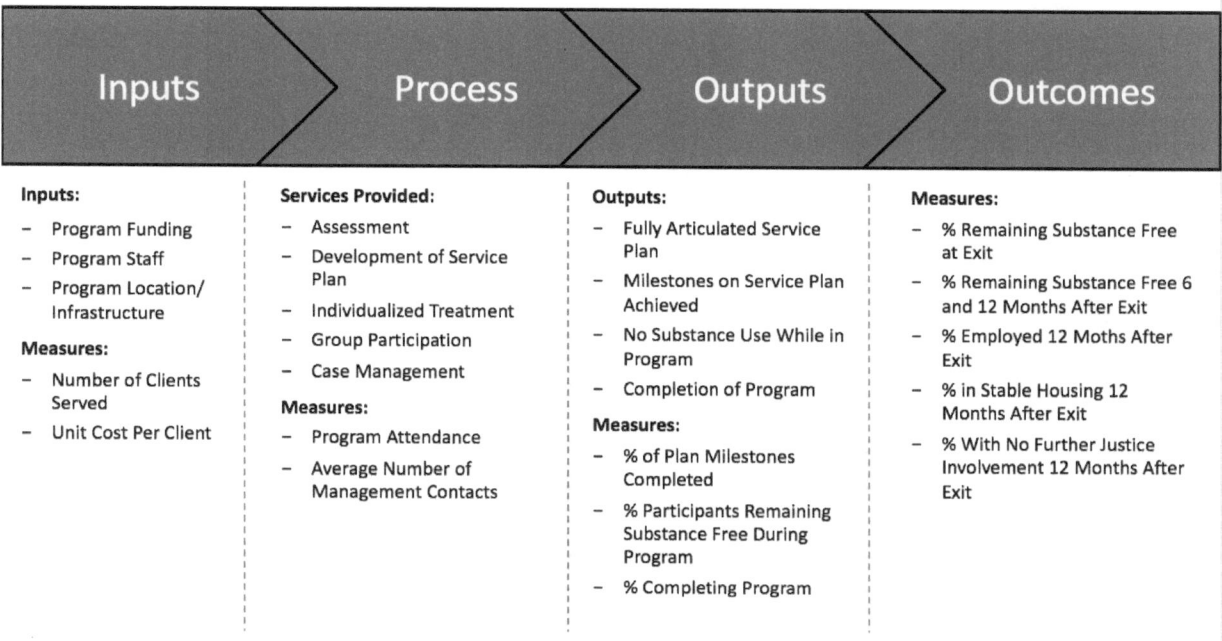

Program Logic Model

| Inputs | Process | Outputs | Outcomes |

Inputs:
- Program Funding
- Program Staff
- Program Location/ Infrastructure

Measures:
- Number of Clients Served
- Unit Cost Per Client

Services Provided:
- Assessment
- Development of Service Plan
- Individualized Treatment
- Group Participation
- Case Management

Measures:
- Program Attendance
- Average Number of Management Contacts

Outputs:
- Fully Articulated Service Plan
- Milestones on Service Plan Achieved
- No Substance Use While in Program
- Completion of Program

Measures:
- % of Plan Milestones Completed
- % Participants Remaining Substance Free During Program
- % Completing Program

Measures:
- % Remaining Substance Free at Exit
- % Remaining Substance Free 6 and 12 Months After Exit
- % Employed 12 Moths After Exit
- % in Stable Housing 12 Months After Exit
- % With No Further Justice Involvement 12 Months After Exit

Scorecards

Another influential approach is the balanced scorecard, created by Kaplan and Norton.[23] Balanced scorecards emphasize a balanced array of measures that include profitability measures, outcome measures and organizational measures like staff turnover and employee satisfaction.

There are several important aspects to a balanced scorecard—

- Scorecards should contain a balanced array of profit, client outcome, and process measures;
- There should be some measures that relate to human resources, like staff turnover or employee satisfaction;
- These measures should be reported together, so you can see how different aspects of organizational performance relate to one another (you may identify, for example, that your profitability is decreasing as employee satisfaction decreases).

---

23   Kaplan, Robert S., and Daniel P. Norton (1992). "The Balanced Scorecard - Measures That Drive Performance," *Harvard Business Review*, January-February. Pp. 71-79.

No matter what performance framework you are using, the notion of a balanced scorecard can and should be incorporated into your measurement strategy... The measures that are emphasized may differ depending upon the framework used, but the basic concept is important and should be utilized.

FIGURE 23 SAMPLE BALANCED SCORECARD

Balanced Scorecard			
Return On Investment	**This Year**	**One Year Ago**	**Five Year Trend**
ROI for Program A	$2	$1.87	
ROI for Program B	$0.11	N/A	N/A
ROI for Program C	$0.97	$0.94	
Customer Satisfaction Index (ACSI)			
Program A	82	78	
Program B	74		
Program C	77	73	
Overall	78	76	
Staff Satisfaction (1 to 5 Scale)	4.3	3.9	
Client Outcomes (For All Programs)			
% of clients staying off drugs (6 months after exit)	70%	64%	
% of clients in stable housing (6 months after exit)	78%	72%	
% of clients employed (6 months after exit)	48%	45%	
Operational Efficiency			
Cost Per Client Served			
Program A	$1,667		
Program B	$2,000	N/A	
Program C	$84		
Average Number of Contacts Per Case Manager Per Month			
Program A	163	170	
Program B	105	n/A	
Program C	N/A		

Figure 23 is a sample balanced scorecard for a large non-profit specializing in substance abuse treatment. As you can see, it has a section for ROI (one public-sector version of profitability), customer and employee satisfaction, client outcomes, and operational efficiency.

Lean and Six Sigma

"**Lean**" is shorthand for "Lean Thinking" by Womack and James[24]. Lean Thinking highlighted a new approach to streamline manufacturing processes, using such concepts as "pull," and "flow." As applied in the public and nonprofit sector, Lean became a new way of thinking about process improvement.

The concepts of pull and flow can be very important to any process improvement effort.

Flow **i**s a concept that emphasizes reducing the batch size in order to eliminate system constraints. *Flow* is achieved when a product or information is produced by moving at a consistent pace from one value-added processing step to the next with no delays in between.

Pull is a methodology by which a customer process signals a supplying process to produce a product or information or deliver product/information when it is needed. The supplying process is not initiated until the pull signal is received. This increases efficiency and reduces the need for holding large inventories.

Together with **understanding value and the value stream**, reducing **non-value added** processing steps and **reducing error rates/defects**, applying principles of pull and flow can create a lean system that is much more efficient and cost effective.

By itself, Lean doesn't really work as a performance measurement development framework (nor was it really intended to). The focus of lean (and six sigma too—see below) is the *improvement project*, not the systematic application of a balanced array of performance measures.

A strange dynamic often occurs when the performance measurement system development is going on in parallel with a lean, or other improvement initiative in an organization. Staff seem to only have so much tolerance for measurement and improvement related projects. If there is a lean project occurring, staff may pay less attention to the measurement project, or vice-versa. They may even say, "we are already doing LEAN!" when approached about participating in measurement development. Clearly, this can be problematic. It is important to show how lean improvement efforts "fit" into broader measurement development efforts.

The central feature of "**Six Sigma (6σ)**" is the notion of "six sigma quality," which emanated from the statistical process control literature and referred to processes producing a high proportion of output within specification (defect levels below 3.4 defects per million opportunities, or DPMO). While this

---

[24] Womack, James P. and Jones, Daniel T., (1996). Lean Thinking: Banish Waste and Create Wealth in Your Corporation. New York: Simon and Schuster.

is a high standard, the goal is to improve all organizational processes—whether they can realistically achieve this level of quality or not. Organizations should look at their most important processes and set an appropriate sigma level for them. It was introduced by engineers Bill Smith and Mikel J. Harry while working at Motorola in 1986.[25] Jack Welch made it central to his business strategy at General Electric in 1995.[26].

Six Sigma was the "next generation" evolution of Total Quality Management (TQM). While not officially part of the Six Sigma, the problem solving tools emphasized in TQM, like cause and effect diagrams, quality function deployment, check charts, pareto charts, and root cause analysis, are often used in Six Sigma projects.

In recent years, some practitioners have combined Six Sigma ideas with Lean to create a methodology named "Lean Six Sigma." [27]The Lean Six Sigma methodology views lean, with it's focus on flow and waste issues, and Six Sigma, with its focus on variation and design, as complementary disciplines that mutually support improvement projects. While conceptually okay, to me this hybrid feels a bit too much like something consultants cooked up to "get business" from those who were initially seeking either Lean or Six Sigma ☺

Results-Based Accountability™

When I am able to recommend a performance framework [as opposed to being told "this is the framework we are using"] to an organization I recommend Results-Based Accountability (RBA™).[28] RBA was developed by Mark Friedman, who worked in the Maryland Department of Health and Human Services for many years, and then for the Ann E. Casey Foundation. Mark developed RBA while at Casey to help public sector organizations, and particularly small non-profits, find appropriate ways of demonstrating their success. RBA emphasizes:

1) Starting by defining the result, or condition of well-being, that a community is trying to achieve

2) Making a distinction between population and performance accountability

---

[25] Tennant, Geoff (2001). <u>SIX SIGMA: SPC and TQM in Manufacturing and Services</u>. Gower Publishing, Ltd.

[26] Pande, Peter S.; Neuman, Robert P.; Cavanagh, Roland R. (2001). <u>The Six Sigma Way: How GE, Motorola, and Other Top Companies are Honing Their Performance</u>. New York: McGraw-Hill Professional.

[27] Harry, Mikel J.; Mann, Prem S.; De Hodgins, Ofelia C.; Hulbert, Richard L.; Lacke, Christopher J. (20 September 2011). Practitioner's Guide to Statistics and Lean Six Sigma for Process Improvements. John Wiley and Sons.

[28] Friedman, Mark (2006). Trying Hard Isn't Good Enough. Santa Fe, NM. Trafford Press.

3) Simplifying performance measurement by distilling measures into three broad categories: How Much, How Well, and Is Anyone Better Off?

4) Selecting the most important population indicators and performance measures; being careful not to saturate the user with too many measures

5) Using the language of "contribution" to link program outcomes to high level population results.

I have found RBA to be a very flexible and useful framework. We at COG have used RBA with the CT General Assembly's Appropriations Committee, various state agencies, and many non-profit organizations. I must admit that when first exposed to this framework it seemed "oversimplified." I was used to the wide array of technical terms applied to the measurement development process. But RBA intentionally avoids this, and if you suspend disbelief and try the RBA approach you will see that this very straightforward approach is easy to apply and communicate. As you will see throughout this book, I still choose to use additional, non- RBA terms in certain situations, but RBA is a great general framework that works well in most situations. RBA is also a comprehensive, internally consistent framework that "holds together" very well. As such, there is no need to "hybridize" it with other frameworks (in fact, Mark strongly discourages this).

FIGURE 24 SAMPLE RESULTS BASED ACCOUNTABILITY FRAMEWORK

Result: All Capital Region Youth are self-sufficient, employed, and achieve educational success.

Self-Sufficiency	Employment:	Educational Success
Primary Indicators: ▪ % at or above 200% of Poverty Secondary Indicator: ▪ % of students on free and reduced lunch	Primary Indicator: ▪ Unemployment Rate ▪ Secondary Indicators: ▪ Youth (16-24) unemployment rate ▪ Labor force participation rate	Primary Indicator: ▪ % with at least an associates degree Secondary Indicators: ▪ % at or above goal on third grade mastery test ▪ 4-year graduation rate ▪ % requiring remedial or developmental coursework in college

Additional Indicators:
- % opportunity youth (% youth 16-24 not in school or working)
- % youth that:
  - do not have stable housing
  - any parents
  - are justice involved
  - have a behavioral or mental health issue
  - have a substance abuse issue

Strategies	System Performance Measures (Cross Program)
Youth Recruitment and Engagement	▪ Number and % of Opportunity Youth served
Enriched Preparation	▪ % of Opportunity Youth needing GED/HS diploma that obtain GED/HS diploma
Occupational Bridging	▪ % of Opportunity Youth with a work experience before age 24 ▪ % moving to training, post-secondary education ▪ % that move to credit bearing coursework
Retention Supports	▪ % of youth served that remain enrolled in college or remain employed

Common Program Performance Measures (as appropriate for program): % entering employment, % earning a credential, % earning GED or HS diploma, % of those entering employment employed 1 year later

Figure 24 above shows an RBA framework I developed with Capital Workforce Partners, a Workforce Investment Board based in Hartford, CT. As you can see, there are three quality of life results CWP programming contributes to: employment, educational success, and self-sufficiency. The primary indicators used to determine the extent to which those results are being achieved are listed for each result area, as well as secondary indicators. Because this framework is intended to apply to multiple community partners, the framework also shows the strategies being used by the partners to contribute to improve those quality of life results. For each strategy, two or more system performance measures were identified as well. Notice the full array of actual PROGRAM performance measures are not listed: those are represented by the "common performance measures" at the bottom of the diagram.

Collective Impact

RBA's emphasis on results, and its conceptualization of *population accountability* makes it consistent with the Collective Impact approach. The term "collective impact" was first applied to this work by John Kania and Mark Kramer in 2011[29]. As its name implies, Collective Impact is an approach, like RBA, that recognizes that it takes more than one organization or program to achieve the results that communities are seeking. It provides helpful guidance on how community organizations can structure partnerships in order to increase the collective impact of its efforts. Of course, measuring this collective impact is an important component of this approach. This measurement approach is like population accountability in RBA. Population indicators are measures of the extent to which a quality of life result is being achieved at the community level. As such, they are a reflection of the collective impact of the collection of partners and programs contributing to that quality of life result.

---

[29] Kania, John, and Kramer, Mark (2011). "Collective Impact," Stamford Social Innovation Review, Winter.

5

MEASUREMENT CHALLENGES

"Celebrate the moment, as it turns into one more, another chance at victory, another chance to score," Rush, *"One Little Victory"*

Over my 25 years working with performance measures, in multiple policy arenas, I have encountered a wide array of measurement challenges. I could probably write a book just exploring these (and perhaps I will someday), but I wanted to share several that I consistently encounter and about which I have some constructive advice to offer. Sometimes overcoming these challenges in the context of a project can make the difference between success and failure; other times they may seem like minor considerations, but I consider these "little victories" as something to celebrate along the way...

Lagging Performance Measures

Many of the outcomes we want to measure take a while to "ripen." For example, we often we want to see, for an employment program, the percentage of those exiting the program that are still employed six months later. Or, for a criminal justice program, the percentage of those completing the program that have not had further justice involvement (for 6, 12, or 24 months after exit). Or, for a substance abuse program, the percentage of clients that have remained substance-free (for 6 or 12 months after exit). This creates a problem when you are trying to create performance reports in real time that provide some information about the outcomes that may be achieved later. One solution is to use a rolling reporting framework:

Two Year Reporting Sequence

Q1   Q2   Q3   Q4   Q2-1   Q2-2   Q2-3   Q2-4

You would report on actual outcomes for Q1 and Q2 in Quarter Q2-1; report on actual outcomes for Q2 and Q3 in Q2-2, and report on the actual outcomes for Q3 and Q4 in Q2-3, etc. However, while this provides actual performance information, it is about outcomes that occurred six or more months earlier. This means that any action taken on the basis of such information is 6 or more months old. For many programs this may not be acceptable.

Intermediate Outcome Measures

A different approach is to specify measures that are predictive of the ultimate but lagging outcome measures of interest. For example, for a substance abuse program, the average number of sessions attended may be a predictor of relapse. Another predictor of relapse may be the number of relapses during program participation. Predictive models can be built that use these measures as predictive of the lagging outcomes. The same can be done for other lagging outcome measures in other policy arenas. For example, recidivism may be predicted by both the % of sessions attended and the number and type of risk factors the client had upon entering the program. For employment outcomes, the percentage of participants completing the program may be predictive of entry into employment; the average number of case management contacts, or the number of different services received may also be predictive of success. For such an approach to work an initial analysis of the relationship between the predictor measures and the outcome measure should be conducted. Simple or multiple regression, logistic regression, and structural equation modeling (SEM) techniques may be useful here.

RBA practitioners may ask "where do intermediate outcomes fit in with an RBA model?' Most "intermediate" outcome measures are either "how well" measures in RBA parlance, or shorter-term "better-off" measures. But I use the term "intermediate outcome measure" to describe the concept because I think the label helps people understand the concept.

Evidence-Based Standards as Intermediate Outcomes

Standards associated with evidence based practices, when the practice is truly evidence based (see Chapter 14) can be used as a predictor of outcomes. Measures of fidelity to the program model, and measures of the percentage of clients getting all of the important elements of the model, can be used as proxies for lagging or difficult to collect outcome measures. Again, for this to work there needs to be an established relationship between these measures and the outcome measures of interest.

System Performance Measures

There are really two kinds of system measures. The first are aggregations, (or "roll-ups" in the vernacular) of the common performance measures applied to programs. For example, if different juvenile justice programs calculate the 12-month recidivism rate in the same way, then these can be aggregated to produce a "system level" recidivism rate for all such programs.

There are other measures which may be appropriate to calculate at the system level that do not have an analog at the program level. For example it may be appropriate to examine co-enrollment measures…the percentage of system participants that are served by multiple programs…this has a different meaning when applied to an individual program. Another example would be "the percentage of system participants that are justice involved"…you may want to try to reduce this percentage at a system level, but for some programs (those intended to serve only the justice involved) this measure would be tautological.

An important point here is to remember that these systems exist, even if they are not formally named or sanctioned. ***Just because there is no legislative committee or oversight council to examine system issues, does not mean these systems do not exist.*** The partners operating in these systems should find ways to come together and begin measuring and analyzing at the system level. You can help them with this!

The following table is a set of common program and system performance measure definitions for youth in Hartford, CT. Notice that the performance measures in the top part of the table are sufficiently generic so that they could be applied to any youth program for which that outcome was a goal. Also notice that many of the measures in the "system performance measures" section of the table are aggregates of the common program measures in the top part of the table. For any system, if service providers can begin to collect common program performance measures, then these measures can ultimately be "rolled up" to the system level.

FIGURE 25 EXAMPLE OF A SET OF COMMON PROGRAM AND SYSTEM PERFORMANCE MEASURES

Measure	Definition
Number of unique opportunity youth participants served	Count of the number of unique opportunity youth participants served during the report period
Number of participants served, by type of service	Count of the number of unique participant served, for each service type, during the report period
Percent of opportunity youth participants with fully developed ISS	Number of opportunity youth participants that have a fully developed individual service strategy divided by the total number of participants
Percent of opportunity youth participants with a work experience	Number of opportunity youth participants that have a work experience divided by the total number of participants
Percent of opportunity youth with basic skills deficiencies that are receiving basic skills support	Number of opportunity youth participants with basic skill deficiencies that have received basic skills support during the program, divided by the total number of opportunity youth participants that are basic
Percent of opportunity youth receiving basic sills support that have improved their basic skill level	Number of opportunity youth receiving basic skills support that have improved their basic skill level during the report period, divided by the total number of opportunity youth receiving basic skills support
Percent of opportunity youth receiving occupational skills training that complete training,	Number of opportunity youth receiving occupational skills training that complete the training divided by the total number of opportunity youth that have either completed or no longer attending training
Percent of opportunity youth receiving occupational skills training that receive a credential	Number of opportunity youth receiving occupational skills training that receive a credential, divided by the total youth receiving occupational skills training
Percent of opportunity youth that complete all program elements	Number of opportunity youth that complete all program elements identified in the ISS divided by the total number of participating
Percent of opportunity youth that enter employment during or following program participation	Number of opportunity youth that have completed or are no longer participating in the program that have entered employment at or within 90 days of program exit, divided by the total number of
Percent of opportunity youth that enroll in post secondary education following program participation.	Number of opportunity youth that have exited from program that enrolled post secondary education divided by the total number of opportunity youth that have exited the program

SYSTEM METRICS

Measure	Definition
Opportunity Youth Participation Rate	Estimated number of opportunity youth in community divided by the number of unique opportunity youth served in al partner programs
Percent of Opportunity Youth Served with ISS	Number of unique opportunity youth served across programs that have a fully developed ISS, divided by the total number of opportunity youth served across programs.
Percent of Opportunity Youth with Work Experience	Number of unique opportunity youth served in all programs that have a work experience divided by the total number of opportunity youth
Percent of Opportunity Youth Served That Earn a Credential	Number of opportunity youth receiving occupational skills training across all programs that receive a credential, divided by the total youth receiving occupational skills training across all programs
Percent of opportunity youth that enter employment during following program participation (cross program)	Number of opportunity youth that have completed or are no longer participating in partner programs that have entered employment at or within 90 days of program exit, divided by the total number of
Percent of opportunity youth that enroll in post secondary education following program participation (cross program).	Number of opportunity youth that have exited from partner programs that enrolled post secondary education divided by the total number of opportunity youth that have exited partner programs.

Measuring the Activities of Community Collaborative Efforts

These can be very challenging efforts to measure. Ultimately, activities of community collaboratives should be measured by examining the outcomes of the services that are provided to the public. However, often the individual services are measured under the auspices of individual programs operated by an individual partner of the collaborative. So, then, what measures should be applied to the activities of the collaborative? The key is thinking about what collaboratives do. Collaboratives leverage resources across partners and programs; they create service strategies and align services; they create initiatives that cross traditional service lines. So measures for these collaboratives may include things like:

- The amount and percent of resources leveraged for system efforts;
- The number of partners participating, and the frequency/intensity of their participation
- The rate of successful referrals between partners
- The outcomes associated with the services that are delivered through specific collaborative initiatives;
- The number and percentage of specific project milestones met by the collaborative, by project type
- A partner assessment (via survey) of the productivity and effectiveness of the collaboration (how much has it actually accomplished? Has the process been efficient or agonizingly laborious?)

Measuring the Activities of Internal Business Units

Activities of internal business services units can be difficult to measure, because there can be lack of clarity about just who the customer of those services are. The primary customer of the business office, or the IT department, or human resources, are the other units of the organization, or the organization as a whole. So measures of their activity may include staff's satisfaction with those services, the responsiveness of those units, or the amount of time it takes for a service request to be fulfilled. However, it is also important to measure how the activities of those units contribute to client outcomes. It may be important to establish that an IT improvement initiative actual contributed to better client outcomes, or that some action of the business office resulted in cost savings that positively affected a program's cost per customer.

Here are some typical measures to use for different internal business units:

Information Technology

- Staff satisfaction with services (helpfulness, responsiveness, did they get the help they needed)
- Average time from service request to problem resolution
- Percentage of project milestones delivered on-time

- Hours of server-downtime per month (or other appropriate period)
- Person-hours saved through implementation of new IT solution
- If responsible for website[30]:
  - Average number of screenviews
  - Average number of pages per session
  - Number of users
  - Number of new users
  - Average Number of sessions per user
  - Average load time, connection time, redirect time, etc
  - Percentage of customers that report website influenced their decision to seek services

Business /Budget Office

- Staff satisfaction with services (helpfulness, responsiveness, did they get the help they needed)
- Average time from budget information inquiry to provision of budget information
- Average number of days from receipt of invoice to payment of invoice
- Number of instances of payment of invoice beyond 30, 60 and 90 days
- Average number of days from requisition to receipt of needed product or service (this could be further broken down into sub-process steps—average time from requisition to ordering; average time from ordering to receipt by organization; average time from receipt to delivery to customer unit).

Human Resources/Staff Development

- Staff satisfaction with services (helpfulness, responsiveness, did they get the help they needed)
- Average time from posting of new position to filling of new position
- Number of employees terminated prior to end of probationary period
- Percent of staff evaluations completed on time
- Percent of staff receiving professional development during report period
- Average number of hours of professional development received by staff

Performance Measurement Unit

- Staff satisfaction with products and services (helpfulness, responsiveness, did they get the help they needed)
- Average time from analysis request to receipt of information

---

[30] There is a vast array of web analytics that can be considered; this is only a sample.

- Number of analytic products produced during report period
- Percent of analytic products available on-line
- Percent of analytic products that staff report they "regularly refer to"
- Average cost savings associated with improvement initiatives supported by the unit
- If public is a consumer of this information, public satisfaction with information provided

For any of these units, if the unit can identify any specific changes it initiated during the reporting period, and identify how those changes translated to better client outcomes, they should do that. Sometimes there are no new initiatives; just the on-going work of the unit. In those cases, the staff satisfaction may be the best indicator of the unit's effectiveness.

Earlier in the book, I mentioned the activity-based costing[31] methodology. ABC allows you to define a set of activities for any activity stream, including those of internal business units. Part of the ABC methodology is defining which activities are value-added, and the proportion of costs of any activity stream that are value-added. Value-added analysis can be helpful in understanding which activities of the business units are seen as adding value to the services provided to the ultimate clients of the organization.

Setting Performance Targets

Setting performance targets can be tricky business. Like performance reports, the way in which you go about setting performance targets for performance measures may differ based on how those targets will be utilized.

If they are being used simply as a management/activity guidance tool, the analysis approach and use can be relatively simplistic. However, if these targets are going to be used to determine whether performance was "acceptable," or if funding is going to be attached to the achievement of those targets, then the approach needs to be more defensible (and probably a bit more sophisticated).

Process Performance Targets

One category of performance targets relate to process. Targets can be set for measures like participant number served, attendance rate, average number of case management contacts, percentage of participants receiving services that contain all of the prescribed "evidence-based" components, etc.

---

[31] Kaplan, R.S. and Anderson, S.R. *Time-driven activity-based costing. Harvard Business Review*, November 2004, Volume 82, Issue 11, p. 131

The most important considerations for these process targets is 1) having adequate historical data, and 2) understanding the cyclical and seasonal aspects of customer flow, if any. If adequate historical data are not available, targets can be set based upon experience and any available benchmark information (based upon prior studies or successful similar implementations).

Outcome Performance Targets

Outcome measures usually require more elaborate analysis. Of course, having adequate historical data is still important, but it is not sufficient. If there is any variation in outcomes by geography or customer characteristics, you may consider the adjusting the performance targets accordingly. Once again, benchmark information from similar programs or the same program in different jurisdictions can be very informative.

Outcome targets can be helpful as end of year measures, or targets that are used to trigger payments in a performance contract. However, keep in mind what I have said about lagging outcomes and what that might imply for using such an outcome as a payment trigger.

Negotiating Performance Targets

Over the years I have been involved in multiple efforts to develop, negotiate, and set performance targets. There are a number of considerations:

- Is there prior performance history available?
- Are there national, state, or system wide targets that need to be achieved?
- Are data available that can be used to adjust targets based upon customer characteristics and economic factors?
- Are there specific federal or state statutes, regulations, or policy missives that guide or limit how or what you do in the negotiation process?

The following is the basic process that can be followed for negotiating performance targets:

FIGURE 26 PROCESS FOR NEGOTIATING PERFORMANCE TARGETS

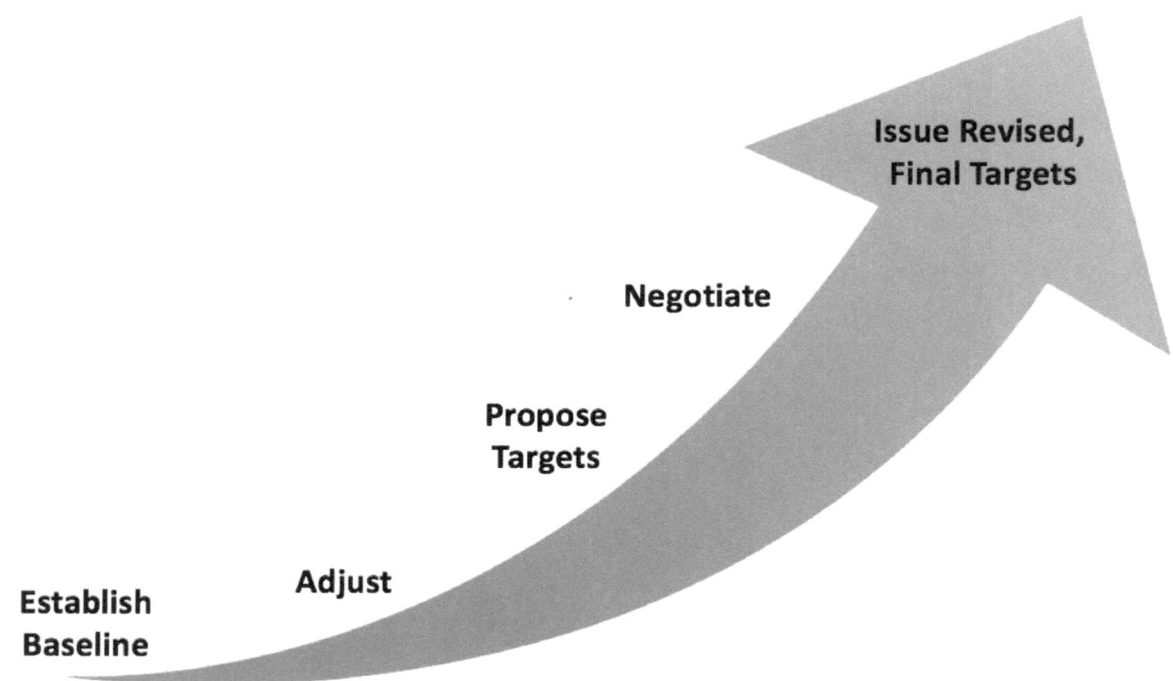

BASIC PROCESS FOR NEGOTIATING PERFORMANCE TARGETS

Issue Revised, Final Targets

Negotiate

Propose Targets

Adjust

Establish Baseline

The baseline for each organization with whom you are negotiating should be established using historical data. In adjusting the baseline, consider any target level that the program or agency has already committed and any basic continuous improvement increment you are trying to achieve, and apply any adjustments based on differences in mix of customers served or economic conditions. Once adjusted targets are proposed, those responsible for meeting the targets should be given the opportunity to provide feedback, and to make their case for any adjustments that should be made. Of course, their case should be data driven, and relate to factors NOT already considered in the initial adjustment methodology. In my experience, staff often do not understand that the conditions they are concerned about are already considered in the proposed targets. Sometimes, however, staff do provide additional information that should be taken into account. When this occurs, the targets should be adjusted accordingly and finalized.

Creating Performance Indices

Performance indicies can be very useful if stakeholders and staff "buy in" to the index and what it represents. The customary and appropriate caution regarding such indicies is that whenever you aggregate or collapse data into an index you LOSE information. I recommend, whenever such an index is reported, to report not only the index but its primary deconstructed components. That way, users can see how the index is moving but also how each of the primary components is moving, and whether there is one or more than one that seems to be driving the variation in the index. One of the nice ways of displaying components of an index, if you have a relatively small number of index components, is by using a radar chart (see Chapter 6).

The primary reason for creating a performance index is to aggregate important measures into a single index that people can pay attention to. They might look at the deconstructed components if they like, but most often they will look and see how the index is doing. Having a summary index at the top of a regular performance report can be a very useful "first approximation" tool for an executive or a manager. For programs and systems where the measurement model is relatively stable, I think such a summary index can be very helpful. However, as soon as such an index begins to suggest a problem, then you must look at the deconstructed dimensions in order to diagnose the problem. You need to determine which elements of the index are driving down overall performance on the index.

FIGURE 27 SAMPLE PERFORMANCE INDEX

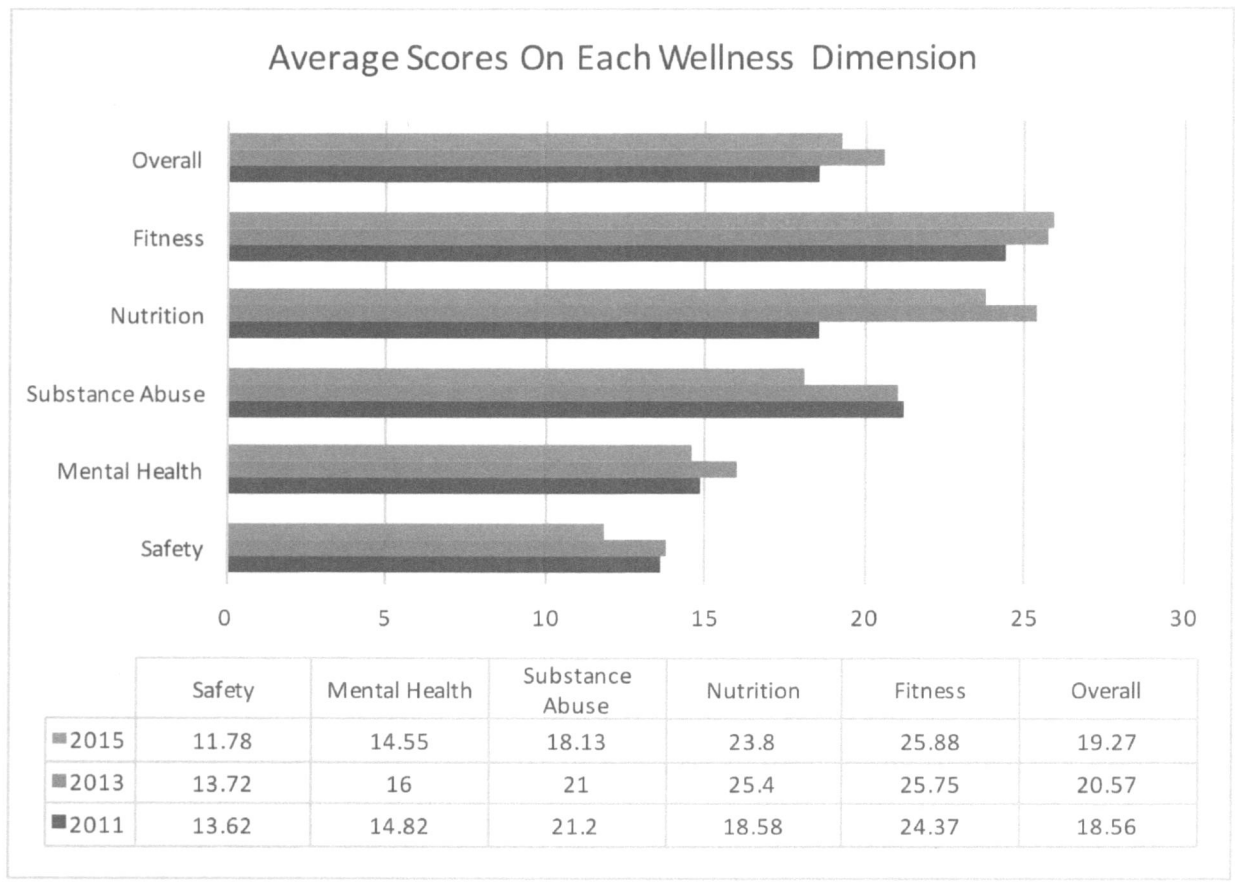

Figure 27 is an example of an "index of indicies"…each dimension is an index composed of several questions from the Center For Disease Controls Youth Risk Behavior Survey.[32] Then, each of these indicies were "rolled up" to an overall index. In this case, the lower the score the better. In the case of this index the index itself is meaningful; it represents the average percentage of youth engaging in negative or risky behavior across dimensions.

Performance Contracting

The need to embed some consideration of performance into contracts for services has been an on-going struggle in the public and non-profit sector. While there have been long standing performance contracting approaches for some kinds of products and services (like rockets, fighter-planes, and

---

[32] Center For Disease Control Youth Risk Behavior Survey. Please note the CDC does not report the survey results as indicies, they report results of individual questions, which is great for diagnostic purposes but of less utility as a community level indicator.

tanks), I have not seen many fully-realized performance contracting schemes for social, criminal justice, or workforce development services).

Part of the issue is the tension between the distribution of funds to these programs due to program need, and the need to hold these programs accountable for performance. If a service provider is performing poorly, and you withhold funding or cancel their contract, what happens to the people they are serving? Usually, there will be service gap of some kind. Also, non-profit providers are important actors and advocates in the community. Withholding funding from them can be tricky politically.

Despite these difficulties, I think there are ways we can move contracts for social services further along the performance continuum. This should start with the development of the RFP and selection of service providers. Requested activities and services should align with the program's intent and with any system strategies. The Request for Proposal (RFP) should be clear about what quality of life conditions are the focus of the RFP. In other words, what quality of life conditions are expected to improve through the provision of the services that are being procured? The real key, I think, is to specify the performance measures that will be used both to evaluate the effectiveness of services but also which ones will be used in the contract management process. If the services being procured are routine, long standing services, then chances are there are performance measures that are commonly applied to those services. Those should be stated right in the RFP. If the services are new, and performance measures have not yet been developed, the RFP should ask respondents to state what measures they would suggest.

Once a service provider has been selected, it is critical that a clear scope of work is developed, one that explicitly links services to be provided with expected outcomes. The contract should specify what services are provided, and if appropriate, how the services will be provided [e.g., if an evidence-based practice is being utilized].

If an organization is issuing multiple contracts for similar services, it is important that the same performance measures be specified across all contracts for similar services. These common program performance measures can ensure both consistency of service and provide a common understanding of outcome expectations. Sometimes, even if services are similar, there will be some differences in the way in which services are delivered or the particular mix of services across contracts. So, it may be appropriate to specify other measures, beyond the common performance measures, that capture these differences. Also, if appropriate, include provisions for how services are delivered, and what outcomes are most important.

These contract development provisions will allow an organization to review expectations with the vendor, specifically including vendor reporting requirements, collaborative efforts at program improvement, contract monitoring requirements, and criteria for contract renewal.

The on-going performance monitoring process should build-in an emphasis on improvement, and a progressive/incremental response to poor performance. There should be requirements for the vendor to create an improvement methodology, with guidance from the contracting organization.

Of course, contract management efforts should be calibrated to the scope and importance of the contract. The larger the contract, or more critical, the more intense the performance monitoring approach should be. Comprehensive performance monitoring (see Appendix D) should include a mix of desk review, in person inspection/observation, and case sample approaches.

The trickiest aspect of performance contracting is determining what measures to use to trigger payment. Include at least one service level measure ("how much" in RBA terms), one quality measure (how well), and one outcome (better off) measure in the array of measures used to trigger payment. Also include a measure of timely and accurate reporting of customer data. The link between payment and performance should be phased in, especially when only cost reimbursement strategies have been used in the past. Contract renewal should be made contingent upon a review of past performance, including a review of the measures used for payment and any other important outcome measures that might not be available during the course of the contract.

FIGURE 28 SAMPLE PERFORMANCE MEASURES FOR USE IN PERFORMANCE CONTRACTING

Purpose of Measure	How Much?	How Well?	Is Anyone Better Off?
Monitoring	Service Level to target	Program Attendance Rates; customer satisfaction (process); fidelity to model	Customer satisfaction (outcome); Outcomes achieved while participating in program; newly identified outcomes achieved in prior period
Payment	Service level	Data entry timeliness; program completion rates	Improvement in assessment scores at exit; short-term recidivism rates
Contract Renewal, Program Evaluation		Cost per Outcome; Return on Investment	Longer term customer outcome measures, like 12 and 24 month recidivism rates; job retention rates; graduation rates

Cost-Benefit and Return on Investment (ROI) Analysis

Cost-Benefit Analysis (CBA) is a term that is thrown around a lot, and is one of those oft-referenced procedures that rarely gets performed in the manner in which it was conceived. Somehow, *any* kind of cost measurement gets conflated with CBA, and somehow when cost data are involved the data are taken far more seriously and generate quicker reactions than other analysis. Because of this, organizations are often reluctant to report cost measures on a routine basis (because of the fear of misinterpretation).

Most cost-benefit analysis is implicitly based on the Kaldor-Hicks Criteria. Kaldor and Hicks argued that policies which resulted in an increase in aggregate real income are *always* desirable because the *potential* exists to make every individual better off.[33]

The traditional cost-benefit approach entails the following:

1. Calculate Costs

Sometimes, this is straightforward if we know the entire cost of the program from its budget. However, sometimes programs include activities paid for by other partners or programs, that is they "leverage" other programing to accomplish what they are attempting to achieve. In these cases, it can be difficult to get a true estimate of the costs of the program.

2. Calculate Benefits

A program or policy may affect many groups, including taxpayers, and program participants. What is the size of the effect for each group? The challenge here can be monetizing the effects.

Cost avoidance is a big category, ripe for monetization. The key question is...what costs would be incurred if a program participant is NOT successful:

- **Would they be hospitalized? (determine average cost of hospitalization)**
- **Would they be incarcerated? (determine average cost of incarceration)**
- **Would they be on welfare or receiving other public benefits? (determine average cost for each kind of benefit).**

And, on the other side, successful participants might:

Pay taxes! (determine average taxpayer contribution (refined by average wage level for participants who are employed).

As you begin an inventory of costs and benefits, be sure to document where all cost and benefit information is coming from. For elaborate models information can come from several sources, and it is easy to lose track.

---

[33]   Boardman, A., Greenberg, D., Vining, A., Weimer, D. (2008) *Cost-benefit Analysis: Concepts and Practice* (4th Ed.). New York: Prentice Hall.

Notice I said "successful participants" above—not all recipients of service complete the service or benefit from it. Therefore, the "success rate" of the service needs to be built into the calculation at some point.

3. Compare Aggregate Costs and Aggregate Benefits?

As you build your cost-benefit model, try to keep the calculations easy to follow. Sometimes it is better to break up complex calculations into sub-calculations in separate spreadsheet cells. That way it is easier to reconstruct what you did in what sequence.

What are the implications if the assumptions are changed or the estimates are varied? Would different information change the bottom-line results drastically, slightly, or not at all?

It is critical that you do not just build a model, come up with a CBA estimate, and say "Voila"….here it is. There are multiple ways to check the assumptions of a CBA model. **Partial sensitivity analysis** is a lot like sensitivity analysis in other predictive modeling…you select one variable and change its value while holding other variables constant, to see how sensitive the cost benefit model is to each change. Another way of checking your assumptions is to do **best and worst case scenarios.** As the name suggests, use the most favorable assumptions about a program or policy's results to create the best-case scenario, and do the opposite for the worst-case scenario. This will provide you with a full range of possibilities, and will help you determine whether the model is likely to shift from a positive net benefit to a negative net benefit just by changing the assumptions somewhat. You can also do **break-even analysis**, so you can determine how large a policy's impact must be for its benefits to equal its costs. There are also more elaborate ways to examine large numbers of scenarios by conducting Monte Carlo analysis, bootstrapping, and other iterative simulation approaches. These can be very useful but also require considerable expertise, and are outside the scope of this book.

Reporting The Results

Of course, you should be careful with any data you present, but CBA results require more than the usual level of care, because it is so likely that they will get 1) frequently repeated and 2) carefully scrutinized.

The tables that report your CBA results should be clear and comprehensive so that people can understand them without reading the accompanying narrative. Consider the following guidelines when tabulating results:

- Always show more than the summary number
- Consider showing a break-out (not too detailed, just major categories, of both the benefit and cost estimates)
- Be very clear about what ever discounting you have applied

There are some great on-line tools that can guide you in doing better cost-benefit analysis.

One of my favorites is CBAbuilder:

http://www.cbabuilder.co.uk/CBA1.html

The following are key formulas for calculating important cost benefit measures:

Key Formulas

- **Net Present Value= (Benefits-Costs (Appropriately discounted))**
- **Cost Benefit Ratio=(Benefits/Costs)**

Return On Investment (ROI) utilizes the cost benefit approach but presents the results in a specifc way:

- **Return on Investment = ((Benefits-Costs)/Costs)**

In my experience, the ROI calculation can be very misleading. When it looks "good" it gets over-quoted, often out of context. We must remember that ROI calculations are developed using the same assumptions as CBA; there are usually many gaps and flaws in our assumption sets. However, when a CBA study gets "boiled down" to a single ROI number, all of the cautions and caveats and deprecating provisos are lost...and people start to "run" with the ROI calculation, using it in everything from press releases to grant proposals to budget requests.

I am not saying we should not attempt these calculations, they add an important perspective to our understanding of how a program contributes to the quality of life results we are looking for. However, I **am** saying that these models are far from perfect, and should be developed and reported with an appropriate degree of caution.

6

THE "OPTICS" OF DATA PRESENTATION

"**Image is everything.**"...*Tennis Great Andre Agassi in Famous Camera Ad*

"**Comparison is the essence of analysis.**"....*Anonymous*

As most of us learn early on, the way that we display data is critical in ensuring its utility and the likelihood that it will be used to inform decisions. I am a disciple of Edward Tufte, a professor emeritus at Yale who wrote a series of acclaimed books on data display. My copy of his first book, "The Visual Display of Quantitative Information," is war-torn and tattered after over 2o years of use. Tufte has several "data display principles" that I always try to adhere to and I advocate most earnestly (see information box).

Tufte's Data Display Principles*

- Show the **data**
- Induce the viewer to think about **substance**, rather that about the method, graphic design, or technology used to produce the graphic display
- **Avoid distorting** what the data have to say
- Make large data sets **coherent**
- **Reveal** data at several levels of detail, from a broad overview to a fine structure (drill-down approaches)
- Encourage the eyes to **compare** different pieces of data

*adapted from Tufte, 1982.

One of his most important principles is "avoid distorting what the data have to say." This distortion can happen in many ways[34], but one that I encounter often is the misuse of scaling on charts. Unfortunately, if you just paint a bunch of data in excel, and tell it to create a chart, the default setting in Excel will generate a chart with a scale that maximizes (visually) the difference between points on the chart. The first chart below mis-represents the degree of change in the variable, because it does not use zero as the starting point. The second chart represents the same data using zero as the starting point. While this may seem very elementary to many reading this, I see this mistake (or intentional distortion) on an almost daily basis.

---

[34] See Edward Tufte's collected works, but especially his first book, "The Visual Display of Quantitative Information."

FIGURE 29 DISTORTION OF DATA THROUGH INAPPROPRIATE SCALING

To avoid this, you should always use a scale with a zero point where appropriate.

There are many software packages that create tables and charts. The most ubiquitous of these is Microsoft Excel. In this chapter I provide many examples of data displays, most of which were created with Microsoft Excel. This was done for several reasons. First, I use Excel a lot and am very familiar with it, so it was the easy for me. 2nd, and more importantly, I wanted to show *that none of these*

displays require specialized software. They all can be done, if all else fails, in something like Microsoft Excel. Of course, other software packages have default charts that you might prefer or have additional capabilities, and therefore it may be desirable to use other software. When creating charts for "glossy" publications, sometimes it is better to create them in a more flexible, visually-oriented software package, like Adobe Illustrator, but for many purposes Excel is fine. Data visualizations in real time using the web are also developed differently. The purpose of this section isn't to show you how to build these charts, but to outline important considerations, and to share a few approaches to the graphic display of data that have served me well over the years.

Creating Performance Reports

Performance reports should conform to Tufte's data display principles[35]. They should take into account the audience and the reasons why the viewer might be utilizing the report. A frequent mistake made in developing performance reports is including too many different measures and too much detail. When possible, performance reports should have a drill-down organizational structure, with a high level summary page or pages, and then increasing levels of detail following the summary. This increased level of detail usually involves disaggregating the measures that are in the summary... reporting the same measures by jurisdiction, by site, by customer group, by customer characteristics, etc. Both the summary and the drill down sections of the report should encourage comparison when appropriate. Comparison can take many forms:

- Over time
- Across and between jurisdictions and overall
- Across and between sites within jurisdictions and overall
- Across and between customer groups and overall
- Across and between customer characteristics and overall
- With "like" jurisdictions from other cities, states, countries
- With "like" programs from other cities, states, countries

Whether you are talking about a report that shows how a community is doing in one quality of life domain, such as safety, or you are reporting the results of a specific program, or you are reporting on the performance of a single agency, there are certain critical principles that should inform the creation of those reports:

1. Select a small number of important measures (for at least the summary pages of the report);

---

[35] Tufte, Edward R., (1983). The Visual Display of Quantitative Information. Cheshire, CT, Graphic Press.

2. The selected measures should provide a balanced set of key details regarding the life domain, agency, or program[36]

3. Show the measures so that they can be reviewed simultaneously to check on the degree of co-variation

4. The report should support and encourage critical comparisons (see above list).

5. The report should always include some explanation of the measures provided. Mark Friedman calls this "the story behind the baseline" and emphasizes the importance of providing some informed analysis/interpretation of each measure.

Please see Appendix E for a sample program performance report using an RBA format. Also note the sample "balanced scorecard" in Chapter 4.

Simple Tables

Another one of Tufte's basic principles is, "sometimes a simple table is better." I have found this to be absolutely true. Sometimes a table can communicate what you need to show better than any chart could. However, there are some important design principles for simple tables:

1) Use common sense, easy to understand labels

2) Always show the 'N"; include numerators and denominators where appropriate

3) Always label the time periods represented in the table

4) Always show all the data related to the analysis…in other words, make sure things total correctly

5) Avoid the overuse of different line types or fonts in tables…it makes them very difficult to read

Labels

Appropriate and understandable labeling in creating tables and charts is probably the most important thing to remember. Any data display you create may be distributed to others outside of its native context. With appropriate labeling and the other rules above, these tables should be able to stand alone. Labels should be easy to read, not too long, and accurate. Try to avoid too many abbreviations, other than obvious (like months or state names) or very necessary ones (like abbreviating scientific names for species).

---

[36] Different performance frameworks have somewhat different recommendations regarding just what to include. See the performance framework discussion in Chapter 4.

Always show the "N"

Another obviously important one, especially when reporting sample data. However, it is also important when reporting percentages. When cell sizes are small, percentages can be very misleading, so it is important to show the numerator and denominator as well.

Always specify the time periods represented in the table.

The viewer should never be confused about "which year are these data from?" Or "What program years does this analysis include?" Sometimes this can be challenging when a mix of data from different program, fiscal, and calendar years is reported, **but you need to find a way to make this clear in the table.**

Always show all the data related to the analysis

Never show "selected" data from a data series in a table. People will think you are omitting data that do not support your case. Always make sure you show all the data for the variables you are representing in the table. Make the data total correctly. If this means including a row called "missing or did not report," include that row.

Avoid Over-Use of Different Line-Type and Fonts in Tables

Stay away from different line types in tables…multiple line types make tables very difficult to read. Sometimes the inclusion of double lines is appropriate, especially in tables where financial data are presented, but even there their use should be limited.

Prototype Charts

I do not have space here (nor do I want) to cover every possible different kind of chart. But, I wanted to share a few important ones that I often use in my work. In building these I try to apply Tufte's principles, along with my own experience with the problems of presenting data (especially creating a chart that will work equally as well as something in a hard copy document, a PowerPoint presentation, or on a web-page). If you are looking for fancy, eye catching, charts in this section you have come to the wrong place. These are functional, basic charts and tables that show the data, do not distort the data, and that serve to present usable data in a straightforward fashion.

Line (Time Series) Chart

One of the charts I am called on to use most frequently is the line or time series chart. This is usually a pretty easy chart to build and understand, but there are a few pitfalls. Figure 30 below is a representation of a VERY SIMPLE line chart. ***It is simple for a reason…it's purpose it to represent the TREND and help viewers understand what is happening over time.*** The individual values are not of critical importance, so there is no need for tic marks, data labels on the line, or gridlines… they all get in the way viewing the trend.

FIGURE 30 DISPLAYING A SIMPLE TREND

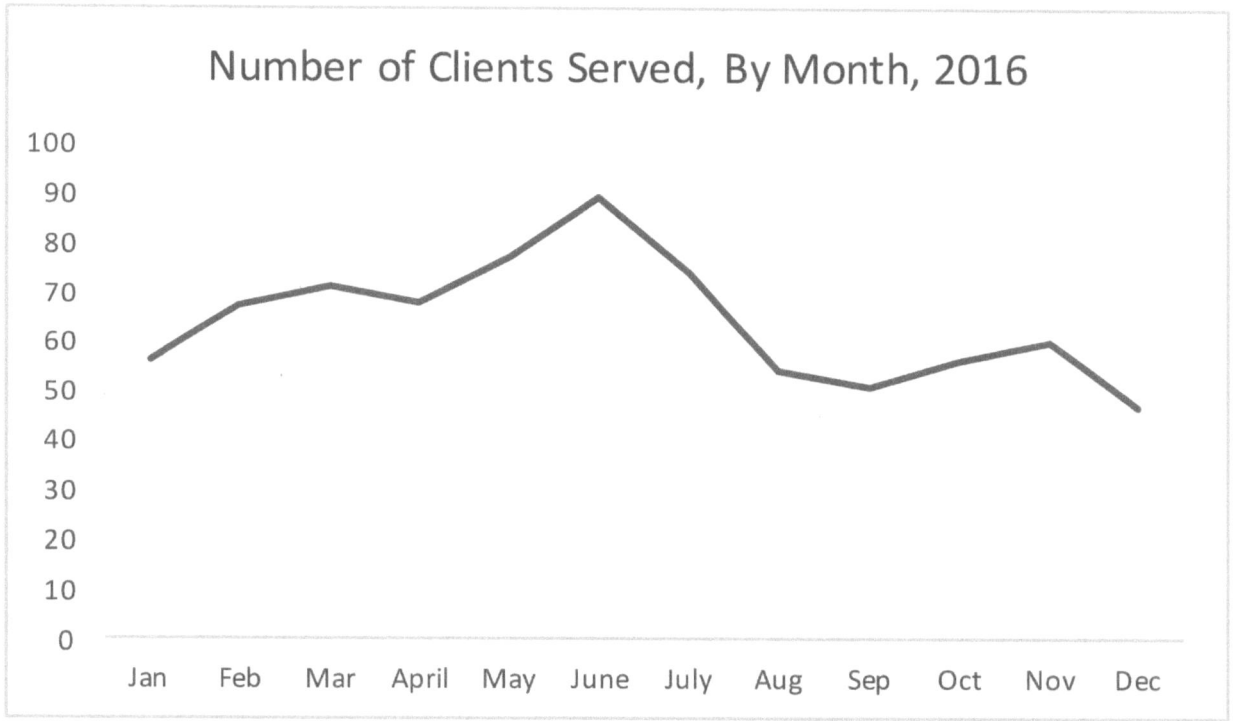

Sometimes you might want to show a similar trend, including both numbers and percentages. This becomes a bit more complicated… Figure 31 shows a line chart that shows the trend of individuals exiting a program, and a trend of the percentage of those exiting that were employed at exit. Since, unlike the first chart, the values have more importance, but you still want to show the trend, we:

1) Show the values for each month in a data table at the bottom of the chart.
2) The data table also afford us the opportunity to create a legend as part of the table, without taking up additional real-estate for a legend
3) This chart has two vertical axes…so that the trend for both the number and the percentage can be viewed appropriately.

FIGURE 31 DISPLAYING NUMBERS AND PERCENTAGES IN THE SAME CHART

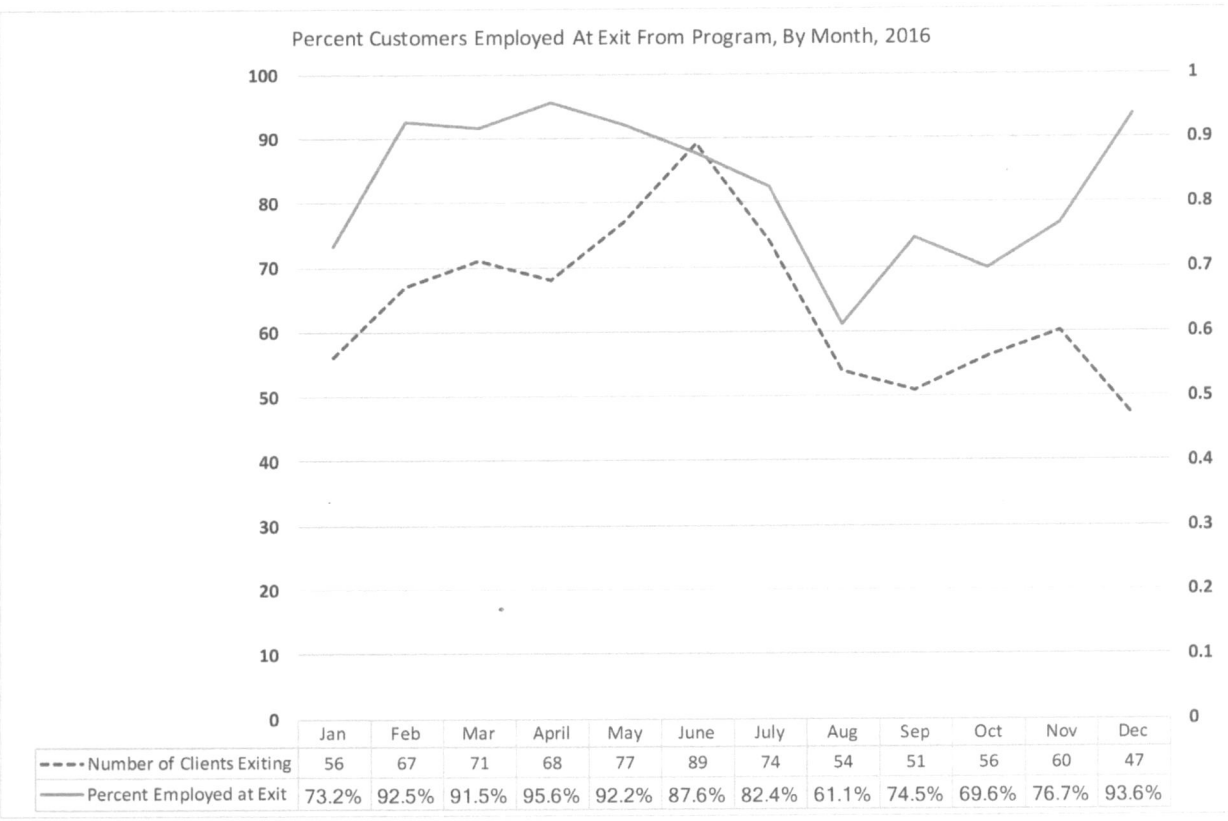

Percent Customers Employed At Exit From Program, By Month, 2016

	Jan	Feb	Mar	April	May	June	July	Aug	Sep	Oct	Nov	Dec
Number of Clients Exiting	56	67	71	68	77	89	74	54	51	56	60	47
Percent Employed at Exit	73.2%	92.5%	91.5%	95.6%	92.2%	87.6%	82.4%	61.1%	74.5%	69.6%	76.7%	93.6%

I often collect survey data using Likert scale questions… When reviewing a single question a simple table showing the frequency of each response category is appropriate. See Figure 32. However, when looking across questions it can be helpful to display the mean of each Likert scale question, to identify those that are significant lower (or higher) than the others. (See Figure 33). If you are developing latent variable models, sometimes it is helpful to show what questions are related to each latent variable (see figure 34).

FIGURE 32 SAMPLE FREQUENCY TABLE FOR LIKERT SCALE QUESTION

3. I found value in the First Aid/CPR Certification

		Frequency	Percent	Valid Percent	Cumulative Percent
Valid	Strongly Disagree	2	5.7	6.3	6.3
	Disagree	3	8.6	9.4	15.6
	Agree	8	22.9	25.0	40.6
	Strongly Agree	19	54.3	59.4	100.0
	Total	32	91.4	100.0	
Missing	System	3	8.6		
Total		35	100.0		

FIGURE 33 BAR CHARTS FOR MULTIPLE LIKERT SCALE QUESTIONS

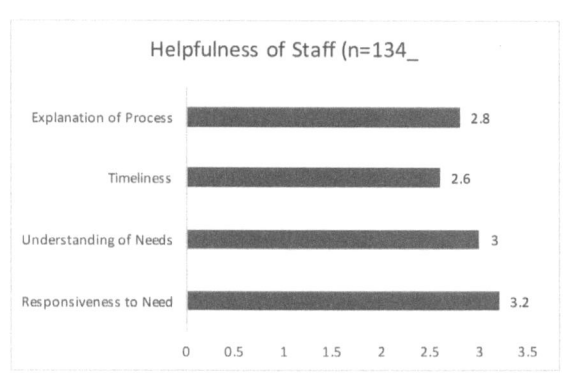

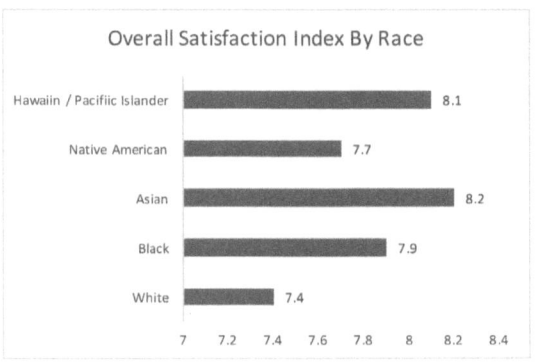

FIGURE 34 EASY WAY TO DISPLAY WHICH LIKERT SCALE QUESTIONS ARE RELATED TO WHICH LATENT VARIABLES

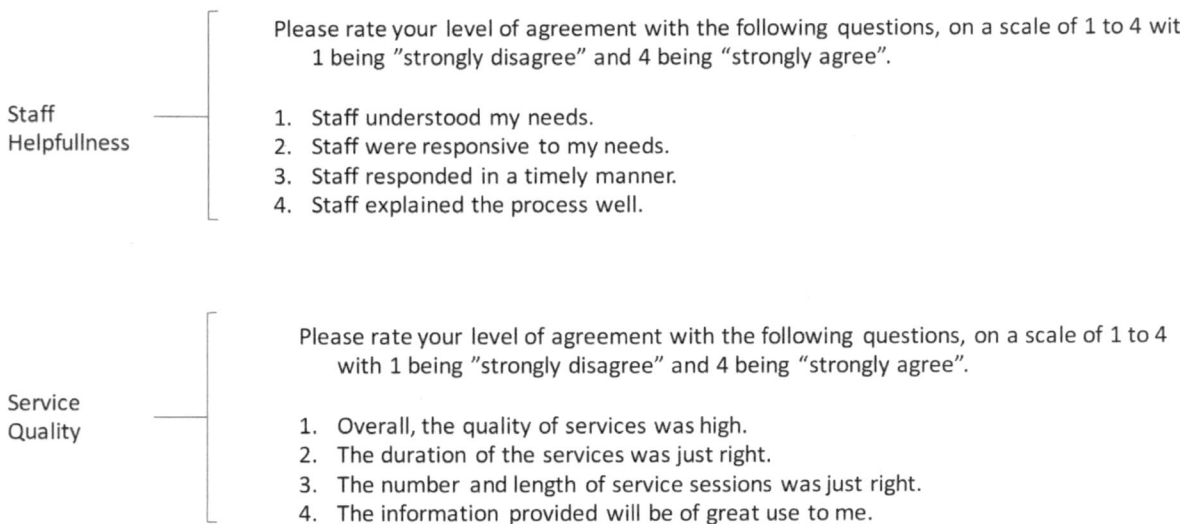

Standardizing Charts With Multiple Data-Series

Sometimes you may have multiple data series that you want to show on the same chart, but each series has very different numerical values. If the trend lines are reported as is, it will be difficult to compare them visually, since the slopes from segment to segment will be much different for one than the other. See Figure 35. To deal with this (especially if the comparison of the trends is what you are really after), you can standardize the values (using percentage change from the first value), anchoring them to the first value of each data series. See Figure 36. This allows you to readily compare the trends. There are also more sophisticated versions of this, where you do the same kind of standardization, but do it for 3, 4, 5, 7 (or more) period moving averages.

FIGURE 35 SAMPLE OF MULTIPLE UNEVEN DATA SERIES

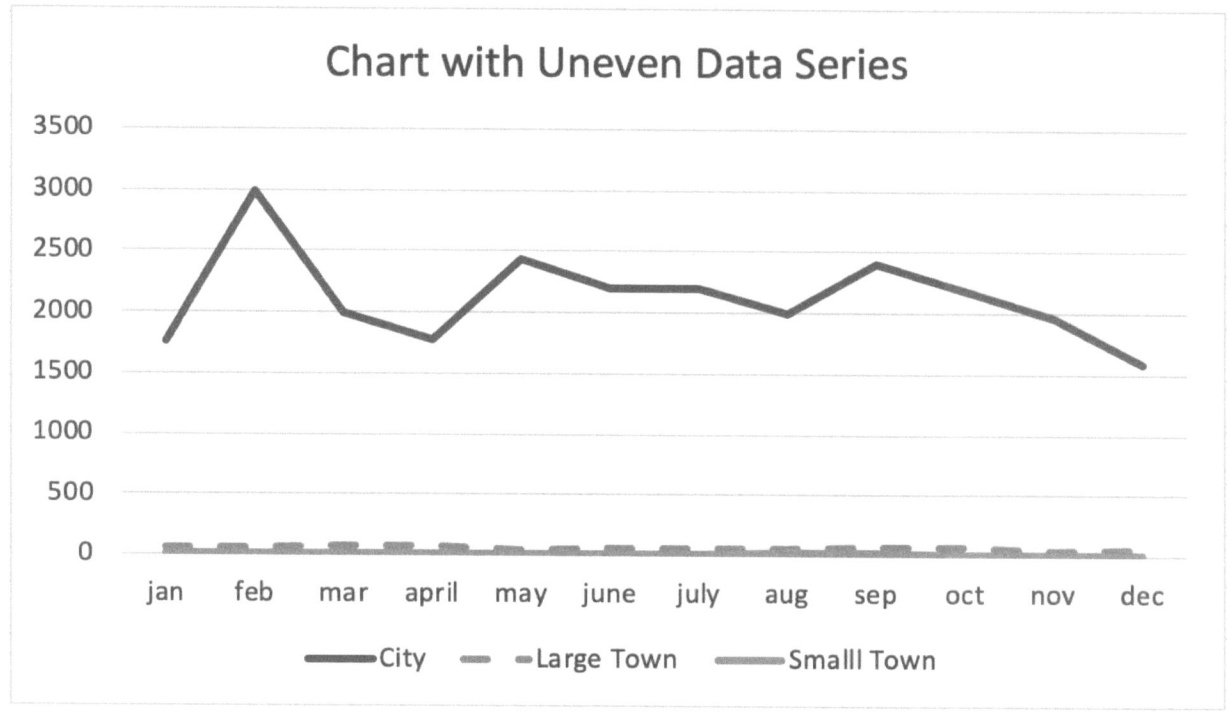

FIGURE 36 STANDARDIZING DATA SERIES TO FIRST VALUE

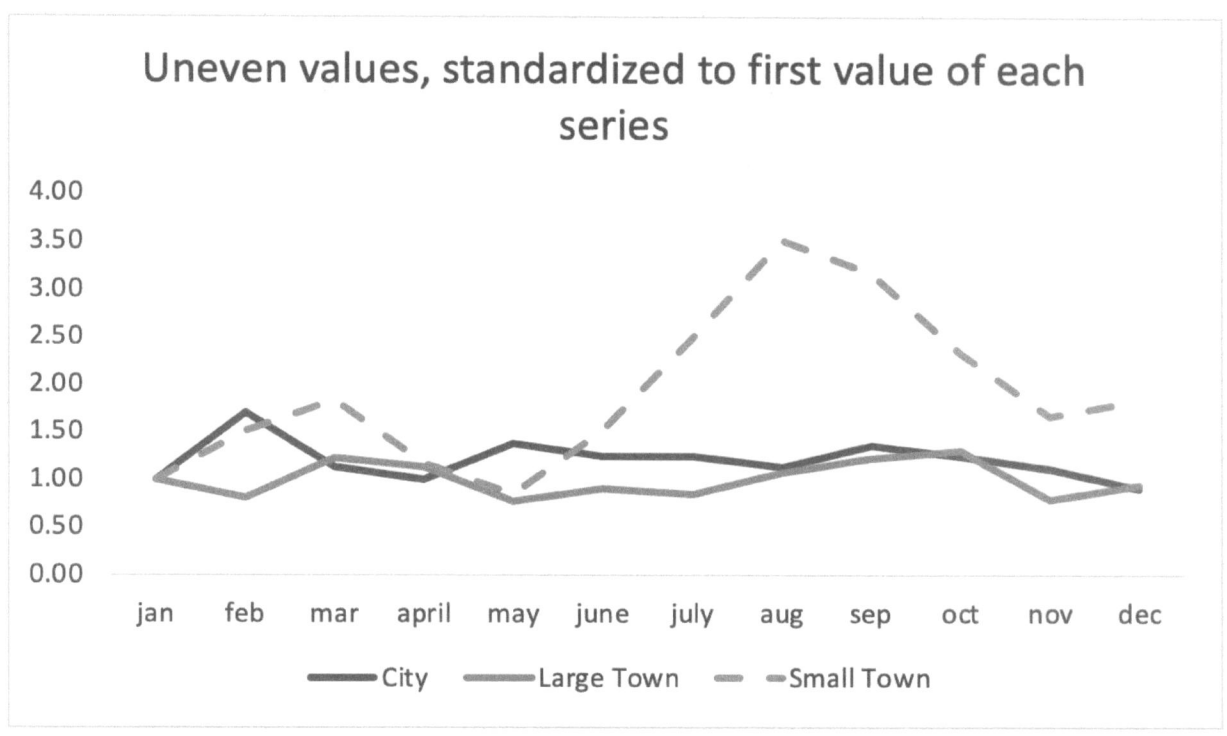

My favorite specialized chart: The radar chart

The radar chart is one of my favorite charts because it allows you to represent multiple measures in one chart. If you standardized the measures to a zero to 100 scale, you can show a past or current state of what is being observed along several dimensions. In the example below, we are showing multiple dimensions of happiness. The first chart shows an individual's rating of happiness on several dimensions prior to participation in a therapeutic program; the 2nd shows the ratings for the same individual following participation.

FIGURE 37 SAMPLE RADAR CHARTS

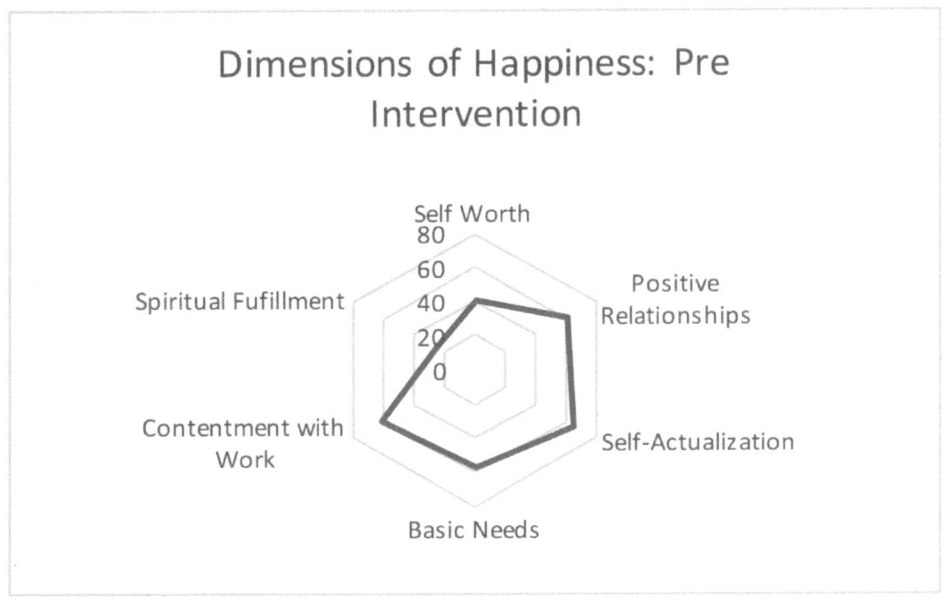

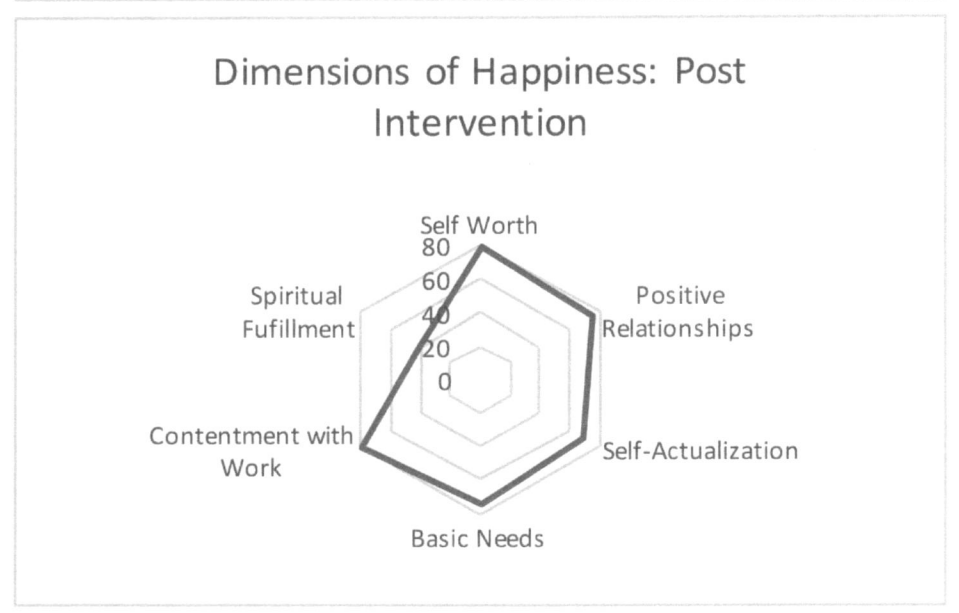

Tufte (and Galileo before him) recommends the use of small multiples (repeated use of simple charts or pictures over time). Radar charts can be used in this way as well. I have used radar charts to visualize the average health and well-being of youth, using the Center for Disease Control's Youth Risk Behavior Survey. The CDC reports the responses to multiple questions related to health and wellness, but does not aggregate them in any way. As a way of showing how a community is doing on achieving health and wellness of youth along multiple dimensions, I used the radar chart to show aggregate data for physical fitness, diet and nutrition, safety, substance abuse, mental health, and life engagement. I believe in this type of chart because we too often fixate on one dimension or another, and we don't step back to see how we are doing across dimensions.

Dashboards

Dashboards can be very helpful in providing a summary snapshot of the performance of a program or system. In Figure 38 below, I created a dashboard of population and system metrics of the Connecticut Juvenile Justice System. This kind of dashboard is useful because it shows the most recent available data, and trend data for multiple measures, so you can see where co-variation is occurring, and where something unforeseen may be driving differences in measures where you may expect to see covariation. An important aspect of a dashboard is the quick flagging of metrics that appear to be moving in the wrong direction (the yellow highlighting in the chart).

The dashboard on the next page is pretty information dense, which can be a good thing when you are providing a summary of an entire system or program... However, it would be too much to look at everyday or even every month. Other dashboards are much less dense, and highlight only the most important measures that might be examined on a daily, weekly, or monthly basis. For many programs this may come down to a few key things: customer flow, budget to actual expenditures, and expected outcomes. That being said, it is important to maintain a certain level of information density. Take advantage of the real estate that you have to work with...whether it is a page in hard copy report, or a webpage.

> *Schackziom Number 3:*
>
> **Information Density**
>
> **it is important to maintain a certain level of information density. Vast amounts of white space are a lost opportunity to include additional data that are relevant and allow the user to make different kinds of comparisons. that otherwise might not get made.**

FIGURE 38 COMPREHENSIVE DASHBOARD

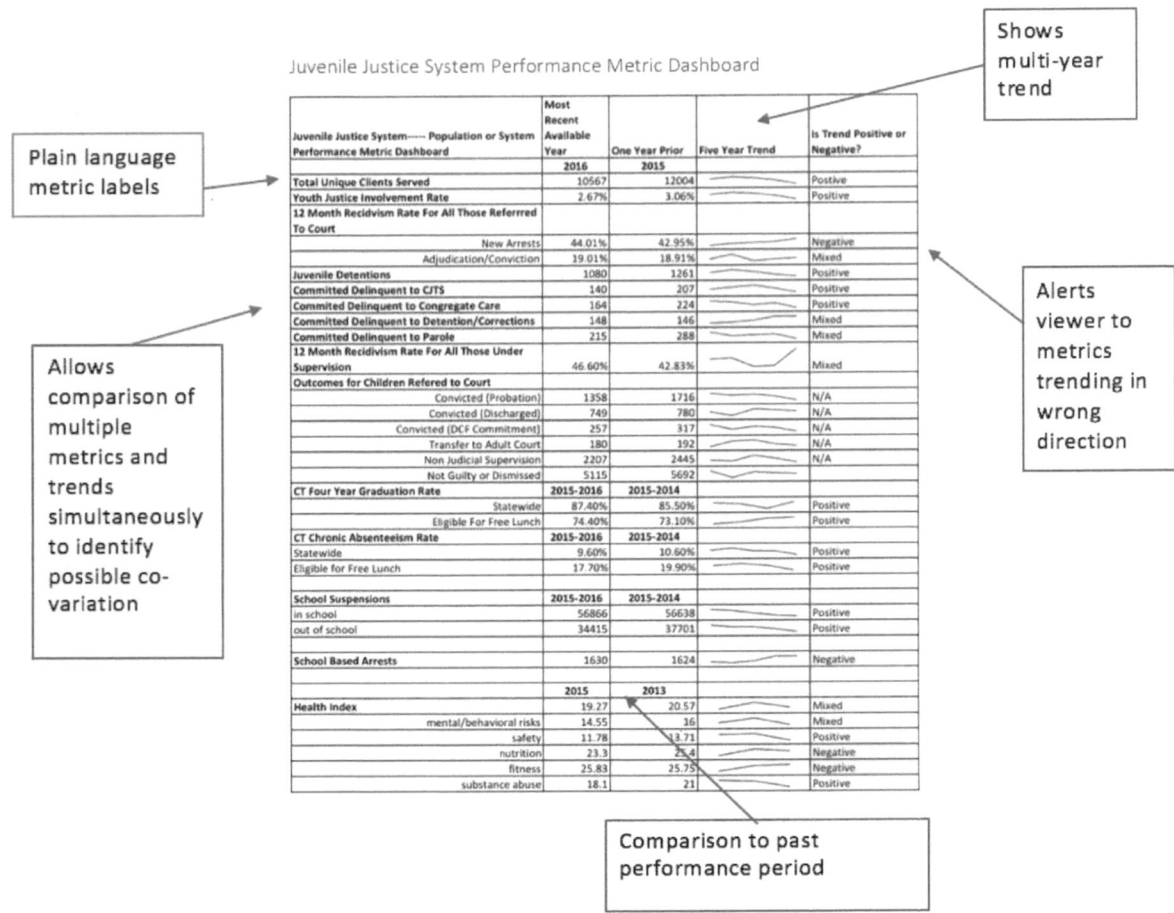

Sometimes you want to be able to quickly see which jurisdictions, sites, grantees, or providers are achieving their performance goals. Many report generation packages allow you to generate displays like the one in Figure 39. This example is from the USDOL Senior Community Employment Program (SCSEP). COG helped SCSEP develop this application, called Infospace. It was developed using SAP Business Objects. This example shows different sub-grantees for the state of Washington, and the percentage of their goal they achieved on their community service measure.

FIGURE 39 DASHBOARD HIGHLIGHTING % OF GOAL ACHIEVED

Period Type: YTD
Period Type: PY2016Final

Grantees	Num	Den	Rate	Goal	% Goal
1 AARP Foundation Programs	2,416	3,820	63.2	54.5	116.0
2 Alabama	34	68	50.0	42.0	119.0
3 Alaska	51	79	64.6	56.0	115.4
4 American Samoa	1	19	5.3	46.4	11.4
5 Arizona	12	43	27.9	43.5	64.1
6 Arkansas	21	45	46.7	47.1	99.2
7 Asociación Nacional Pro Personas Mayores	93	269	34.6	42.6	81.2
8 Associates for Training & Development	59	113	52.2	57.0	91.6
9 California	48	225	21.3	44.3	48.1
10 Colorado	15	36	41.7	49.9	83.6

Nationwide Rollups | **All Grantees** | All Grantees Over Time | Sub Grantees | Sub Grantees Over Time | National Grantees by S

Customer Flow

Customer flow can be depicted in many ways, depending on whether you are looking for something on a daily, weekly, or monthly basis, vs something that you may look at quarterly or annually.

The following is an example of how you could depict customer flow on a quarterly or annual basis. Notice it depicts, in sequence (from the first activity undertaken through exit from the program), the number of clients at each stage of the program, and shows how this differs from the previous year. It also depicts "client drop off" at each stage...from recruitment to eligibility determination, from assessment to service, and from service to completion and outcome.

FIGURE 40 CUSTOMER FLOW TABLE

Customer Flow Table	This Year	One Year Ago	Percent +/- from 1 Year Ago
Recruited	875	925	-5.4%
Determined Eligible	654	763	-14.3%
Assessed	610	715	-14.7%
Service Plan Developed	540	632	-14.6%
Received Service	534	625	-14.6%
Completed Program	490	510	-3.9%
Employed At Exit	376	416	-9.6%
Percent of Those Recrutied Determined Eligible	74.7%	82.5%	-9.5%
Percent Determined Eligible Assessed	93.3%	93.7%	-0.4%
Of those Assessed, % Plan Developed	88.5%	88.4%	0.1%
Of those with Plan, % Served	98.9%	98.9%	0.0%
of those with Plan, % Completing	91.8%	81.6%	12.5%
Of those Served, % Employed at Exit	70.4%	66.6%	5.7%

However, for a quick, more visual look at customer flow on a more frequent basis, you could do something like this

FIGURE 41 CONDENSED CUSTOMER FLOW DISPLAY

	This Month	Montly Target	% of Monthly Target Achieved	Year to Date	Year to Date Target	% of Year to Date Target Achieved	Annual Target	Projected Recruitment This Year	Monthy Trend
Recruited	31	25	124.0%	110	125	88%	300	264	
Served	80	75	106.7%	95	100	95%	275	250	

Outcomes Achieved	Number of Youth	Percent					Annual Target	% of Annual Target Achieved	
Youth wiith less than 3 missed school days	65	81.3%					85.0%	95.6%	
Youth with no disciplinary incidents	67	83.8%					85.0%	98.5%	

Notice that the above example provides the viewer with multiple comparisons…For the "recruited" and "served" measures, it provides a comparison of what the program did this month with its monthly target; what has been done year to date with where the program expected to be year to date, and how close the program is to its annual target. **Sparklines** are a useful feature in Excel that provide "mini-charts" for each of the measures. While not a fully realized trend chart, they provide a "sense" of the trend for comparative purposes.

Sometimes, a very simple graphic can serve to depict customer flow. Something like this could also be shown multiple times in a report, to remind the reader of the "service context" for another analysis being presented.

FIGURE 42 SUMMARY CUSTOMER FLOW DISPLAY

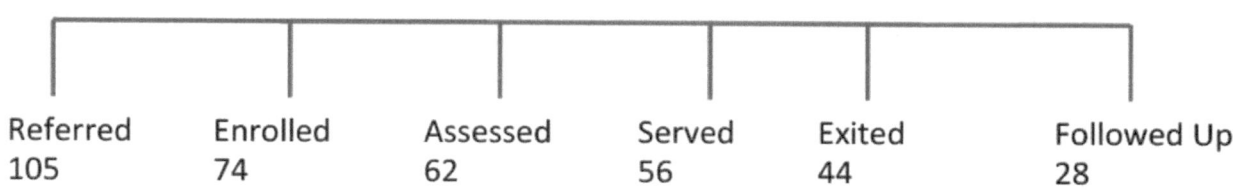

Customer Flow (Year to Date)

Referred	Enrolled	Assessed	Served	Exited	Followed Up
105	74	62	56	44	28

It is sometimes useful to create customer profiles—customer sub groups with specific characteristics that either a) occur frequently or b) have very different outcomes than other groups or the overall rate. Once these customer groups are identified, they can be consistently shown. Not only can you show how many customers fit these profiles, but also how their outcomes compare to the outcomes for all customers.

FIGURE 43 SAMPLE CUSTOMER PROFILES

	Total	Number Entering Employment	Percent Entering Employment
Younger (under 25) African American Males with no HS Diploma	80	20	25%
Older (over 25) Hispanic Females with Children	45	15	33%
Justice-Involved Veterans	10	5	50%
All Other Clients	95	44	46%
All Clients	230	84	37%

Below is another example from the SCSEP Infospace system, here, the outcome measure (in this case entered employment) is depicted for males (49.5% for PY 2015 final) and females (52.4%). These kind of reports can be generated in real time and linked directly to the production database.

FIGURE 44 SAMPLE CROSS TABULATION OF GENDER AND OUTCOME

Age At Enrollment	01. Male		02. Female	
	Count	Rate	Count	Rate
By Gender:	11	18.0%	37	22.6%
55 - 59	5	21.7%	15	21.7%
60 - 64	4	20.0%	14	29.2%
65 - 69	1	9.1%	6	17.6%
70 - 74	1	25.0%	2	25.0%
>= 75	0	0.0%	0	0.0%

The next page shows another version of a program performance dashboard, for internal management use. At a glance, it shows customer flow, budget to actual program expenditures, two important process measures (case management contacts and days absent from program), and a critical outcome measure.

FIGURE 45 SAMPLE PROGRAM PERFORMANCE DASHBOARD (INTERNAL USE)

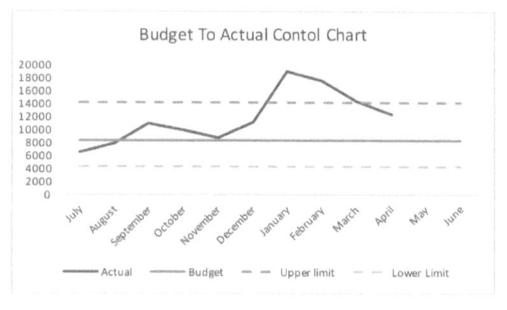

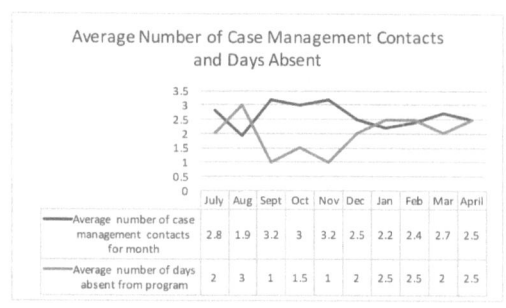

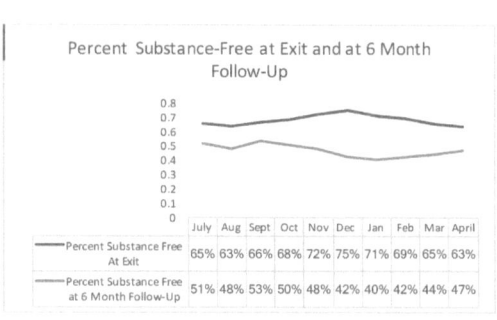

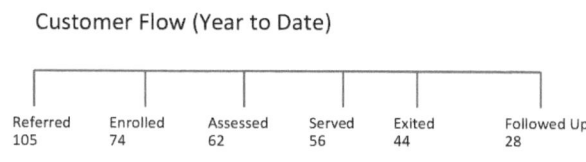

Population-Level Reports

At the community or population level, reports usually show population level indicators. They may include some system performance measurement information as well. The Charter Oak Group helped the Connecticut General Assembly apply Results-Based Accountability to the budget process over a 10- year span. If you go to the Connecticut General Assembly Appropriations committee website, you can see the evolution of the effort and the reports that were generated. Some of those reports are population- level reports, like the reports of the early childhood cabinet. Other are performance level reports. A related effort was the Children's report card, developed by the Children's Committee of the legislature and delivered on the web via the Result's Scorecard, a software package developed by Clear Impact to be consistent with the Results-Based Accountability framework.

Many of the population level indicators used in these reports can be compiled from the US Census, the Bureau of Labor Statistics, or the Center For Disease Control. Additional data may be available from state or local agencies. In many states, there are collaborative efforts to make these data available on-line. In Connecticut, the Connecticut Data Collaborative -- ctdata.org – has several large data sets from state agencies as well as some US Census and other data available.

Dealing with Small Cell Sizes

One of the issues that often comes up with population level data for smaller jurisdictions is the problem of small cell sizes. For surveys such as the American Community Survey (ACS), the annual sample sizes for small jurisdictions can be very small. One way of dealing with this is to use multi-year averages. In fact, the US Census will not release data for very small jurisdictions except as multi-year averages (due to privacy concerns).. The ACS has data for many variables available as 3 and 5 year averages. Even when not compiled for you, annual data for small jurisdictions can be "rolled up" into multi-year averages that are more stable and analyzable.

FIGURE 46 ROLLING MULTI -YEAR AVERAGES TO ADDRESS SMALL CELL SIZES

	2010	2011	2012	2013	2014	2015	2016	2017
Number recidivating	3	8	4	7	5	6	9	7
Number sent to JRB	7	14	9	11	8	11	15	13
Rolling 3 Year Rate			50.0%	55.9%	57.1%	60.0%	58.8%	56.4%

As Figure 46 shows, this approach can be used where the cell sizes for any one year are too small to be reliable. Instead, a "rolling" 3-year average is used. The cell size for 3 years of data is larger and more analyzable.

Here is a partial example of a population level report I developed for Move Up! --an adult literacy collaborative based in Hartford.

FIGURE 47 PART OF ADULT LITERACY DASHBOARD

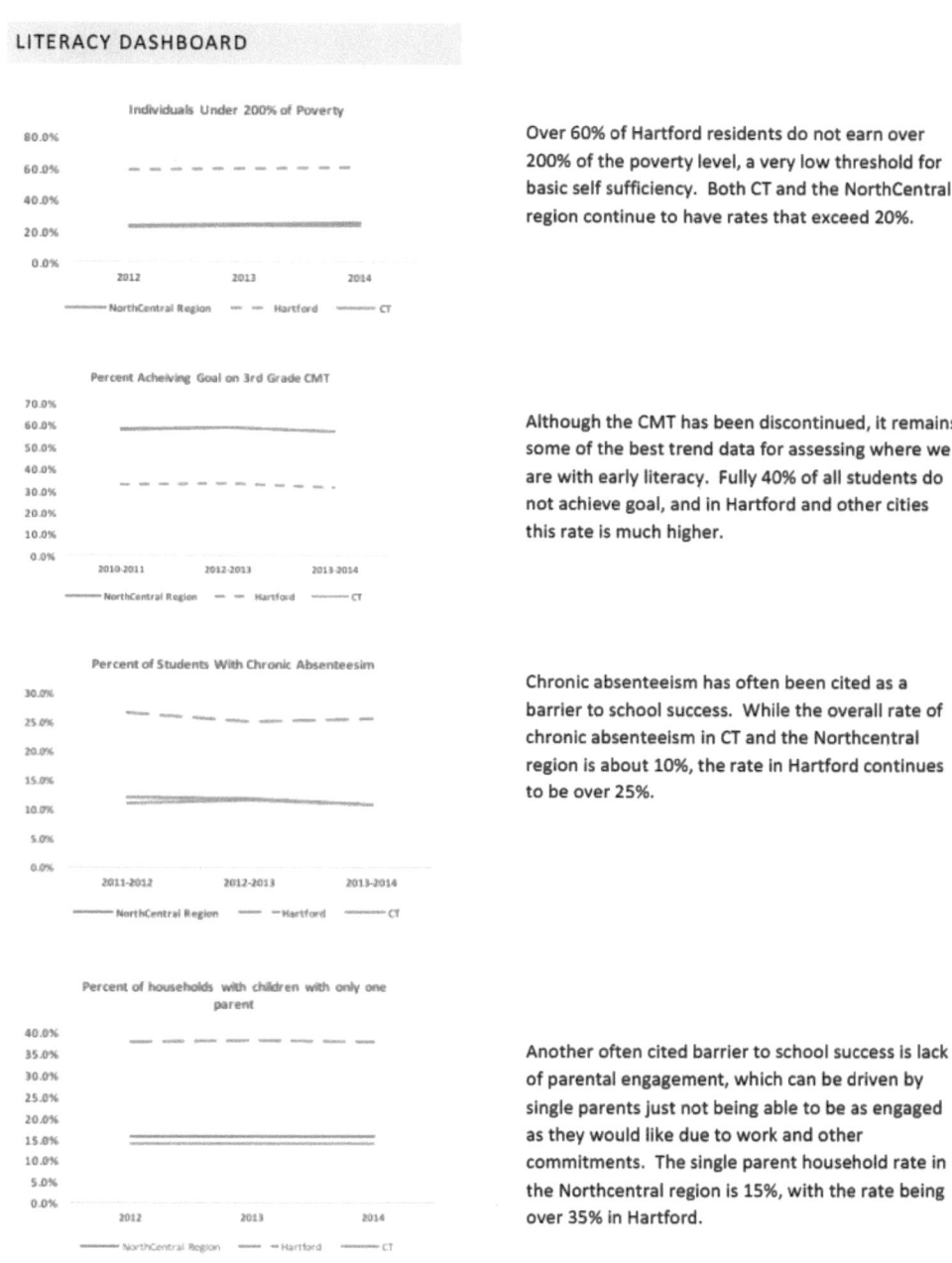

LITERACY DASHBOARD

Over 60% of Hartford residents do not earn over 200% of the poverty level, a very low threshold for basic self sufficiency. Both CT and the NorthCentral region continue to have rates that exceed 20%.

Although the CMT has been discontinued, it remains some of the best trend data for assessing where we are with early literacy. Fully 40% of all students do not achieve goal, and in Hartford and other cities this rate is much higher.

Chronic absenteeism has often been cited as a barrier to school success. While the overall rate of chronic absenteeism in CT and the Northcentral region is about 10%, the rate in Hartford continues to be over 25%.

Another often cited barrier to school success is lack of parental engagement, which can be driven by single parents just not being able to be as engaged as they would like due to work and other commitments. The single parent household rate in the Northcentral region is 15%, with the rate being over 35% in Hartford.

Please note that the four indicators shown show the overall trend, and include a brief narrative that highlights what is called "the story behind the baseline" in RBA terms. Notice the level of information is much more "macro" than the more detailed customer flow and customer characteristic tables shown earlier. This report was later "web-enabled" using Tableau, an on-line report generator that is easy to use and can be used to build fairly-complex and elaborate data narratives.

Telling Complex Data Narratives

There are several relatively new on-line tools for creating presentations. We are all familiar with PowerPoint, which despite its flaws continues to be used because of its availability and general ease of use. We are also familiar with how hideous PowerPoint presentations can be, ranging from having almost no content (lots of pictures and one "thought nugget" per slide, to each slide having 10 or more bullet points with lots of text in a small font, which can be read by no one. When well executed, power point presentations can be effective, but there are real creative and structural limitations to what PowerPoint can do (at least easily).

Prezi and Tableau are two on-line tools that are much more flexible, and allow you to use a "storyboard" approach for your complex data narratives. A "storyboard" approach allows you to develop an appropriate sequence that leads the audience through variations of the following components;

1. the purpose of the analysis, and essential context for the analysis
2. analytic design and data sources used
3. basic descriptive information (macro to micro)
4. essential comparisons (including hypothesis tests)
5. any integrated modeling
6. findings and recommendations

Tableau is great if you want to build a story that includes multiple data displays quickly. You can import data from an excel spreadsheet and multiple other sources. Tableau has a great engine for creating all different kinds of data displays, and these displays can be put into a format they call a "story."

Here is an example of charts done in tableau that are part of a whole series on adult literacy. Together they form a story. A weblink can be created so that people can access them on-line.

FIGURE 48 SAMPLE WEB-ENABLED TABLEAU CHART

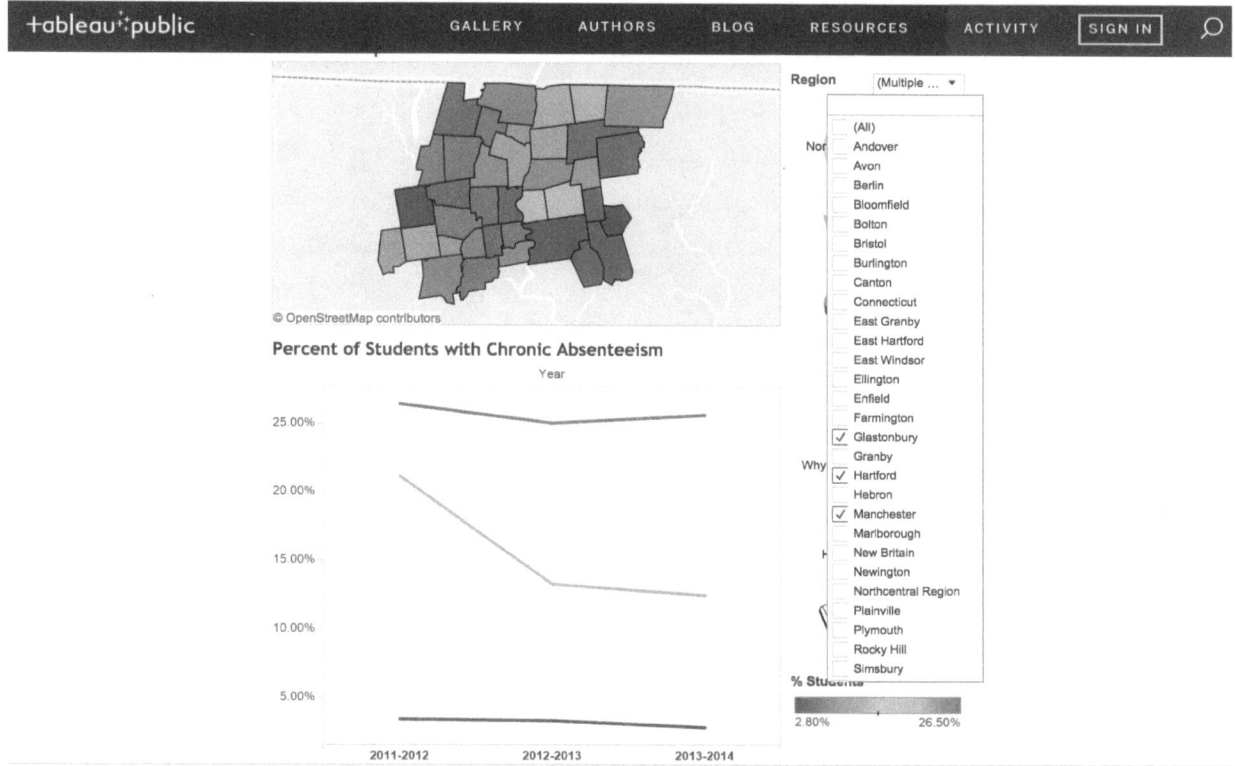

FIGURE 49 ANOTHER TABLEAU CHART

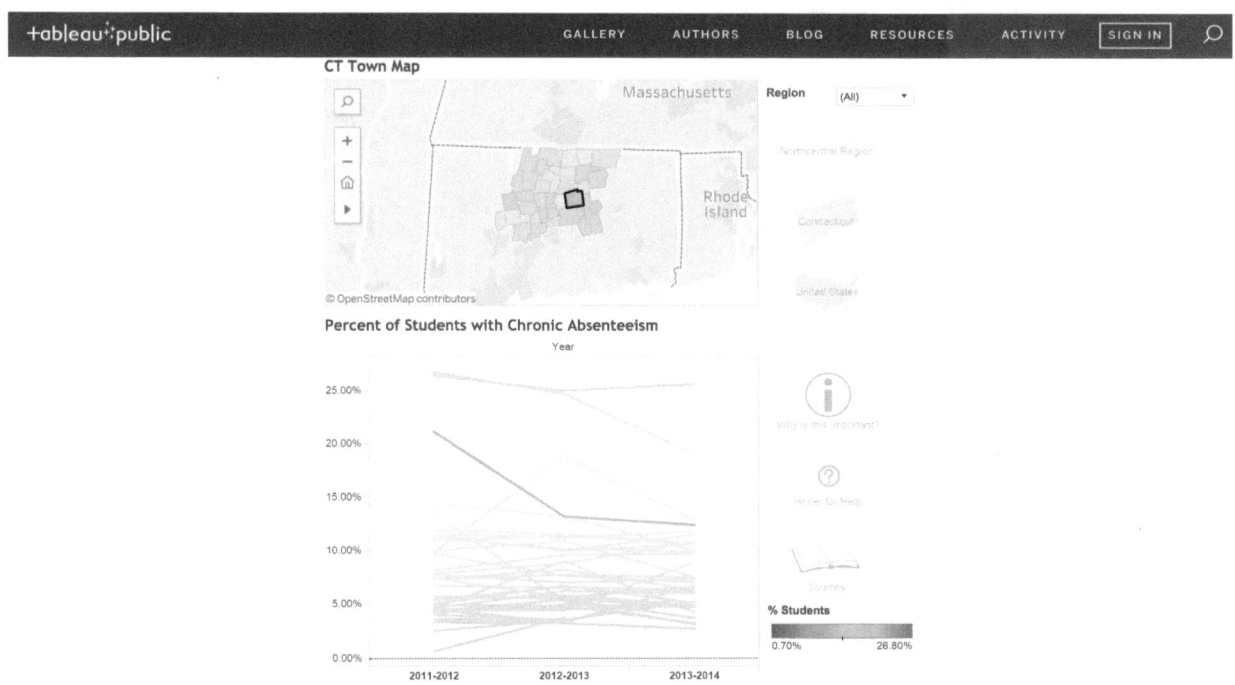

With this chart, the user can click on the individual town on the map, and view the trend for that town. The user can also compare a town's rate with the state and national rate as well, or to the rates of similar towns.

Prezi is another tool I use for telling complex data narratives. It works like powerpoint, but you can move from slide to slide and from section to section in very interesting ways, and you can animate the entire presentation in a much more compelling way than Powerpoint allows you to do. While I can't really demonstrate the animation, follow the link in the footnote to see what I mean.

Prezi always starts with an overview or "portal" page where you can access the other pages in the presentation. [37] The overview slide is very useful as a summary of what is being shared, and how the topics are related. From this slide you can move to content slides, which, again can be connected in an organic way from the overview slide rather than simply sequentially like Powerpoint.

Like Powerpoint, the slide can combine text, tables, charts, pictures, etc. To conclude: for me, the key to successfully telling a complex data narrative is in the **sequencing** of the information, and **providing the appropriate context** for the data being presented.

A cautionary note on the story telling approach. The story telling/story board approach, which can be very powerful and compelling, is probably not the way to think about all performance reporting. ***Sometimes you are not sure of the story y*et.** Routine performance reports support analysis that develops INTO a story. Sometimes you have to look at data that may be relevant but do not turn out to be central to the story. Sometimes the disaggregation of data show some interesting differences; sometimes not so much. But you need to look at all potentially relevant data before you boil the findings down to a "story." Don't jump the gun. However, once you have a story to tell, the storyboard approach can be a powerful way to tell it.

---

[37]   Please check out the following link to see the above mentioned presentation "live" to get a better sense of how Prezi can be useful. https://prezi.com/view/g8wWQ4r61lzabxm3NXUr/

7

DECISIONS, DECISIONS....

....“If you choose not to decide, you still have made a choice”.... Rush, *“Freewill”*

“Facts are stubborn things.”....John Adams

Important Decision Concepts

Data analysis and data reporting are only useful if they help inform decision making. Sometimes we data scientists speak and act as if an analysis or report is an end in itself... that there is some virtue in doing it even if we stop there, and do not use it. But deep down, we all know that if an analysis or report is not used, it is of no utility (hmmm...that is sort of like saying if I don't drink this juice, it hasn't been drunk... but you know what I mean).

There are many reasons for conducting analyses or presenting data. The easiest one to get out of the way is the regulatory or statutory requirement... I owe much of my work to such requirements. I have participated on workgroups that helped operationalize measurement requirements for federal programs, such as the Workforce Investment Act (WIA-now WIOA). I have helped develop entire performance management systems for federal programs, such as the Senior Community Service Employment Program, and for entire systems, such as the Connecticut Juvenile Justice System. Usually, these requirements are intended to hold jurisdictions or grantees accountable for the program dollars provided to them. Even though these are program requirements, and that is why I am hired to support the effort, the requirements are intended to support underlying decisions, such as the decision to continue funding the program, or decisions related to expansion, replication, or management of a program.

Another reason to do data analysis is to help support decisions related to changing programs or policies. Data analysis supporting program evaluation helps answer the question, “would participants in this program have succeeded without the presence of the program?" Data analysis related to changing policies answer questions like, "how much will we save by implementing this policy change?" Or, "how will program performance change if this policy or process change is implemented?"

Sometimes, data analysis is done to diagnose performance problems, or to identify what services or customer characteristics are most highly associated with successful outcomes. Clearly, this kind of analysis can inform possible decisions to emphasize certain services, or to change the service structure to better deal with customers with certain characteristics or risk factors.

Many of the above reasons for analysis are not always articulated as decisions, but they support decisions nonetheless. When you think about them as decisions, and think about the analyses you do as supporting decisions, it is important

> **Schackziom Number 4: Dr. Schack's Pantheon of Glorious Decision Therorists**
>
> **Herbert Simon: Satisficing**
>
> **Charles Lindlbom: Successive Limited Comparisons**
>
> **Daniel Kahneman, Amos Tversky and Paul Slovic: Decisions Under Uncertainty: Heuristics and Biases**
>
> **Egon Brunswik: The Lens Model and Ecological Validity**
>
> **Cohen, March and Olsen: Garbage Can Model**
>
> **John Boyd: OODA Loop**
>
> **Sun Tzu: The Art of War**

to remember some of the basic things we know about decision making. I am including these important decision concepts because I have found that this is one area that many data scientists have not had exposure to, and they can be very helpful in grounding our work in good theory.

One of the most important concepts is **satisficing**, first described by Herbert Simon, the Noble prize winning economist and public administration scholar.[38] Simon compares satisficing with a "rational comprehensive" approach to decision making, where the analyst/decision maker tries to gather information about all possible dimensions of a problem and all possible solutions. However, as Simon points out, for complex problems (and even most simple ones), this is a fool's errand. It just takes too long and too many resources, and you still may miss something. This condition Simon calls "bounded rationality." So instead, you try to assemble data on the dimensions that matter the most, and the solutions that are most feasible, and that is usually good enough. This process Simon calls *satisficing*. ***In the real-world of decision making, satisficing is the only approach that is practical.***

Early on in my graduate academic studies I happened upon work by Kahneman, Tversky, and Slovic.[39] Their work on decision heuristics has been very useful to me as a data analyst, both to remember as

---

[38]   Simon, Herbert A., (1947). <u>Administrative Behavior</u>, New York, Macmillan.

[39]   Kahneman, Tversky, and Slovic, (1977). Judgment Under Uncertainty: Heuristics and Biases, New York.

I am doing the analysis, but also to remember as I present the data to decision makers. Kahneman, et al. identified decision heuristics, such as anchoring, availability and adjustment, as rules of thumb that people use when confronted with uncertainty and incomplete information.

People routinely use the **Representativeness** heuristic, in which "probabilities are evaluated by the degree to which A is representative of B, that is, by the degree to which A resembles B." This causes insensitivity to the prior probability of outcomes, insensitivity to issues of sample size, and even leads to misconceptions of chance. Kahneman, Tversky, and Slovic provide the example of someone who is given a description of a company and is asked to predict its future profit. If the description of the company is very favorable, a very high profit will appear most representative of that description; if the description is mediocre, a mediocre performance will appear most representative. If people predict solely in terms of the favorableness of the description, their predictions will be insensitive to the reliability of the evidence and to the expected accuracy of the prediction.

Availability refers to people assessing the frequency or class of an event by the ease with which the instances or occurences can be brought to mind. For example, one may assess the risk of diabetes among over-weight people by recalling such occurrences among one's acquaintances. This leads to biases due to the retrieveability of instances, the effectiveness of the approach used to identify alternatives, and by the degree to which contingencies can be imagined. I find analysts are not immune here…the variables they choose for their models are often the ones that are easily retrieved, or the ones they have used in prior analysis.

Adjustment and Anchoring refers to making estimates by starting from an initial value that is adjusted to yield the final answer. Bias is introduced because different starting points yield different estimates, which are biased toward the initial value.

With only a little imagination, we can see how these heuristics come into play in the analysis process, and the presentation and use of the results of analysis.

As we develop analytic designs, we often rely on how THIS analysis resembles some OTHER analysis we have done. This can lead us to develop the analytic approach before we have fully considered the questions to be answered. As suggested by the profit prediction example, our analytic predictions may be influenced by some descriptive component of the problem, even if the numbers say different.

We can also imagine how we may tend to include variables in our analysis that we use frequently, and/or for which we can readily get data, sometimes omitting variables that we may have to think harder about, or that we haven't seen used in prior analysis. Of course, we all can relate to anchoring….we rarely drift far from our first approximations….even when significant adjustment is called for after the receipt of new information.

Another important concept, related to anchoring, is Lindblom's concept of **successive limited comparisons**. Lindblom wrote about this in the context of budget development, in a famous article called "The Science of Muddling Through,"[40] showing that most budgeting is not "zero-based," but is based upon what was done the previous budget period. Successive, limited examination of options based upon what was done in the prior period anchors the analysis. ***This allows for very complex budgets to be updated in a manageable way, but also substantially limits budget discussions.***

Let's try a little thought experiment. Imagine being a state legislator sitting on the legislative Appropriations committee. You are a part time legislator, who is a real estate agent when not doing legislative stuff. You just spent the fall running for re-election, and you focused on selling a few properties to have money for a good holiday season. The new legislative session has just begun and the governor has just released his proposed budget. This budget is roughly a 3 billion budget, that is broken into a little under 50 separate agency budgets. You have approximately 3 weeks to review the budget before budget hearings begin….

No way, right? Not if you were going to try and deconstruct each budget, understanding the reason for each funded program, whether the program was achieving the expected outcomes, and try to understand each proposed change. Lindblom's point is that instead of trying to do that, we essentially assume the history of each agency budget as a given, and look to make small adjustments at the margins. We anchor our decisions in our past spending history; the decisions we make are limited to small adjustments to each line item. Using this model we are much less likely to eliminate line items or programs completely.

When my business partners and I were working with the CT General Assembly to apply performance measurement to the budget process, this was one of our biggest challenges. Think about it. First, *how do you develop performance data for each program within each of 44 agencies*? We are talking about hundreds of programs here. How does a legislator find the time to look at all that performance data? How does the appropriations committee, which holds 30 minute to 1 hour long budget hearings for each agency, consider performance information during the hearing and in subsequent "work sessions?"

While we never discovered the ultimate answers, we did develop some promising approaches, including a "program report card" format that gave legislators the important performance information they

---

[40] Lindblom, Charles E., The Science of Muddling Through Public Administration Review, Vol. 19, No. 2 (Spring, 1959), pp. 79-88

needed to make decisions about continuing to fund programs. Using RBA's seven performance question approach[41], COG (together with the Office of Fiscal Analysis, the Connecticut legislatures non-partisan budget office) developed a process where prior to a budget hearing legislators would be briefed on the program report cards that were developed, and would have questions prepared that related to those report cards. Agency staff were told to be prepared to answer the seven basic questions (and one additional question) for any of the programs discussed at the hearings. These eight questions were:

1) To what quality of life result(s) does program contribute?
2) What are the performance measures you use to determine how well the program in operating?
3) What performance measures do you use to determine whether anyone is better off?
4) How are is the program doing on the most important of these measures?
5) What role do (or can) partners play in improving on these measures?
6) What are some of the actions that can be taken to improve on those measures?
7) What do you propose to do (include recommendations for low cost or no cost solutions) and...
8) If program funding needs to be reduced, what actions can be taken for ensuring the program maintains the current level of service to the public.

The key aspect to all of this is that only some programs were examined in detail. Each agency was asked to prepare program report cards for two or three programs. Sometimes the Appropriations sub-committee was interested in a particular program, and that program was designated as one of the programs that required a report card. Other times, when there was no such designation, the agency chose which programs to report on.

The first year this approach was tried, the report cards varied considerably in quality. As time went on the report cards improved, especially if an agency "bought in" to RBA and used the approach internally. Examples of these included the CT Judicial Branch, Court Support Services Division, the CT State Department of Education, and the CT Department of Families and Children [there may be others, these are the agencies I have had significant interaction with regarding RBA]. Some of the other agencies treated the request for report cards as a compliance exercise, and were less successful. The CT General Assembly Appropriations committee website has an RBA page that contains links to many of the report cards submitted over the course of this project.[42]

Another decision concept that has helped me over the years is one developed by one of the most influential modern American military thinkers, John Boyd. Boyd, who was air force fighter pilot,

---

[41] See Friedman, Mark (2005), "Trying Hard Is't Good Enough," Sante Fe, Trafford Press.

[42] www.cga.ct.gov/apps

developed a decision process model called the O-O-D-A loop. Understanding the OODA loop can inform how and when you present your data.

FIGURE 50 OODA LOOP

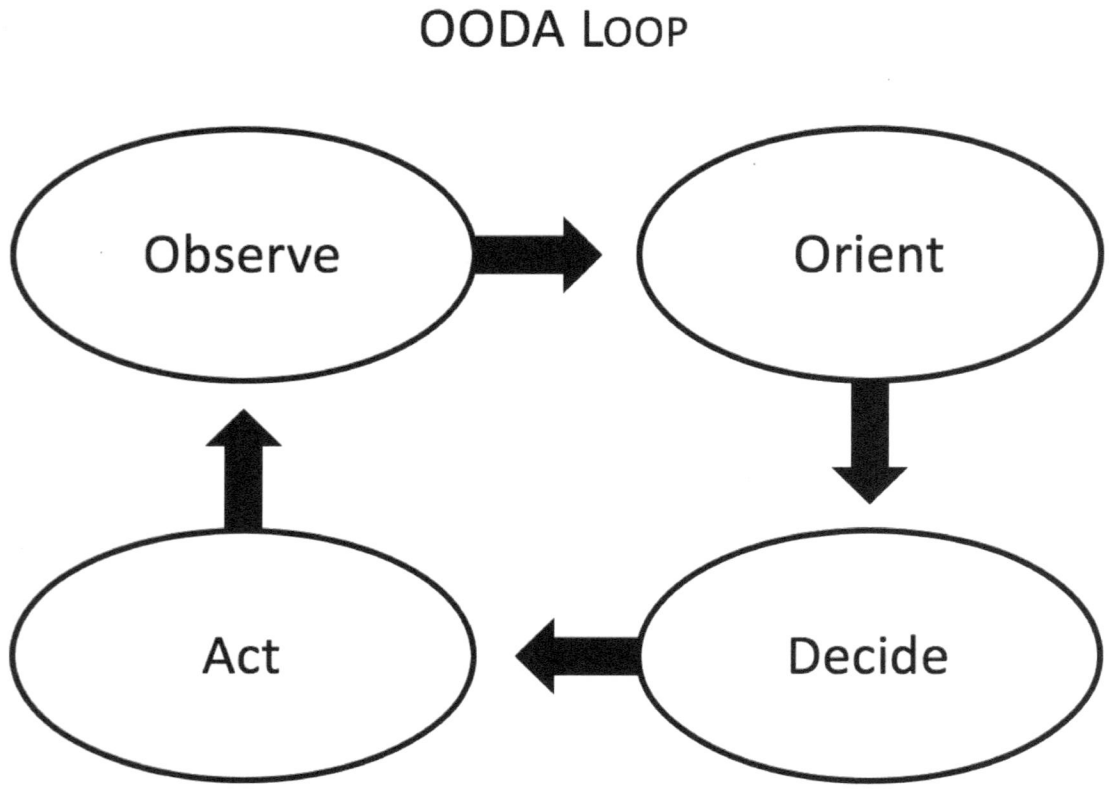

OODA LOOP

Boyd emphasized that decision making usually is an aggregation of many OODA decision cycles. He emphasized the importance of the "ORIENT" stage of the cycle, and that orientation is not a single-instance stage, but a more iterative stage of calibration and adjustment. In the military context, Boyd emphasized getting "inside" an opponent's "decision" cycle…both by anticipating what he is going to do, but also by doing unexpected things, and deciding and acting quicker than he can. I believe these concepts can inform our work as data scientists, especially when we think of the data and processes we use to 'orient' ourselves and our data users. I also think this can inform the way we use information to help us adapt, and to help us innovate.

Another four-letter process, the Plan-Do-Check-Act cycle of Walter Shewart (as elaborated by W. Edward Deming, who preferred Plan-Do-Study-Act)[43] and Joseph Juran, is the primary way in which process and policy changes should be developed, tested, and improved.

FIGURE 51 SHEWART CYCLE

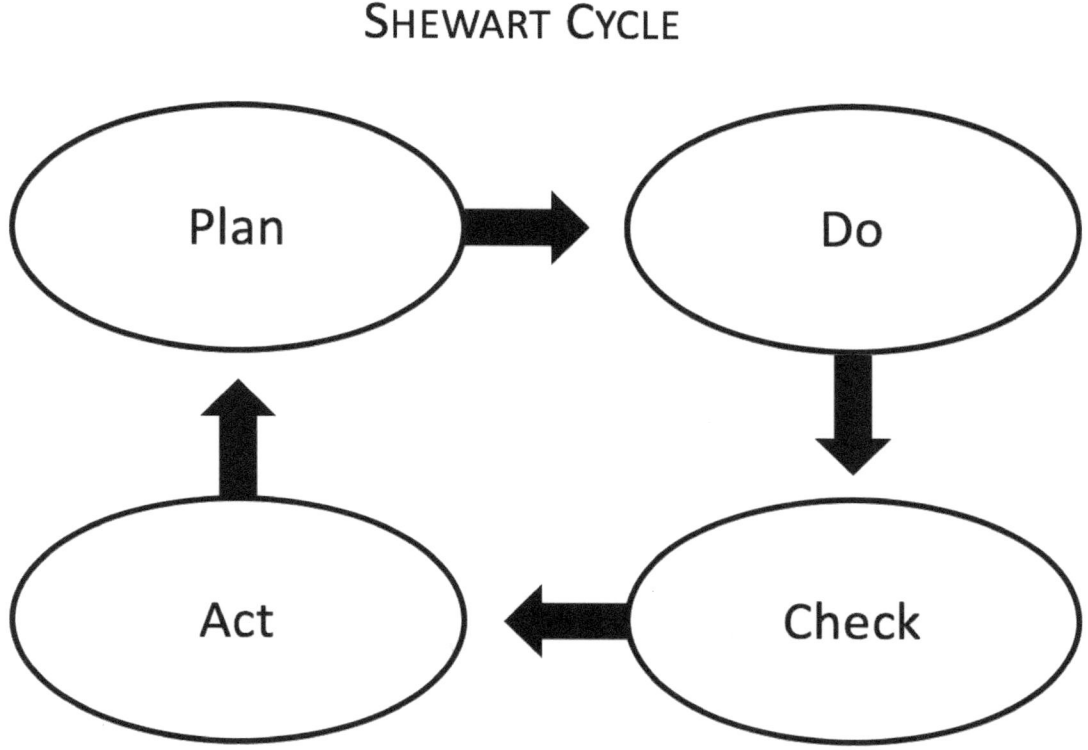

SHEWART CYCLE

The "plan" stage represents either the initial development of a process or policy component, or the initial response to feedback that a process or policy is not working. "Do" represents either the initial implementation of a process or policy component, or the implementation of a "fix" developed after feedback. "Check" means just that..checking to see whether the approach worked. What is sometimes missed here is that measurement can and should be used as part of the "check" process. Finally, "Act" represents determining whether additional action should be taken (that is, planning another change), and initiating that process. **This process is iterative, and on-going, and should never be considered "complete."**

---

[43]   See Moen, Ronald "Foundation and History of the PDSA Cycle" for a fascinating account of the evolution of this tool. From Shewart to Deming to Ishikawa to Deming...fun stuff.

Another one of my annual reads is Egon Brunswik's writing on perception.[44] Egon Brunswik was a cognitive psychologist who wrote in the 1940's and early 1950s, before he sadly committed suicide. Besides having a name that conjures images of a deranged lab assistant enjoying a game of bowling, Dr. Brunswik has been very influential in the realm of decision theory and judgment. Egon developed the Len's Model, which describes the very attenuated way information used to make decisions makes it to our brain for processing. Brunswik also developed the concept of ecological validity. He emphasized the need capture the effect of the environment or context within which a phenomenon is being observed.

FIGURE 52 BRUNSWIK'S LENS MODEL

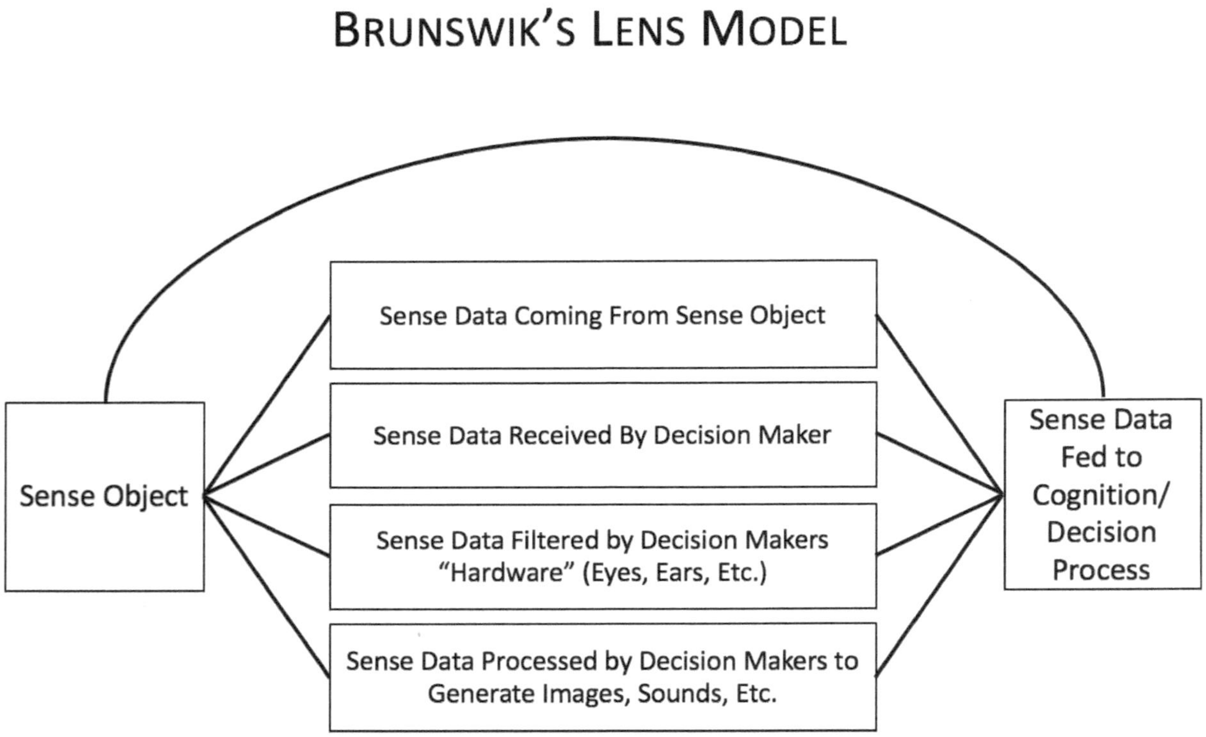

BRUNSWIK'S LENS MODEL

I like Brunswik's model[45] because it reminds me of the long metaphysical philosophical tradition, from Plato's Parable of The Cave to Kant's *Ding Un Sitch* (thing in itself), where "real" objects, unknowable directly, emanate sense data that we can apprehend and utilize. It reminds us how attenuated our sense of the universe is, and reminds us that the data we hold so dear are only some dim reflection of reality.

---

44 Brunswik, Egon (1956). Perception and The Representative Design of Psychological Experiments, Berkeley and Los Angeles, University of California Press.

45 Please note that the depiction of the model in Figure 54 is not a traditional presentation of the model. I created this version because I think it is a bit easier to understand than the model as traditionally presented.

For emergencies (and trips to the beach) I have what they call in special operations a "bug-out" bag... In this bag, together with sun screen, a parafoil kite, binoculars, and a yo-yo is the only book in the bag, Sun-Tzu's *The Art of War. Sun Tzu* has a lot of very interesting things to say about information, analysis, and decision making:

"The victorious military is first victorious and after that does battle. The defeated military first does battle and after that seeks victory."

Here Sun-Tzu is emphasizing the importance of planning, and assessing the situation, and being ready. We need to remind clients of the value-added of the information we provide to the planning process, and make sure we are involved throughout planning process, not just the initial stages of it.

"Knowing the other and knowing oneself, In one hundred battles no danger. Not knowing the other and knowing oneself, One victory for one loss. Not knowing the other and not knowing oneself, In every battle certain defeat."

Here Sun-Tzu is arguing that knowledge protects one from danger; the general must know both himself and the other, and his environment. As data scientists, we have a crucial role to play in providing that knowledge.

"Foreknowledge cannot be grasped from ghosts and spirits, cannot be inferred from events; cannot be projected from calculation. It must be grasped from people's knowledge."

Sun-Tzu reminds us that one can be sure of the future only through knowledge that is immediate, concrete, and detailed. It's best source is direct perception (human intelligence). This is important for us, as analysts, to remember. Our predictive models, trend analyses, and fancy data presentations can only bring the decision maker so far, and sometimes more immediate facts or circumstances will (appropriately or not) be given more weight in the decision process.

> **Schackziom Number 5:**
>
> Cross-functional or multi-partner workteams often begin with what seems like a systematic decision process that gets abandoned as time goes on, relying instead on a loose *"preponderance of opinion"* that leads to resentment, an artificial reduction in the number of options considered, and an ultimate choice which may be somewhat workable but far from optimal or even satisfactory.

Group Decision Processes

I have done a lot of work with community collaboratives over the years, as well as with policy groups that involve multiple state agencies working together at a system-level. Decisions emanating from these collaboratives or multi-state agency working groups are different than those coming from a single organization; even if the collaboratives have chair-people, these chairs often do not have any real, additional decision power than the other members of the group. There is an approach to making decisions in this context called "decision conferencing," which I have successfully used to facilitate group decision making.[46] The most important part of decision conferencing is that the real decision makers need to be in the room[47]…otherwise whatever decision comes from the group can be overturned by the "real" decision maker. The decision-making group should include everyone who should be a party to the decision. The problem (whatever the decision-making group is trying to decide) then needs to be modeled. I have often used a multi-attribute utility model, or similar model, for this purpose.[48] This usually means articulating the decision problem, and identifying the possible alternatives to be considered and selected. Then each alternative is evaluated using a mutually agreed upon set of factors. Each factor is then weighted in terms of its importance. Then each alternative is scored on each of the factors. Each person in the group can vote, both on the importance of the criteria as well as the score of each alterative on each factor. If the group are in the same room, wireless "clickers" can be used so they can cast their votes. The results of the voting can be projected onto a screen.[49] Sometimes it is good to do this in phases…First have the group rate the importance of each factor, and then have the group score each of the alternatives on each factor]. The group can see which alternative got the highest total number of points, which got the highest score on each factor, and which got the highest average score across factors. The cost of each alternative can also be estimated, and the scores of each alterative can be assessed in terms of score vs. cost.

---

[46] Phillips, L. D. (1989) 'People-centered group decision support'. In G. Doukidis, F. Land, & G. Miller (Eds.), *Knowledge-based Management Support Systems,* Ellis Horwood, Chichester.

[47] Moore, Allen B. and Feldt, James A., (1993). Facilitating Community and Decision-Making Groups. Malabar, FL, Krieger Publishing.

[48] MAU models are just one of many models that can be used in decision support and group decision specifically. See Baird, Bruce. (1989). Managerial Decisions Under Uncertainty: An Introduction to the Analysis of Decision Making. Wiley and Sons: New York. I highlight this approach because I have found it to be applicable in many situations.

[49] This process can also be executed using a video or internet conference format.

FIGURE 53 EXAMPLE OF MULTI-ATTRIBUTE UTILITY MODEL

	Cost	Durability (% of Ideal)	Weighted Score	Authenticity (% of ideal)	Weighted Score	Handling (% of Ideal)	Weighed Score	Aesthetics (% of Ideal)	Weighted Score
Weights		1		0.75		0.75		0.5	
Longsword A	380	60	60	50	37.5	60	45	90	45
Longsword B	350	75	75	80	60	60	45	50	25
Longsword C	450	75	75	75	56.25	75	56.25	60	30
Longsword D	150	50	50	50	37.5	40	30	90	45

	Weighted Total	Cost / Weighted Score	Rank Based on Overall Score	Rank Based on Cost / Score	Average Rank
Longsword A	187.5	2.03	3	3	3
Longsword B	205	1.71	2	2	2
Longsword C	217.5	2.07	1	4	2.5
Longsword D	162.5	0.92	4	1	2.5

Figure 53 above is an example of a multi-attribute utility model. I used something I love, longswords, as an example. As you can see, there are four possible longsword choices. The four factors on which they are rated are durability, authenticity, handling, and aesthetics. My sword user-group rated each alternative on each factor. They also rated the importance of each factor, with durability being the most important, authenticity and handling 75% as important as durability, and aesthetics as half as important as durability. The ratings across factors are totaled. Cost, of course, is also a consideration. You can create a cost divided by the weighted score variable as well. Then you can rank the alternatives by both overall score and cost/weighted score, and average the ranks. As you can see, Longsword B had the highest average rank, while Longsword C had the highest overall score and Longsword D had the highest cost/weighted score. The decision would probably go to Longsword B.

There are software packages, such as **Hi-View** and **Equity** developed by the London School of Economics[50], that are designed to help you build these models on the fly in a decision conference, but I have able to do this just using Microsoft Excel. This kind of process can generate considerable buy-in from the participants, and it can be much easier to reach consensus. From a consulting perspective, there is some, but a reasonable amount, of pre-work involved. You need to arrange for a room, a laptop, the LCD projector, and the wireless clickers. You need to create an articulation of the decision problem, a list of possible alternatives, and a list of possible factors that can be validated with the group. If doing this as a web conference, you need to arrange for the web conference capacity and make sure all of your files and related documents are displayable and work correctly.

---

[50]   See http://www.catalyzeconsulting.com/software/equity3/

I strongly recommend considering this type of decision conference approach for your multi-agency workgroups and collaboratives. While workgroups often "get there" in the end, in my experience they often begin a process with a systematic approach and abandon it as time goes on, relying on a loose "preponderance of opinion" to dominate the decision process. This "preponderance of opinion" can often be a reflection of "groupthink"[51] This often leads to resentment, an artificial reduction in the number of options considered, and an ultimate choice which may be workable but may not be even close to optimal. Decision conferencing can also be used within organizations, especially when important decisions requiring the buy-in of multiple department or unit heads are being made. In this context, it is important for the head of the organization to be there, but should agree to a) adhere to the decision that develops out of the process, and b) to act as just another participant in the process and not try to influence with process through the exercise of power. Sometimes organizational leaders cannot agree to operate this way, and it is better to conduct the decision conference without their attendance. In these cases, the leader should 1) agree to consider the output of the decision conference, and 2) if the ultimate decision is not consistent with the decision conference outcome the leader should be prepared to adequately explain the reasons for the final decision.

Integration of These Decision Theories

While I do not offer one unified decision approach here, I do advocate internalizing the insight these theories provide. Taken together, they offer a deep understanding of the nature of individual and organizational decisions, the limitations inherent in human decision processes, and the importance of embedding this understanding into the way we think of our data analyses and how we present data in support of decisions.

Chapter 8 is devoted to another important concept, first identified by Cohen, March, and Olsen, in their decision article, "The Garbage Can Model of Organizational Choice." …

---

[51]   Janis, Irving L. (1982). *Groupthink: psychological studies of policy decisions and fiascoes.* Boston: Houghton Mifflin

8

SOLUTIONS IN SEARCH OF PROBLEMS....

The Chinese ideograph for "Crisis" is a combination of the symbols for "danger" and "opportunity"...*chew on that for a* while....:-)

Cohen, March and Olsen developed a theory of organizational choice called, "The Garbage Can Model of Organizational Choice."[52] Other than being a colorful metaphor, the model IS useful because it describes the many inputs into the organizational decision process (the garbage can): resources; personal, unit, departmental and organizational agendas; problem interpretations; and my favorite, solutions in search of problems. These solutions are offered up by one or more

> **Schackziom Number 6.**
>
> **Fully diagnose a problem before rushing to implement a solution. Look carefully at solutions that involve information technology, training or marketing, particularly when they are proposed before a problem has been diagnosed.**

sponsors in an organization, and it often seems as if they are offered no matter what the problem is...that the sponsor(s) are more concerned with implementing the solution than with solving whatever problem is being discussed. The problem becomes a means to an end, the end being the implementation of a *favored solution*. I have observed this phenomenon many times over my career. As problems are diagnosed, there are some types of solutions that tend to be "offered up" even before the problem diagnosis is complete. Certain kinds of information technology, training, and marketing solutions often fall into this category.

Information Technology Solutions

In our high-tech, application driven age information technology solutions can be the great panacea. If a process isn't efficient, it should be computerized! If a computer software being utilized has deficiencies, it should be replaced, often with a customized solution! This is something to be particularly wary of. Software packages that are supposed to be off the shelf, but that are sold with ability to be customized,

---

[52]   Cohen, March, and Olsen (1972) Administrative Science Quarterly, Volume 17, No.1 Pages 1-25.

can result in serious cost escalation problems. Time and again I have seen organizations spend thousands of unanticipated dollars on customization, sometimes to get applications to do things that one would think they should do already, like generate basic reports. As data scientists, we have to be particularly concerned that these solutions come with the ability to create useful data extracts and reports. Often, however, it is unclear that these information technology solutions are really what is needed. It is critical that organizations complete the diagnosis of a problem before an IT solution is contemplated. It may be that the relevant current IT application works just fine, or can be adjusted slightly without the often considerable expense of replacing it. Or, the problem may not require an IT solution at all; a change in policy or practice may be the appropriate solution.

A relatively recent version of this problem is the excitement generated by the suggestion that "we should build an app," often one that can be used on a portable smart device. And there is a lot of room for innovation in this area. It is very "hip" to include the development of a smart device app in many grant proposals. But the same logic still applies: Does the problem we are trying to address really call for an "app?" or is the perceived need to seem current and innovative driving the development decision rather than the true diagnosis of the problem?

At the risk of being truly sacrilegious, I believe that even artificial intelligence or machine learning solutions can fall into this category. It is very tempting, once you are exploring machine learning tools, to cast about looking for new problems to apply them to. By all means do so. But, don't automatically think "machine learning" whenever a problem is encountered. There are many analysis problems that do not require that kind of heavy hitting diagnostic…and still others for which we simply do not have enough training data to utilize these approaches in a valid way. And similar to the "app" craze, we are now in the "bot" craze, where artificial intelligence applications (in miniature, often referred to as "robots" or "bots") are now being applied to a myriad of problems. While there is nothing wrong with this when it is appropriate, I suspect there are many such efforts that are 50 pound solutions to 10 pound problems.

Training Solutions

When organizational outcomes are not being achieved, or staff not behaving as expected, often the first solution offered is "staff training." "If staff were better trained they would know how to do this." However, like IT solutions, sometimes staff training is not at all what is needed. Perhaps, instead, they need a closer or different kind of supervision. Perhaps they need a different policy or practice to implement. Or a different kind of data report or analysis to guide their decisions? Even when training seemed appropriate, I have seen too many training efforts that are too generic, or lack actionable elements that participants can take back to work and implement.

Marketing or "Awareness Building" Solutions

I often consult to community collaboratives that are trying to achieve better quality of life results for their communities. Rather than focus on improving the services that are provided in the communities, these collaborative sometimes focus on marketing or "awareness building" solutions. "If our residents knew about the services we have available, more of them would use these services and better outcomes would be achieved." First, use and good outcomes are two different things, which these collaboratives often confuse. Second, with limited resources it is unlikely that "building awareness" is going to have much leverage to improve these results. Instead, actionable, real improvements should be developed and implemented.

Reorganization

This solution is really a "hail-mary" play.….organizations that are in serious trouble often contemplate reorganization. But, as Elliot Jacques pointed out, often reorganization is implemented as way to *appear* to do something drastic while not changing the underlying set of policies, practices, and processes very much, if at all. If reorganization is truly needed, the reorganization needs to "get at" the underlying polices, processes and institutional norms that have led to the organizational problems in the first place. Simply consolidating a few departments, renaming some units, or otherwise "rearranging deck chairs on the Titanic" will not do the trick. Any pervasive dysfunction has to be removed, and that requires leadership, culture change, and data driven improvement strategies. Reorganization should be the LAST thing considered, rather being thought of as an easy fix.

It is usually easy to recognize a symbolic rather than actual reorganization… for a reorganization to be real, the actual structure and flow of work in an organization has to change. Sometimes when you look beneath the veneer of a reorganization, all that has happened is that the same units and departments have been relabeled, and a few managers have swapped jobs. This is not a reorganization, but it might play one on TV ☺.

9

THAT'S IT! WE'LL BLAME EVERYTHING ON POVERTY!

Three Diagnostic Domains: Policies and Process, Customer Characteristics and Environment

People love excuses. And poverty is a big one: If a program is not achieving its expected outcome, if a community is not achieving a quality of life result that it is looking for, very often people point to continued poverty as the reason for a lack of success. While there is often some truth to this, over emphasizing it can create problems. If performance problems are due to poverty, and the program (or the community) is not ready to tackle "bringing an end to poverty," this reduces the ability of the group (whether it is a problem-solving team for a program or a community collaborative) to transcend this issue and think of other things that might help (or even think of incremental steps that can begin to address the poverty issue).

> **Schackziom Number 7:**
>
> **When diagnosing performance problems, make sure you think of three important domains:**
>
> ✓ **Policies and Process**
> ✓ **Customer Characteristics**
> ✓ **Environmental Factors**

One important approach in analyzing performance is to think of three core diagnostic domains: policy/process, customer/client or population characteristics, and the environment. This allows you to "group" potential causes for performance problems by these three domains, and think beyond any one of them. Causes related to poverty can be spread across all three of the domains, but there will be other, non-poverty related causes that can be identified as well. Including process is very important, because staff tend NOT to believe that their process is the problem...yet it could be, or it could be one of several causes that should be explored. Sometimes simple things like ensuring participants receive reminder texts for their next appointment, or changing a policy related to when a child is referred to court after a school-related incident, can be critical to improving performance on related outcome measures.

Policies and Process

When I first started working as a performance analyst, Total Quality Management (TQM) was still very popular. TQM arose out of the efforts of American industry to catch up with Japan's manufacturing processes. Since the 50s, American engineers like W. Edwards Deming and Joseph Juran helped Japanese companies become more efficient, and ensure the production of quality products. When American industry was foundering in the late 70s and early 80s, these "elder statesmen of quality control" brought these techniques back to the US and helped American industry transform their processes. TQM had many different dimensions and emphasized a lot

> ***Schackziom Number 8:***
>
> *Process mapping is a great way to:*
>
> *1) gain an understanding of the processes used in a program;*
> *2) identifying important decision/transition points which are good opportunities or measurement, and*
> *3) identify parts of the process that no longer make sense or could be made more efficient*

of different things, including using data to improve processes. TQM also emphasized working in teams. TQM had several team-oriented diagnostic tools, such as force-field analysis, cause and effect (or fishbone, or Ishikawa) diagramming, interrelationship di-graphing, and process mapping.[53] I still advocate the use of these tools when diagnosing performance problems, even though they are not as "new" or "innovative" as they seemed when TQM was first introduced. One of these tools, process mapping is a great way to:

1) gain an understanding of the processes used in a program;
2) identifying important decision/transition points which are good opportunities or measurement, and
3) identify parts of the process that no longer make sense or could be made more efficient.

Process mapping can be used to think through possible factors affecting performance...it is a process for thinking about process ☺.

---

[53]   Check out Brassard, Michael and Ritter, Diane. (1994). The Memory Jogger II. Methuen, MA, Goal /QPC. for a succinct, solid explanation of these tools.

FIGURE 54 SAMPLE PROCESS MAP

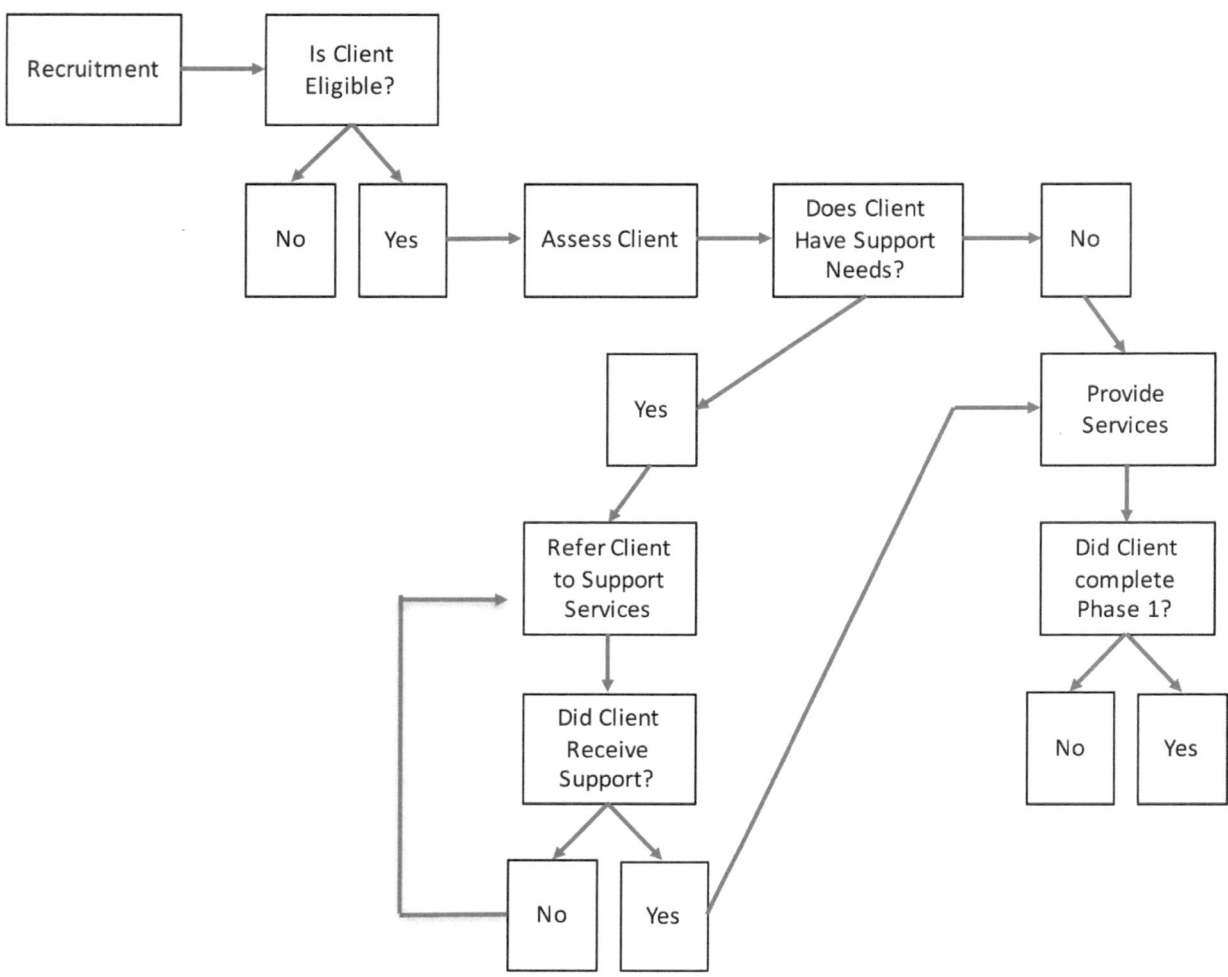

If you look at the sample process map above (Figure 54). You can see how each decision or transition point suggests an important measurement point. For example, the transition from recruitment to eligibility determination can be measured as the % of those recruited that were determined eligible. The following table shows each transition/decision point in the diagram and a possible process measure:

FIGURE 55 MEASURES DEVELOPED FROM PROCESS MAP

Transition / Decision	Possible Measure
Recruitment-Eligibility	% of those recruited that were determined eligible
Eligibility-Assessment	% of those determined eligible that were assessed
Assessment-Support Needed?	% of those assessed requiring support services
Support Needs-Referred For Support Services?	% of those requiring support needs that were referred for support services
Referral For Support Services- Services Provided?	% of those referred to support services that receive support services
Assessment-Services Provided	% of those assessed that receive program services
Services-Completion	% of those receiving services that complete Phase 1 of program

There is an obvious pattern here. I am not suggesting that all of these measures are necessary or equally important, but they are all potentially important and are easily identified through process mapping.

Customer Characteristics

The second key diagnostic domain relates to customer characteristics. It is almost always true that programs work better for some kinds of customers than others.[54] This can be due to many different factors related to the customers themselves. They may not be ready for a program (academically, emotionally, behaviorally, or family-status wise) and/or they may have one or more risk factors (homelessness, disability, substance abuse, teen pregnancy, justice involvement, school dropout, literacy or numeracy problems, PTSD, ADHD, the list goes on and on). Disaggregating performance data by key customer characteristics can help you identify which risk factors are held by a high percentage of customers, and which may be associated with significant differences on key outcomes. It can also help you design programming that addresses these risk factors. This can be done by creating new, targeted programming or by implementing design changes into the core programming.

This process of disaggregation can be tricky. It is possible to disaggregate outcome data by gender (for example) and not find a real difference. You can also disaggregate the data by ethnicity and see no difference, but when you look at the outcome data by ethnicity and gender, you might find that Hispanic females have very different rates than non-Hispanic males. So it is important to look

---

[54] See Pawson, Ray (2006). Evidence-based Policy: A Realist Perspective. Sage Publications, Thousand Oaks, CA.

at multiple variables and multiple levels of disaggregation to get better understand the relationship between these customer characteristics and outcomes.

Ultimately, you can develop customer profiles, where customers with the combination of characteristics that most affect outcomes are grouped together. These profiles can be tracked over time (especially pre-post intervention) and reported in performance reports to help sustain attention to the groups that have lower performance levels. (Please see Chapter 6).

Economic and Environmental Factors

Even when a program is well conceived and implemented, and works well for the customers it serves, program outcomes can be affected by factors outside control of the program, unrelated to customer characteristics. Economic factors, like a recession occurring, or a large employer closing in the community can have a serious impact on the effectiveness of a program. Environmental factors can have a similar impact. The occurrence and aftermath of a natural disaster, or the urban decay associated with the systematic loss of key industries, or issues like the poisoning of a community's drinking water, or the loss of irrigation water to a drought…all can affect the effectiveness of a program. Other factors, like the lack of available transportation or medical care, can also have an impact. These environmental factors are often overlooked when diagnosing performance problems, and when creating data models that represent the interaction of outcomes, services, and participants. Brunswik's work on representative design and ecological validity can be informative here; Brunswik emphasized the need to sample environments as well as participants to better understand the effect of environmental differences on outcomes.

As suggested in the last chapter, diagnosing performance problems needs to begin with an examination of the data that establishes the problem, rather than ANY potential solution that may ultimately be considered.

Whatever performance framework you may be utilizing, establishing that a problem actually exists should be the first step…there is nothing worse than working on a non-existent problem! Once that is established then you move to diagnosing the problem, using the three big categories of possible that I have suggested as a starting point…once you have diagnosed the problem, then move to looking into possible solutions.

10

OPERATIONALIZING, COLLECTING, AND ACCESSING DATA

"Data, data, data, I cannot make bricks without clay." Sherlock Holmes (as portrayed by Robert Downey, Jr.).

"The plural of anecdote is data…"…Anonymous

We data scientists love data. And it is sweet when we have data handed to us…data that have been previously collected, with nicely defined data elements in a nicely accessible database. Unfortunately, life doesn't always work that way. Sometimes the data we want

> **Schackziom Number 9**
>
> **You can't report data that do not exist.**

are out there, but there is no easy way to access those data. Sometimes data from multiple sources, with different data elements and formats, need to be integrated before we can do our analysis. And sometimes the data do not exist. In all my years as a data scientist, I have never seen anyone successfully and truthfully report data that do not exist. Sometimes people will speak as if that is possible, but I guarantee it is not. Because this is true, as data scientists we are often asked to develop data collection approaches to get the data that are needed. This may be the development of a survey process, or the development of "case management" software that includes the collection of quantitative data on clients, such as gender, age, race, ethnicity, education, income, services provided, and outcomes achieved.

Operationalizing Data Elements and Measures

In developing these data collection approaches it is necessary "operationalize" the data elements that will be collected. This means clearly defining what each data element is, what type of data element it is (nominal, categorical, scale, or continuous), and what the possible values are for that data element. Having an easy to understand and use data dictionary for any such data collection system is critical

121

(and often missing). Take the time to create one. You will save yourself and others a great deal of time and effort. Data elements are often collected not so they can be reported in isolation, but because they are part of a performance metric that will be calculated. Again, performance metrics need to be operationalized. A classic example is an entered employment rate for those participating in a vocational training program. How might that be calculated? Do you only count those who complete the program in the denominator of the measure? Do you only count those that have a certain number of days of employment? Do you count temporary jobs? When do you check to see whether someone has become employed? How do you check? With the participant? With the employer? Using unemployment insurance wage records? Do you count participants that entered employment prior to completion? What do you do about participants that drop out early in the program? Do you include them in the denominator? Does it matter why they dropped out? Another good example is the many different possible ways to operationalize recidivism measures…is recidivism (for programs intended to prevent further justice involvement) measured as any re-arrest since program participation? Or is it counted only for a re-adjudication or re-conviction?. Do you count it at 6 months from program participation? 12 months? 24 months? Do you use the date of enrollment to start counting? Or the exit date of the program? From these examples, and many others, you can see how critical it is to be clear about how specific measures are operationalized.

It is usually straightforward to operationalize data elements and performance measures. For data elements, you need to define the following:

1) Name of the data element
2) The width (number of characters or digits of the data element and the number of decimal places
3) The type of data element: string, numeric, comma, dot, date, scientific notation, currency, restricted integer (an integer with leading zeros)
4) The kind of measures (nominal, ordinal, or scale)
5) Actual question used to collect data element…e.g., what is your date of birth?
6) Acceptable values for the data element (e.g., month-day-year..mm-dd-yyyy)
7) Any issues with collection or interpretation

A Note on Excel Spreadsheets

Excel spreadsheets are everywhere, and can be very useful in a myriad of ways. Excel is often the first software organizations use to collect data on their customers and the services they provide. Structured correctly, with appropriately specified data fields and appropriate edits, drop down menus, and security, they can be fairly robust and provide relatively clean data for analysis. However, this is often NOT done very well, if at all, and can lead to serious data problems.

The most common problem with using an excel spreadsheet for data collection is that the data fields are not specified correctly, or consistently. If a column is created for race, for example, and there are no drop downs for the race categories, you can end up with a column that has multiple labels for the same thing (e.g., white AND Caucasian, or Black AND African-American). This makes analyzing the data challenging. Worse, you can end up with labels like (Black Hispanic, or Black Male), even when you have other columns for ethnicity and gender. This can be very difficult to analyze when you want to get separate counts for race, ethnicity and gender categories. Another area where this is problematic is when you do not pre-specify names for services—you can get all kinds of values in service fields that are not consistent. All of these problems are multiplied with basic spelling and other data entry errors.

Another common problem is that date fields are not created correctly...if you leave a date field free form it can be input inconsistently and end up as a string variable, which can be challenging to convert to a real date for analysis. Having a field called age is also problematic, unless specified correctly... like age (in years, at time of enrollment)..because staff can interpret "age" in lots of different ways.

Another spreadsheet nightmare is when the same spreadsheet is distributed to several different service sites for data entry purposes. Any data element specifications or edit issues will be multiplied by the number of sites where data entry is occurring. This leads to nightmares when you try to combine the data across sites.

A fundamental database concept is the concept of "one to many" relationships...where one record, for an individual, needs to be matched to many records...for example, services. Generally, you need a unique identifier for the individual, and the same identifier attached to each service record for that individual. Then analysis software, like SPSS, can create aggregate variables for each type of service provided to each individual. This is only doable with the unique identifier. Having multiple records for the individual (such as the same name and participant characteristics listed more than once in a table) can create problems when you try to match them to multiple service transactions. It is important to de-duplicate the individual records first.

Figure 56 sample data dictionary (partial)

#	Element Name	Common Definition	Data Field	Allowable Values
1	First Name	Participant's legal first name	Text	
2	Middle Name	Participant's middle name or initial	Text	
3	Last Name	Participant's legal last name	Text	
4	Date of Birth	Participant's date of birth	Date	MMDDYYYY
5	Social Security Number	Participant's social security number	Text	9 characters
6	Gender	Participant's gender identity	List	Female Male Other identify preference/Prefer to self-identify Prefer to not self-identify
7	Hispanic or Latino	Participant identifies as Hispanic or Latino ethnicity	Y/N	Yes (Hispanic or Latino) No (Not Hispanic or Latino)
8	Race	Participant's race identity	List	African-American or Black American Indian or Alaska Native Asian Caucasian or White Multi-racial Native Hawaiian or Other Pacific Islander Other
9	Street Address	Participant's street address of residence (number, street,	Text	
10	Zip Code	Participant's zip code of residence (generates city and state)	Text	5 characters
11	Email	Participant's email address	Text	
12	Home Phone Number	Participant's home phone number	Numeric	10 characters
13	Cell Phone Number	Participant's cell phone number	Numeric	10 characters

For performance measures, you should define the following:

1. Name of the measure
2. How the measures is calculated…what data elements (and their source(s)) are used for the numerator and denominator, are there any other elements to the calculation
3. Is the measure a snapshot in time or does it compare time periods
4. What kind of measure is it…how much, how well, or better off (in RBA terms; or you can use input, output, process, outcome)
5. How often is it reported (periodicity)
6. Any issues with collection or interpretation
7. Any source for benchmark information (comparisons from "like" jurisdictions or "like" programs)

Integrating Data From Multiple Sources

Many times data scientists need to integrate data from multiple sources in order to conduct an analysis. ***Unfortunately, it is almost never true that two data sources have data elements that are defined exactly the same way.*** These data sources may also be in different formats. One could be a relational database, another could be an excel workbook with multiple tabs, another could be a flat .csv file. Our job as data scientists is to overcome these obstacles and integrate the data for analysis. There are multiple ways of doing this. There are now software solutions called "middleware" that draw from each of the individual data sources and create an integrated set of data. These are very useful, and if an organization or collaborative has enough resources, and the information need is important enough, then I would advocate the pursuit of such a solution. However, if the data integration problem is for a one-time, ad-hoc analysis (or if the organization lacks the resources for a more elaborate solution), I would advocate a different approach...bringing the data sources down to the lowest common denominator. It is usually fairly straightforward to create flat-file data extracts out of relational databases; If you can do this for each data source, you can then integrate the flat files from the relational database, the multiple excel sheets, and the isolated .csv file using something like SAS or SPSS. These software packages have tools that help you with any conversion issues you might have (like data elements that are defined somewhat differently). *While not as elegant as a data warehouse or middleware solution, this approach has served me well over the years as more elaborate approaches collapsed of their own weight.* I am not saying this is the best solution—some of the middleware approaches that are being developed now are very flexible and effective...but I am saying that such data integration can be done in the absence of higher-tech solutions.

I am currently working with a collaborative that is developing a middleware solution to integrate youth data from multiple providers that have multiple systems for multiple programs. I am serving as a "validator" in this process, using the low-tech approach above to validate the results of middleware aggregation process. This reminds me of the old story about Paul Bunyon with his Ox, Blue, competing against a steam driven logging machine. In the end Bunyon loses, but demonstrates the great capacity of the individual...in my case, I will also lose...but in doing so I will have validated the middleware approach and everyone will be more confident in the middleware results. Since I am doing this work prior to the data being integrated using the middleware, I can also identify issues and challenges that I can share with the middleware developers.

Sample -Based Data Collection

Sometimes the volume of data is so large that it is impractical to use all of the data available (especially if it has not been previously collected and digitized). In such cases, a sample based approach can be used. The most ubiquitous examples of this are sample surveys: surveys that ask about people's opinions, product preferences, potential voting behavior, or experience and satisfaction with a product or service. We will get into survey research considerations later in this chapter.

It is important to remember, however, that surveys are not the only kind of sample based data collection. Program participant records can be sampled for adherence to an evidence-based practice; court records can be sampled to determine outcomes of cases where an eyewitness identified the perpetrator; Medical records can be sampled to determine patterns of care. In order to do this kind of data collection, you need access to the records. You need at least a rough estimate of the number of records from which you are sampling. At that point, you can determine the number of records you need to sample. You also need to create a protocol for examining the records you are sampling.

Lot Quality Assurance (LQAS)

Sometimes we are looking to determine whether or not the group of things we are measuring is "OK" or not. We are trying to make a simple thumbs up or thumbs down decision regarding a sample that we are examining. LQAS[55] is a methodology that allows for the use of very small samples to make such judgments. It was developed by industry as a quick way to determine whether a whole sample, or lot, of a product met a basic criteria. It is important to note that LQAS will not provide much detail or precision, because as soon as you add more variables to your data collection scheme you are moving away from the assumptions of LQAS. If you want more precision or more detail, typically larger sample sizes are usually required. HOWEVER, the approach can be very useful when you are you are looking at a single yes/no question, and you want to quickly determine whether the whole group of records you are sampling from is or is not in a certain state. This approach is now often used in the public health policy arena to quickly determine whether a certain condition exists using a relative small sample.[56]

Survey Research

I have designed, administered, analyzed and reported a lot of survey data over the years. Most of data were collected using paper surveys, data entered or scanned into Excel or SPSS and then analyzed. Some were telephone surveys, others utilized internet survey tools like Qualtrics or Survey Monkey. Survey-based data collection approaches are a key tool in the data scientist tool kit. Like I have said about other topics, this book is not a book about survey research, and I will not attempt to treat this topic in a comprehensive fashion. However, there are some things I have learned about survey approaches that I would like to share.

Convenience samples can be okay.

A "convenience" sample is a sample that does not conform to the requirements of a systematic random sample, but it may be the best that can be done at the time. For example, you may collect surveys

---

55   See Dodge H., and Romig, H. "A method of samling inspection," Bell System Tech Journal, 1929, vol.8 pg. 398.

56   See Pagano, Marcello and Valadez, Joseph J., *International Journal of Epidemiology*, Volume 39, Issue 1, 1 February 2010, Pages 69–71.

from as many clients that are leaving a doctor's office as possible, over the course of a week. While this is plenty of data to analyze for many purposes, it is not random. This limits the generalizability of any data analysis using those data, and the analyst needs to try to understand the types of biases that were introduced by using this sample approach. HOWEVER, these data may be very valuable nevertheless.

There is a big difference between surveying for management purposes and surveying for academic purposes. Often, truly random sample survey approaches are not very feasible in the field. If the client wants to conduct a survey to get a "sense" of customer attitudes, their experience, or satisfaction, then a convenience sample may be perfectly okay. A good rule of thumb is the more important the managerial decision (especially if it involves expending or dispensing (or withholding) dollars), the more systematic (and adhering to random sampling approaches) the approach should be. The same is true of generalizability—if you want to be able to generalize from the results of the survey, systematic randomization becomes more important.

Moving Beyond Simple Customer Satisfaction Questions

There was a while when customer satisfaction was the "in thing," and customer satisfaction surveys proliferated. However, it was soon discovered that if all you ask about is whether an individual is satisfied or not, it becomes difficult to understand what is driving that customer satisfaction. Also, you are expending considerable effort to contact the customer and then asking very little. If you are able to get in touch with the customer, LEVERAGE that contact! While you can't have a never ending survey, DO ask additional questions that will get at the customers' experiences. Ask about key dimensions of service quality. Also, if appropriate, ask about the outcomes of the service…for in many instances a survey may be the only way you can obtain that information as well. Finally, remember that satisfaction is really a latent variable, and you should be asking multiple questions to get at whether the customer was satisfied. The American Customer Satisfaction Index (ACSI)[57] is a good example of how multiple questions are used to measure a latent satisfaction variable. Another reason why the ACSI may be valuable is that is used across many industries and organizations and sectors and can provide very valuable data with which to benchmark your progress.

---

[57]   See http://www.theacsi.org

Integrating survey and service record data

One very powerful approach to developing a better understanding of the relationship between the services a client received (including duration and dosage of services), the client's experience with services, and client outcomes is to integrate survey and service record data. To do this, you need to collect both customer survey data and client services records, and connect them. This is impossible to do after the fact, with an anonymous survey. You need to anticipate that you will be doing this, and somehow put an identifier on the survey, or otherwise connect the survey with the client's service record. This is easier to do if you are using an electronic survey, that can electronically linked to service record. However, if you are doing a follow up paper or phone survey, you will need to make sure the identifier is carried on the survey response so that it can be connected to the service record later.

Once you have connected the survey data with the service records and customer demographic variables, you can look for key drivers of customer satisfaction for different customer groups; what mix of services influences customer outcomes, and whether this differs by customer group. You can also look at the relationship between the customer experience and customer outcomes. You can ultimately build predictive models to determine how likely different types of customers are going to be successful, or what type of customer is most likely to seek out a service or purchase a product. Linking survey data and service record data is very powerful, but is difficult to do without deliberate planning on the part of the analyst.

Integrating Quantitative and Qualitative Data

This leads to a broader question of how do you integrate quantitative data (like data on service transactions, customer characteristics, and environmental factor variables), and qualitative data (such as data from individual and group interviews, focus groups, observation, open ended questions on surveys, testimonials from community leaders, employers, etc).

Sometimes is makes sense NOT to try to integrate these data at all, but use the qualitative data to enrich your understanding of your quantitative findings. Other times, however, you may want to try to categorize/code your qualitative data so that you can create categorical variables out of them, and place them in your data set. Remember, this can only be done if you have this information collected in a way that you can link the qualitative data with the quantitative individual records. This sometimes can be accomplished, but often the qualitative data is not collected in a way where it can be linked to service record.

However, it still may possible to code the qualitative information in a way that will allow you to analyze it using quantitative methods. In particular, visualizing your coded data may help you see patterns that are otherwise opaque.

Mixed Methods Research

The combining of qualitative and quantitative data is an example of a "mixed methods"[58] approach to research and analysis. In order to gain a comprehensive understanding of a service, program, or policy, mixed methods are usually the way to go. Mixed methods (such as a combination of observation, interviewing, surveying, and quantitative analysis of service records) provides a rich array of data to analyze. As I mentioned above, the qualitative data can provide context and inform the quantitative analysis. If you are serious about using a mixed methods approach, you should carefully plan out how you will collect, compile and analyze each component, and how you will synthesize the results.

---

[58] See Cresswell, John (2013), Qualitative Analysis and Research Design: Choosing Among Five Approaches, Los Angeles, Sage Publications.

11

LINKING PLANNING, BUDGETING AND PERFORMANCE MEASUREMENT

"I plan ahead, so I don't have to do anything right now..." *Earl talking to Val, Tremors*

Ever since my early days at CTDOL[59], I have been fascinated with the relationship between an organization's budgeting process, its planning process, and the performance measures used to manage their programs and demonstrate their success. At CTDOL and elsewhere, I saw that frequently there was NO relationship. The three processes were conducted completely independently. There are reasons for this of course. The budget process has a particularly tight timeline. The budget is often developed by the business office with little or no input from program managers. The planning process, while usually participatory[60], is often conducted at a different level of analysis and may or may not have any dollars associated with the full array of planning recommendations. The performance measures are usually those that are required by the funders, and if others are used for management purposes they seldom reach the eyes of the executive team. This pattern can go on indefinitely. However, it is almost self-evident that it would be better if these processes were linked...plans and performance measures would inform the budget process, and there would be an awareness of the proportion of an agencies budget was related to a set of programs (and their performance measures), and planning would include a recognition of the cost of the options being considered during the planning process.

So, how can this be accomplished? First, the staff doing the development work in the three areas have to TALK to one another. It isn't necessary that the units doing the work be physically integrated, but they need to recognize that they are doing work that needs to be linked. They should be sharing preliminary product with each other, and participate on each other's work teams. The documents/ reports themselves should include information from the other development efforts. The budget

---

[59] Schack, Ronald W. (1999). "Linking Process and Outcomes: Performance Measurement at the Connecticut Department of Labor," *PA Times*, May.

[60] The degree of participation depends upon planning method, organizational culture and leadership style.

should include (or at least be informed by) performance measures for the agency and programs[61]; and the planning documents should include budget estimates. Where possible, performance reports (particularly reports used in planning processes) should include the cost measures, and the total cost of the program being measured, and the percentage of the organization's budget represented by the program. This helps set the context for any viewer. See Appendix D for a visual representation of a performance report that includes budget data.

System-Oriented Budgeting, Planning, and Performance Management

One of the most difficult structural hurdles to overcome in my work with the Connecticut General Assembly's Appropriations Committee was that programs that contributed to similar quality of life results (such as early childhood, or juvenile justice, or the environment, or workforce development) were funded with line-items within agencies spread all over the budget. This meant that they were rarely considered together as system. They were not costed as a system, nor did they have cross-program strategies that were expressed and evaluated during the budget process. This meant that Lindblom's description of "successive limited comparisons" ruled the day. The success of the "system" depended upon the success and funding of individual programs decided upon piecemeal in the budget. During the implementation of RBA, there were several "system" level hearings held that were attempts to (at least on a limited basis) bring programs and agencies that contributed to the same quality of life result together, sometimes with each program providing a program report card. Other times a systems-level report card was developed and shared with Appropriations committee members. However, these were usually one-time, ad hoc events. In the end, the budget process carried on as it had previously. Real change in this area would involve re-organizing the budget document (and process) into systems, and then considering and funding each system appropriately. This would require significant support by the CT General Assembly and the executive branch to achieve. While this has not occurred, there are examples of successful "systems" policy approaches. Through my work with both the Justice Education Center, Inc., and the Tow Juvenile Justice Institute at The University of New Haven, I have acted as staff to the Juvenile Justice Policy Oversight Committee (JJPOC) (and its predecessor, the Juvenile Justice Policy Oversight Coordinating Committee, the JJPOCC). The JJPOCC, in an effort to "Raise The Age" of juveniles from 16 to 18, established a "services" workgroup, staffed by The Justice Education Center, Inc., and facilitated by me. This workgroup specified common performance measures for each of several "domains" of service—prevention,

---

[61] This may not always be possible, but performance measures can be reported in a clear and understandable manner to budget decision makers, in a timely way.

diversion, intervention, education/training, and re-entry. The identification of these measures was informed by the contemplated changes to the service structure.

These systems-oriented committees (joint judicial, executive, and legislative committees) have taken a systems oriented approach to juvenile justice planning, including developing an RBA framework for the entire system (including identifying common systems-level performance measures—check out the report card example in Chapter 6)[62]. There have also been efforts to develop funding/costs estimates for the entire system. I believe that this kind of systems-oriented approach should be taken for each "system" within government (transportation, public works, public safety, environmental protection, etc.). While this approach is not quite the direct link to the budget that a total restructuring of the budget might achieve, it is a viable and systematic approach that could greatly improve the linkage between planning, budgeting and performance measurement. However, just setting up a committee is not enough. The committee has to ENGAGE in an examination of the data, and ensure that this is incorporated into its planning and budgeting recommendations.

Budget Performance

Analysis of budget data is a specialized field, and in some ways it falls between the cracks of what certified public accountants (CPAs) do for audit purposes, and the general preparation and tracking of the budget that the budget or business office of an organization does.

I have often been called upon, as a data analyst, to "take a look at the budget" to look for potential cost savings, to assess "what shape" the organization or jurisdiction is in, or to determine what the status of specific program funding is at a specific point in the program year.

I have found several recurring patterns in budgets that you should be aware of, if you ever find yourself in this position.

Inappropriate classification of expenses

There are many reasons that this happens, but you should be ready to look for it and point it out to your client. Many federal and state programs have provisions that do not allow funds to be used for any purpose other than those specified in the grant. Sometimes, however, federal and state funding can be some of the most stable funding an organization receives. It is natural for an organization to tend to use the federal or state money it receives to pay for other program expenses where the funding

---

[62] See Results-Based Accountability Implementation Plan For The Juvenile Justice System, Presented to The Juvenile Justice Oversight Coordinating Committee (JJPOC), March, 2016. Developed by The Charter Oak Group, LLC.

for those other programs has not yet been received. This is a no-no, but it can happen inadvertently and can be hard to spot. You need to look at all the dollars coming into the organization, when deposits were made, and when payments went out, to check whether payments for non-federal or state programs were made when there were not sufficient non-federal or state deposits made to support them.

FIGURE 57 INAPPROPRIATE CLASSIFICATION OF EXPENSES

	Total Expected Revenue	Revenue Received To Date	Expenditures To Date
Grant A (Federal)	100,000	80,000	55,000
Grant B (Foundation)	50,000	25,000	30,000
Grant C (City)	25,000	0	15,000
Total	175,000	105,000	100,000

As you can see in Figure 57, while this organization seems to be doing okay (revenue received to date is higher than expenditures to date), two of the programs have received less revenue than they have expended. Looking at things on a cash (rather than accrual) basis, the only way that both of these things are true is if revenue from GRANT A has been used to fund activities in GRANT B and GRANT C. This could get this organization in hot water in the long run.

Uneven payments throughout the year

One of the challenges of managing a budget is to make sure you are spending money in a controlled manner, spreading out the cash throughout the program year. Sometimes, if a program has a slow start up period or problems with recruitment, program expenditures will lag behind expectations. This can begin to be problem if you are entering the third quarter of a program year and are only beginning to expend dollars.

You can check for this by doing a budget to actual expenditures chart:

FIGURE 58 BUDGET TO ACTUAL EXPENDITURE CHART

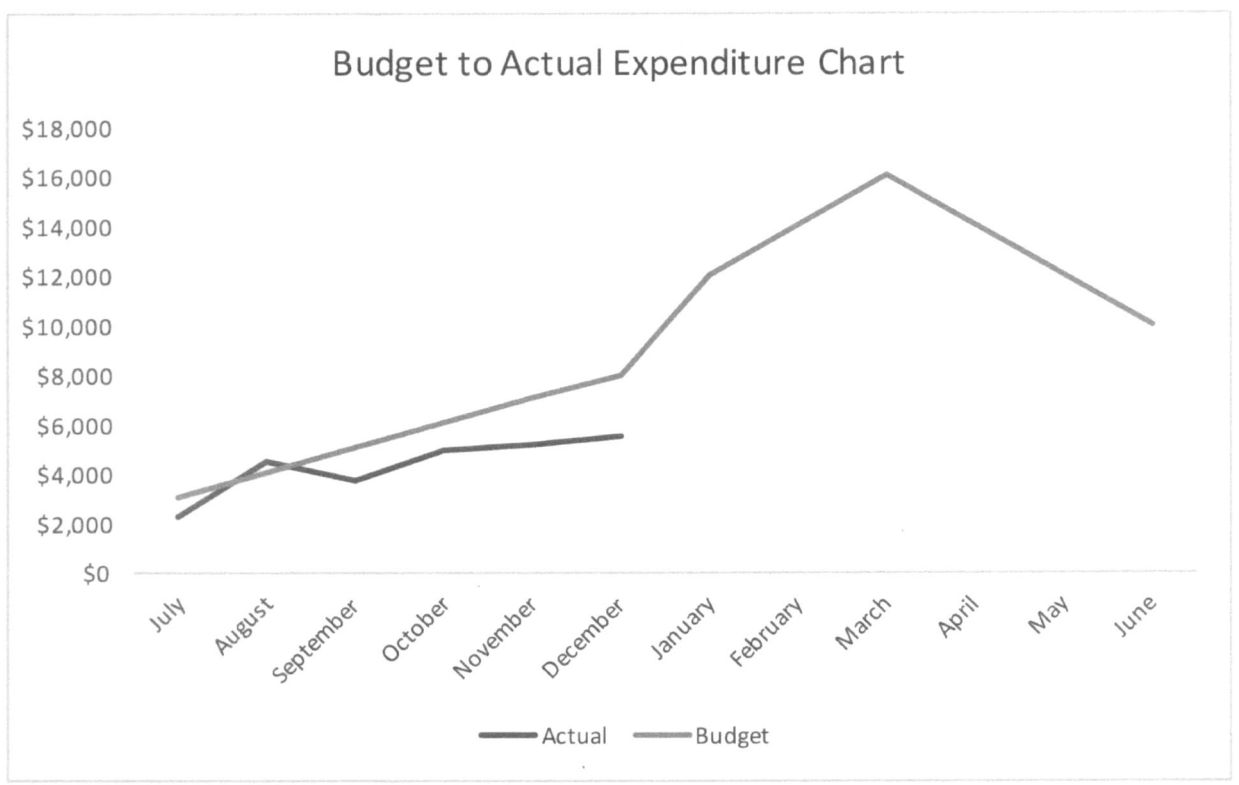

Notice in Figure 58 that the budget already takes into account the seasonal nature of the program, and yet expenditures are still not what they are expected to be. The opposite, of course can also be true, as in Figure 59.

FIGURE 59 BUDGET TO ACTUAL EXPENDITURE CHART

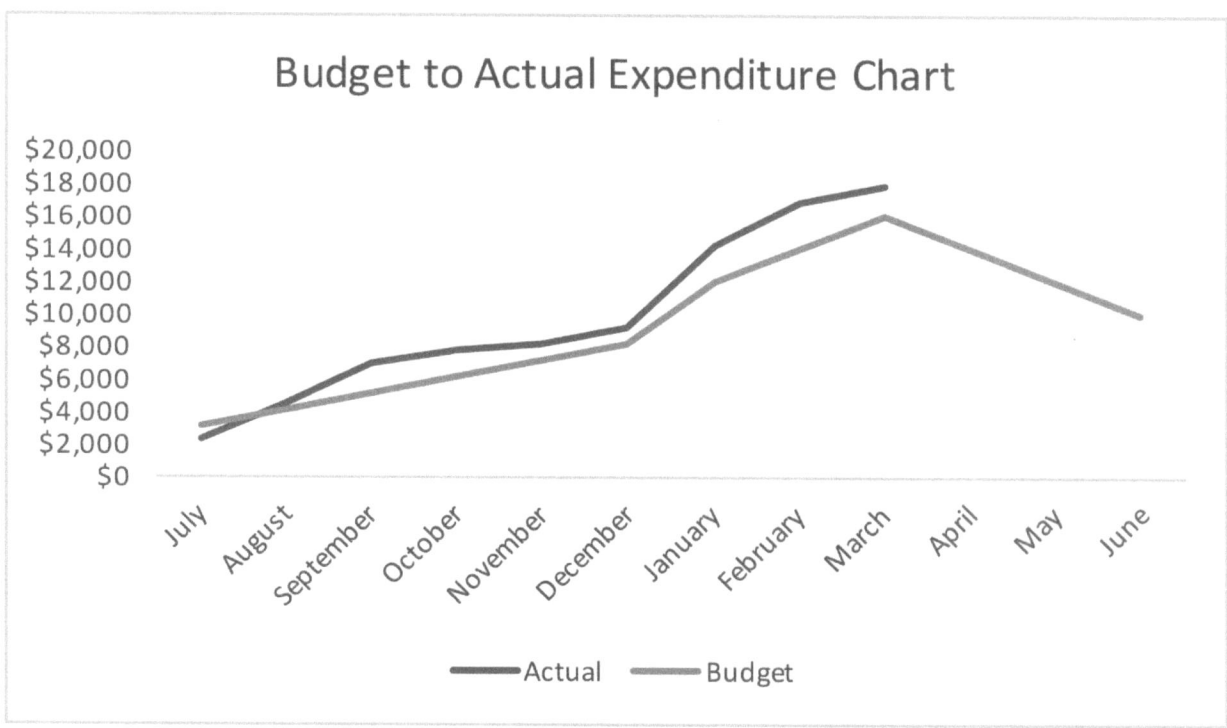

Figure 59 shows that program expenses are consistently higher than the monthly budgeted amounts. There will be trouble at the end of the program year!

Sometimes we don't have history to rely on in terms of projecting a monthly budget. We can use a budget to actual control chart (see Figure 60) to determine whether the monthly spending pattern is outside of normal variation. You can add and subtract 2.5 standard deviations from the actual monthly average, and use these values as an upper and lower control limit. Please note that the estimated expenditures per month (a straight division of the program budget by 12) is also plotted. This can be helpful because it lets you know when an expenditure level is truly outside normal variation, and a red flag should be raised. Sometimes this is known and perfectly understood, but other times this kind of a trend may not be noticed by management without a little help from a valuable data display.

FIGURE 60 BUDGET TO ACTUAL EXPENDITURE CONTROL CHART

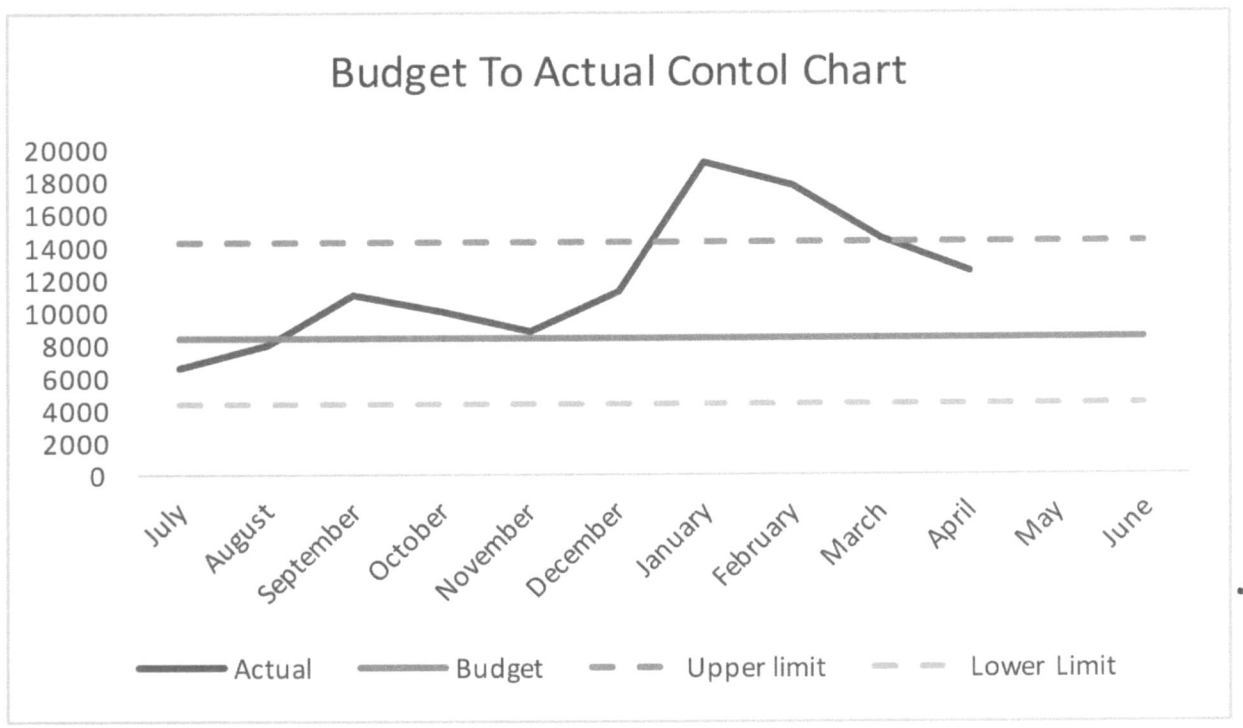

I have also been asked to assess the financial condition of a city. There are some traditional measures of financial condition that help in this regard:

- Unreserved fund balance vs. gross expenditures
- Fixed costs vs. total costs
- Intergovernmental revenues vs. total revenues
- Is there a deficit?
- Use of short term notes increasing?
- One-time revenues vs. total revenues

Figure 61 below is a sample "synthesized" table from a Comprehensive Annual Financial Report, or CAFR," for an imaginary town. I use the term "synthesized" because you usually do not find all the information in this table in one table in the CAFR, it comes from several tables. However, I put it in one table for example purposes:

FIGURE 61 SAMPLE "SYNTHESIZED" TABLE FROM CAFR

Town of Schackville-Baggins	in thousands (000)			
	2012	2013	2014	2015
Revenues				
Property Tax	50000	52000	55000	57000
Sales Tax	75000	74000	73000	74500
One Time Revenues (Foundation Grants)	4223	5656	6655	6598
Interbovernmental Revenue	45000	56254	64235	69899
Total Revenue	174223	187910	198890	207997
Expenditures				
Salaries and Fringe	118756	135654	145555	171232
Contractual	32000	36000	39000	42000
Travel	500	520	540	565
Materials and Supplies	1517	1917	2034	2545
Debt Services	2551	2880	3110	4956
Total Gross Expenditures	155324	176971	190239	221298
Revenues-Total Expendiures	18899	10939	8651	-13301
Total Short Term Notes	0	2123	4121	6223
Total Unreserved Fund Balance	18899	10939	8651	0

If you calculate the above measures for this town data, you can see that the Town of Schackville-Baggins may be in trouble. For example, they are running a deficit in the most recent year; their unreserved fund balance has steadily decreased; they have been increasingly relying on intergovernmental revenue and short term notes, and they have a high proportion of fixed costs.

Of course, these measures should be examined in the economic and demographic context of the town. Indicators like the % of residents earning less than 200% of poverty, the unemployment rate, and the condition of the property and business tax base should be examined.[63]

This is just the tip of the iceberg as far as such analysis goes, but it gives you an idea of the approach that should be taken, and may suggest a new realm of analysis for the nascent data scientist.

---

[63] For more on additional indicators and approaches to evaluating financial condition, please see "Evaluating Financial Condition (2000). International City/ Management Association.

12

THE "POWER" OF DATA

"I'm young, wild, and I'm free…I've got the magic power of the [DATA] in me"… [with apologies to the band Triumph]…

Effect Size and Significance Testing

One of the recurring problems that I see with data analysis is ignorance of (or misunderstanding) of effect size, and the distinction between effect size and statistical significance. As I have emphasized earlier, this is not a statistics text, and I will not be providing a comprehensive treatment of either of these topics, but I do want to try to provide a plain language explanation of the distinction and some important things to remember about these concepts.

> **Schackziom Number 10:**
>
> **Never rely on statistical significance testing alone. Always look at the size of the effect as well as testing for significance.**
>
> **But, don't disregard statistical significance testing either…it can provide valuable insight when examined together with the size of the effect.**

The key distinction is that an effect size measures the **magnitude of the effect** being observed, while a significance test indicates the *likelihood that the observed effect is due to chance*. For decades, statistical significance was the most important measure for a study, because if you could report that a difference was statistically significant, the thinking went, you could report that the difference you found was real (and therefore publishable).

However, there was a real problem with this, as Jacob Cohen pointed out[64]. Something could be found to be statistically significant, but be of very little practical importance (have a very small effect size). Also, when you test for statistical significance, you set a threshold for significance (the p-value). This is usual set at .05 or .01, but in either case it is an arbitrary threshold. A very large, and potentially

---

[64] See Cohen, J. (1988). Statistical power analysis for the behavioral sciences (2nd ed.). Hillsdale, NJ: Erlbaum.

important effect could be observed, but could be dismissed if one relied solely on the arbitrary statistical significance threshold.

FIGURE 62 EXAMPLE OF LARGE EFFECT, NO STATISTICAL SIGNIFICANCE

	Outcome Variable	Effect Size	Significant at .o1 level?
Treatment N=28	78%	+30%--large effect	No, p=.07210
Control=N=25	48%		

FIGURE 63 EXAMPLE OF SMALL EFFECT, STATISTICALLY SIGNIFICANT

	Outcome Variable	Effect Size	Significant at .o1 level?
Treatment N=350	72%	+4%--small effect	YES, p=.00012
Control=N=350	68%		

As you can see from Figures 62 and 63 above, the traditional way of looking at these findings would assert the very small effect in Figure 63 was something to pay attention to, while the much larger effect in Figure 62 was of little interest because it was not statistically significant. This is wrong on both counts. For most treatment interventions in social science, a 4 percentage-point difference between the treatment and the control may be disappointing.[65] While the results in Figure 62 would have to be viewed with caution because of the small cell size, they would still be encouraging because of the size of the effect, and relatively small p value, despite not being statistically significant.

Unlike some researchers, *I do not believe we should completely abandon statistical significance.* I believe it is useful, when considered together with effect size. When a researcher has both pieces of information they can understand and explain their results in a more practical and actionable way.

---

[65] However, sometimes small effect sizes can be important...but go with the premise for example purposes.

This suggests a problem that often arises in our new technology driven data world. Given the ease of generating cross-tabulations and other multivariate displays using ad-hoc database reporting tools, you often end up with a display like this:

FIGURE 64 SAMPLE OF TABLE WITH MANY POSSIBLE SIGNIFICANT DIFFERENCES

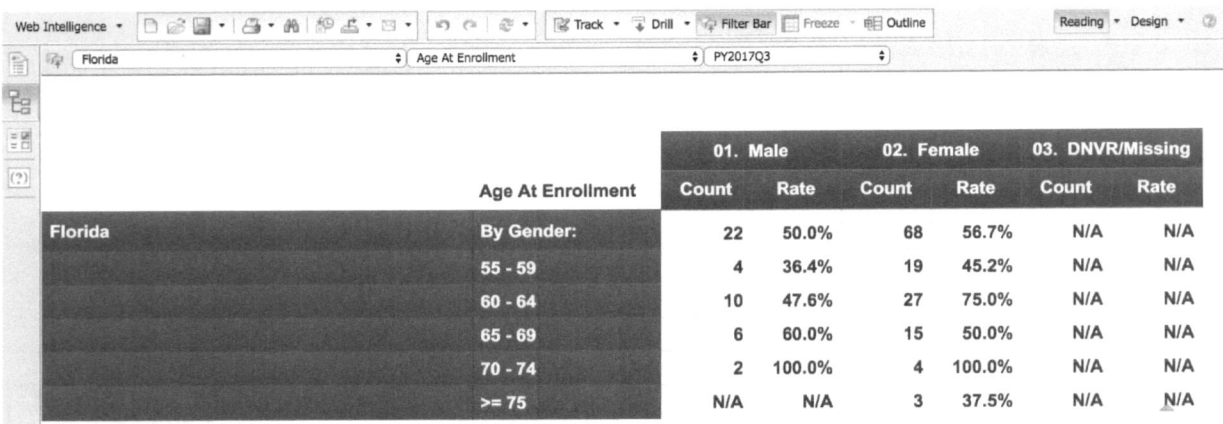

The problem is, how do you tell which of these differences matter? Sure, the percentage of people entering employment who are male and between 60 and 64 is much lower those that are female, but is this a significant difference, based on such a small cell size? When these ad-hoc reporting tools provide these comparisons, but there no way to determine the significance of those differences, they need to be viewed with considerable caution.

Could someone please explain statistical power? Do I really have to worry about it?

Another mis-used and mis-understood concept is the concept of **statistical power.** What do we mean by this, and does it have any bearing on the kind of analysis that I do?

Ensuring your study has adequate statistical power is kind making sure you are wearing a belt and suspenders… it is a rigorous examination of the adequacy of the sample. Statistical power depends upon:

1. sample size,
2. the size of the effect you are trying to detect,
3. the alpha criterion [defines the risk of committing a Type I error (or the probability of incorrectly rejecting the null hypothesis). Normally alpha is set at .05 or lower and statistical tests are assumed to be non-directional (two tailed)].

4. The power of the statistical test [Statistical power refers to the chosen or implied Type II error rate of the test…if the acceptable level of this rate is .2, then desired power is .8]

Notice the four elements listed above. **If you're analysis does not have a sample component, you really can't calculate statistical power for your analysis.** The same is true if you do not really know the size of the effect you are trying to detect. In these cases, you cannot technically calculate statistical power and you should move on to other considerations[66] like specific threats to the validity of the analysis (see Chapter 4).

But, if your analysis does have a sample component, and you want your analysis to be able to detect small effect sizes, you really should consider statistical power carefully.

Calculating Statistical Power

Please take a look at Figure 65 below which recommends a sample size for a specified number of predictor variables if you want to detect a small, medium, or large effect. Notice, the smaller the effect you want to detect, the larger the sample size you need; the more predictors involved, the larger the sample size you need. For most academic studies, you probably want to detect even small effects; but for many other applications it may be appropriate to look for only large effects. Since this requires greatly reduced sample sizes, it is an important consideration that can save considerable resources.

---

[66] although you could use the universe of data you have, treat it LIKE a sample, and do a power analysis…but remember that this is not technically correct…but it could be practically useful.

FIGURE 65 RELATIONSHIP BETWEEN PREDICTORS, EFFECT SIZE AND SAMPLE SIZE

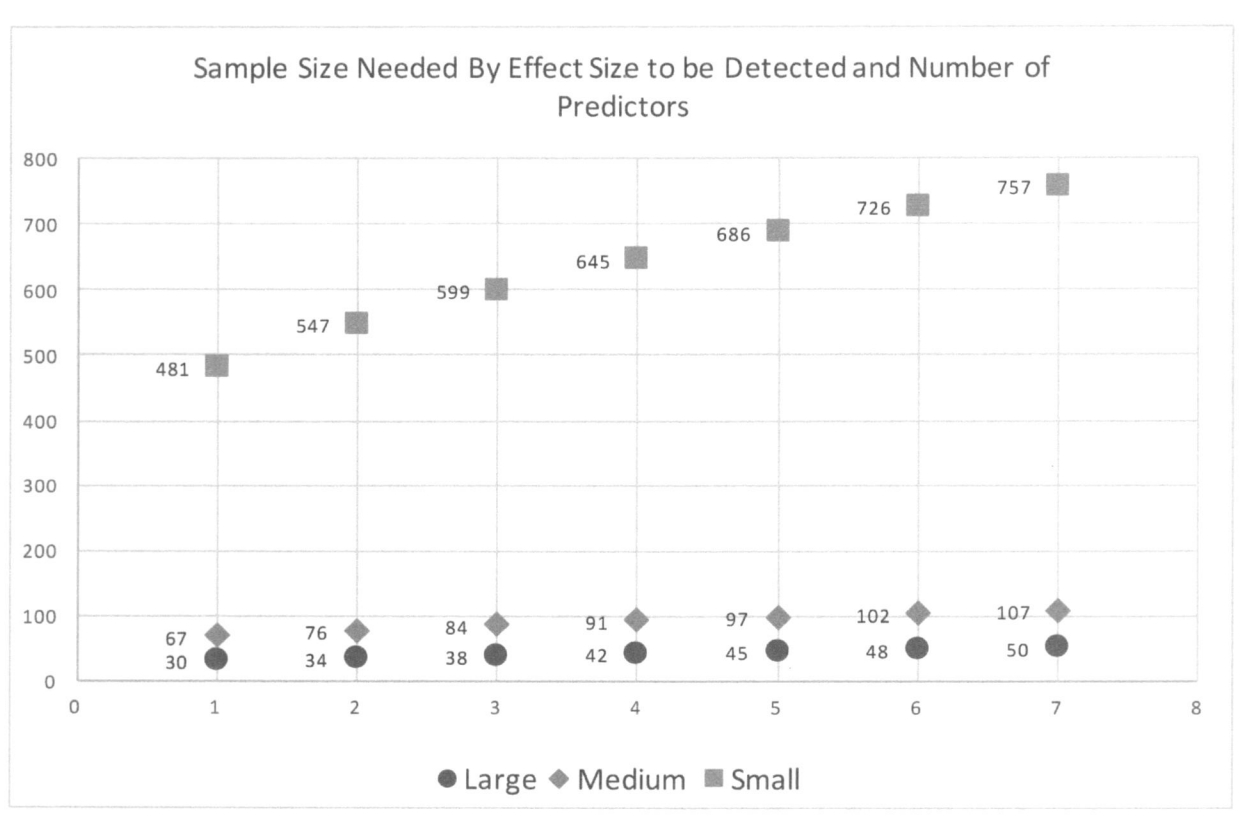

13

THE POTENTIALS AND PERILS OF BIG DATA

"If your time to you is worth savin'...Then you better start swimmin' or you'll sink like a stone....For the times they are a-changin'.... Bob Dylan

Big data are here! It is estimated that the amount of data available on servers in the world double every 20 months.[67] That is terrifying. A lot of the recent growth in the data science field is due to need for more capacity to analyze huge data sets...some are resident on organizations' servers, some resident on servers of internet organizations that have a great opportunity to obtain data from their users... organizations like Google or Facebook or Amazon. Even in federal and state government(s), there are efforts to connect enormous client data bases, like the databases of DMV customers, databases of gun permit holders, of welfare recipients, state pensioners, Medicare and Medicaid recipients.

While the statistical foundation for many of these analyses can be fundamentally similar to those used with smaller data sets, connecting and analyzing these databases require a different set of tools and approaches than those used with smaller datasets. There will continue to be more and more opportunities to engage with big data. There are approaches being developed now that will allow the quantitative data in these massive, connected data bases to be analyzed using a "relational search" approach.[68] Users will be able to type questions, like the ones I posed at the beginning of Chapter 3, into a search-engine like front end, and using a relational search algorithm the application will return the numeric results, in table or chart form. An even more advanced form of this is "voice activated search, using natural language processing. [69]A manager will be able to say to his smartphone, "how many of our clients 16-24 years old are disabled?" and then continue his voice activated analysis with, "of those, how many are employed?" This begins to touch on the outer reaches of my conceptual bubble...I feel like I am living in 1960, with rockets exploding every other time we try to send one

---

[67]   Witten, I, Frank, E, and Hall, Mark. (2011). "Data Mining, Practical Machine Learning Tools and Techniques." Morgan Kauffman. Burlington, MA.

[68]   See "Relational Search: A New Paradigm For Data Analytics," Thoughtspot, 2017.

[69]   See https://www.tableau.com/sites/default/files/pages/838266_2018_bi_trends_whitepaper_1.pdf

up, and someone is trying to tell me that in less than 10 years one of my fellow countrymen will walk on the moon.

With all the opportunities that big data afford, I feel compelled to discuss a few important big data considerations:

A Caution Regarding Exploratory Analysis

A lot of big data analysis is exploratory in nature, rather than confirmatory [see Chapter 3]. As such, it is susceptible to the identification of spurious correlations, as well as to capitalization on chance. As I suggested in Chapter 3, if unexpected (but potentially important) relationships between variables are discovered through big data analysis, it is important to develop a reasonable explanation (a tentative "testable proposition" for the relationship, and, ***using other data***[70], determine whether the relationship persists. If you suspect a spurious correlation, try to identify that significant omitted variable or variables that might be driving the relationship. Again, create a new, testable proposition that includes the omitted variable(s), and see what you find.

This does not mean, however, that your exploratory data analysis is not valuable. We are connecting vast data sets in new and inventive ways, and we cannot always anticipate what we will find. ***We just need to proceed with some discipline and caution.***

Analysis Techniques with Big Data

Unfortunately, most traditional statistical analysis software packages cannot handle big data. That is changing, but many of these packages just can't operate on the scale of truly big data. However, there are analytic packages, like "R" and "Python" that can "sit on top" of distributed database structures like HADOOP and can provide analytics like the ones I have discussed in this book.[71] While the data sets being analyzed are vast, in the end the analytic issues found with smaller data sets still apply… such as the considerations regarding validity, reliability, visualizing and presenting data and the measurement challenges I have discussed.

Sometimes we do not have the luxury of being able to leverage a powerful distributed database structure when we are applying certain methods like machine learning. However, many statistical methods require all the machine-learning training instances to be conducted at one time. There

---

[70]   An oft-used approach is to hold back half your data for confirmatory test.

[71]   Prajapai, Vignesh 2013. "Big Data Analytics with R and Hadoop." Packt Publishing, Birmingham.

is still hope, however. You can use a small subset of a larger data set for training. This often is a practical solution. However, sometimes this is not desirable because you lose information when you apply subsampling. Don't worry too much, though…the predictive capacity of a training model often flattens out long before all the training data are incorporated into it.

Another possible approach is Parallelization. This is another way of reducing the time complexity of learning. The idea is to split the problem into smaller parts solve each using a separate processor, and combine the results together. A simple way to apply any algorithm to a large data set is to split the data into chunks of limited size and learn models for each one, combining the results using voting or averaging. [72]

Data Mining

Like the term "benchmarking" data mining is a very abused term. The kind of mining we are talking about is not done with a shovel, helmet, and headlamp (although that would be cool). Nor is it just "looking for data in unusual places." Data mining is about looking for patterns in data. Large quantities of data are electronically stored and the search for patterns is automated (or close, you could say semi-automated).

Beyond the identification of patterns and the development of predictive models, applying machine learning to the task of data mining can be valuable because the decision trees, or other structural descriptions, that are developed add to the knowledge base. They help us understand our world, beyond the "predictive value" of the endeavor. This is something that we need to help the world understand. We are not just building "black box" predictive mechanisms (although some data scientists might in fact take that approach—"it doesn't matter why it works"….which is instrumentalist and opportunistic, but not wrong)…***we have the opportunity to describe our world in ways we were never able to in the past…because we have the data to do it.***

The Lure of Big Data

As the title of this chapter suggests, I believe "big data' approaches have enormous potential. And the speed of development of big data, artificial intelligence, and machine learning approaches is astounding. I also believe, however, that many organizations can benefit from the availability of big data without going through the expense of developing an in-house big data analytic infrastructure.

---

[72] Witten, I, Frank, E, and Hall, Mark. (2011). "Data Mining, Practical Machine Learning Tools and Techniques." Morgan Kauffman. Burlington, MA.

There are many "big data data sets" available on-line, along with on-line tools for exploring these data. For many kinds of questions, especially public policy questions, these big data sets provide a wealth of information for exploration and policy analysis.

It IS appropriate for large federal and state agencies to develop in-house big data infrastructure, but I would offer a word of caution here. Most smaller organizations, especially non-profit organizations, probably should not focus on developing the kind of in house expertise that is required to develop an in-house big data infrastructure. ***For many organizations, big data applications may become another one of those "solutions in search of problems" (see Chapter 8) that get pursued because the organization wants to appear to be innovative or to "keep up with the Joneses," or because the problem is characterized or diagnosed incorrectly.***

I am not discouraging exploring the use of big data, or saying organizations should not try to learn what they can, I am merely emphasizing caution before expending a lot of resources on developing in-house big data infrastructure that when most organizations do not need to do so. Instead, they should focus on learning what big data resources are already out there, that they can leverage and benefit from. Also, I would wager that most smaller public and non-profit organizations have a lot of work to do to get their own data house in order, just to generate basic data to manager programs and demonstrate success. While they should keep an eye on big data developments, they need to "put one foot in front of the other…before they start walkin' cross the floor . ☺

I have not really discussed the relatively recent, massive impact of machine learning and artificial intelligence on the use of data, data analysis, and decision support. There is a tremendous amount of literature on these subjects. These approaches are already changing our profession, and will continue to do so. I encourage anyone interested in data science to explore these areas. In fact, this is what now comes to mind when people think about data science. Try out machine learning approaches on a small scale; start with simple learning tasks and take it from there. Just a caution: Algorithms are everywhere, and unless we are the ones developing the algorithms, when applied they can become another set of "black boxes." It is crucial that we understand how the algorithms we use are structured, what assumptions are utilized, and what biases are "cooked in" to the algorithms. This is particularly true of the algorithms which are embedded into our analytic software and analysis routines.

14

THE SCIENCE OF DISCONTENT

"Mankind has but one science, the science of discontent"...Frank Herbert, Dune

The science of discontent...sometimes data science seems like this. Humans are rarely happy with their current state, and if they are, it is usually only for a short time. Humans are driven to change, to discover, to innovate, and to do this well, they need....data! While we may not always act on the information, we are constantly asking "is what we are doing good enough?" "Does this program really work?" "Are we spending too much for too little return?" "If this approach worked in Hoboken, will it work in Aspen?" Systems, studies, and various research approaches are used in answering these questions, and along the way things can get rather confusing....

Program Evaluation vs. Performance Measurement

Something that often confuses my clients (and occasionally fellow data scientists), is the difference between performance measurement and program evaluation. Performance measurement is the development of metrics for an activity or set of activities. There is a wide array of possible measures, but these boil down to: input, output, process, and outcome measures...or, as Mark Friedman describes them, how much, how well, and is anyone better off?[73]

Program evaluation is more difficult to nail down, because there are different kinds of program evaluation.[74] There are process evaluations and outcome evaluations. There are formative evaluations and summative evaluations. Often, when people speak of program evaluation, they are speaking of an attempt to determine whether the outcomes associated with an intervention (or treatment) would have occurred in the absence of that treatment. Over the years, I have seen people attempt to discredit

---

[73] See Friedman, Mark (2005), Trying Hard Isn't Good Enough, Trafford Press.

[74] For a comprehensive review of evaluation, See Rossi, Peter, Freeman, Howard, and Lipsey, Mark (2004). Evaluation: A Systematic Approach. Sage Publications. Thousands Oaks, CA.

whole performance measurement systems because the system could not answer this question. While this question is important, it is **not** appropriate to expect performance measurement system to be able to answer this. This is because it takes a specialized approach, called a random control trial, or RCT, to answer this question to the satisfaction of critical observers.

Unfortunately, the random control trial can be resource intensive, and impractical or impossible to conduct for many public programs. So, less intensive or less restrictive approaches are utilized, such as quasi experiments using comparison groups, but these are all "second-best" approaches.

How is performance measurement related to all of this? Well, the outcome measures used, even in random control trials, are performance measures. Often performance measures that have already been developed and collected are incorporated into a comprehensive program evaluation, as are process measures and the results of customer surveys.

Also, other than to answer that very important question, the RCT or similar approaches are not usually necessary, and cannot be sustained in most cases anyway. Most performance measures are routinely collected by computer data collection systems that collect data as customers are served. As shown earlier, an array of measures can be developed by identifying the transition points in a process and making sure data are collected at those points. A performance measurement system should tell you the number and type of people served, the number and type of services provided, some key information about how those services are delivered, and the question most stakeholders care about… are the expected outcomes being achieved?

Mark Friedman, creator of RBA, points out that these outcome, or better off measures, can also be used to show how an individual program, agency, or service system CONTRIBUTES to the quality of life results communities seek at the population level. This language of contribution is very important, because it demonstrates the value of the program in the context of wider community efforts.

The Amazing Morphing Program Problem

This reminds me of a challenge that I have encountered several times over the years. Sometimes, as you begin to conduct an evaluation of a new program (especially a comprehensive evaluation with both process and outcome, formative and summative components) the program will begin to morph even as you are documenting its processes and measuring its activities. I set out to evaluate a youth character development program, the initial emphasis of which was working with coaches to help them be more positive role models to their team members, as well as finding ways of conveying a set of core character values to the participants. However, as the momentum and support for the program increased, the approach was soon applied to non-sport related groups, such as in after school programs and even in the classroom. Some of the program implementations were short, summer sport-related leagues, while others were full year, entire school program. At some point, a health-wellness component was added that could be used in an in school or afterschool setting. The point of describing this is, as you can imagine, that no one evaluation approach could ever capture all of these different manifestations. They all operated under the auspices of what I will term an "umbrella" program, but they differed considerably in terms of the services provided, the dosage and duration of the program components, as well as the expected outcomes. The difficulty is similar to the old adage of the frog in the boiling pot of water…if you happened upon this situation after it was fully developed, you would run away [or, create an appropriately elaborate project scope]—just like a frog immediately jumping out after being placed in a pot of boiling water. However, if you are already engaged in an evaluation that is supposed to document process changes, you can get caught in the trap of trying to "revise" the evaluation scope as additional components are added—just like the frog that boils to death when placed in warm water, with the temperature made hotter but very slowly. As you can probably tell, I have been boiled to death a few times. My advice in these situations is to NOT try to capture of the manifestations using one approach, or even **call it** one evaluation project.

Of course, you can document the addition of the program components in your formative and process evaluation, but do not try to adapt your original outcome evaluation tools to the new components on the fly. The new components deserve a well-conceived evaluation approach that requires more time and resources than you can provide them given the original scope and nature of the evaluation project.

The Perpetual Evaluation of a Promising Practice

A related problem is that of the "Perpetual Evaluation." As I suggested in my distinction between performance measurement and program evaluation, program evaluations are usually single-shot studies, or at the most episodic snapshots. I would argue there is no such thing (or there should not be such a thing) as "continuous" program evaluation. Instead, a program evaluation should be used to document processes and establish that the program has the expected effect. At this point, routine program performance measurement should take over, and regular performance reporting should provide managers and stakeholders with all the information they need. If the program has changed considerably over time, or is being applied to a new target population or in a different setting, then additional program evaluation is appropriate. However, as you can probably tell, I have been in situations where the client came to expect annual program evaluation reports, which, I believed, were too resource intensive to produce and added little additional value over and above the routine performance measurement that was in place.

Of course, this suggests that a natural adjunct to a program evaluation is the establishment of a (or validation of an existing) performance measurement system for the program. If this is done correctly, with an appropriate array of measures being selected, the data collection mechanisms put into place, and appropriately designed performance reports generated on a regular basis, with a strategy for USING those reports, then it is less likely that a continual evaluation reports would be expected or needed.

Performance Measurement vs. Performance Monitoring

This is another distinction that often gets confused. Performance measurement systems can be developed by organizations doing the work, but they can also be developed by agencies funding the activities. When funding organizations review performance data, either remotely or on site, this is usually called *performance monitoring*. The term performance monitoring is also used in the context of contracted services, when the organization issuing the contract reviews performance data to determine whether the provisions of the contract are being met. For some kinds of publically-funded services, performance monitoring approaches can be elaborate. There are different types of monitoring, such as fiscal compliance monitoring, monitoring for compliance with program provisions and rules, and performance monitoring (are targets for how much service is being provided being met? Are expected outcomes being achieved?).

Sometimes, these different monitoring efforts are done by different monitors, at different times, some remotely, so on site. Sometimes, one, big comprehensive monitoring is conducted. I have included a typical "comprehensive monitoring policy" (see Appendix D) so you can get a sense of what a typical monitoring review entails, and so you can see how it differs from routine "performance measurement" activities.

A related issue that creates much confusion is the distinction between the development of a performance framework, or even a set of routine performance reports, and the creation of a robust data system (at the organizational or system level) that can support a wide array of different kinds of inquiry and data analysis. When you set out to develop a performance framework or set of reports, or even conduct a program evaluation, it is driven by a core set of research questions (or key performance questions). However, sometimes there is a desire to create a data approach or system that allows for the use of data to answer a wide array of questions, some of which have not yet been fully articulated. In these cases, what is critical is that the possible categories and types of questions are anticipated, and that the system approaches utilized are flexible enough to support those kinds of inquiry.

Circularity in Application and Report Development

I have been involved in several application and report development projects where my part of the project was to ensure that the reports were user-friendly and meaningful. I was representing the end user in this role. However, I was not actually doing the application development, nor did I have direct access to the data. I was functioning at a mezzo-level, writing report specifications that would be re-written by systems developers that would then be implemented by programmers. This is not that unusual a role for a data analyst. Often, a software package (with its own development team) has been purchased, and someone like me is hired to be that end user representative, because I have both knowledge of the program (the program of services, not a computer program) and I have knowledge of performance measurement and statistics. As you can probably tell, this mezzo-level function can be quite challenging. ***That is because the communication chain can become quite complex***:

Program Manager (Client) → Data Scientist (Me) → Development Project Manager →Systems Developer → Applications Developer(s) ← Database Manager ← Application Project Manager

Like all games of telephone, information can be lost or confused at each step. And discussions take place between dyads and triads of individuals, sometimes leaving out key participants. Sometimes there is a clear process, defined perhaps by the project manager, that is an attempt to clarify the project scope and tasks. These are usually done before work has begun. However, as work progresses there are usually changes to the scope and tasks. This can create delays and misunderstandings, but is impractical to assume (or mandate) that they will not occur. Also, for some reason, suddenly what was once clearly understood by everyone sudden becomes opaque, for if the team recognizes everything clearly they have to admit they did not anticipate something, or that something wasn't adequately designed and articulated.

One of the steps where trouble often arises is the translation between the technical specifications the analyst (me) writes and the technical specifications a systems developer may write. While they may appear to say the same thing in slightly different language, it is not until the technical specifications are realized that you can be sure. ***Insist that early validation and testing of these specifications are built into the development process*** …do not wait for "user acceptance testing" near the end of the process (when there is often so much pressure to release the product that concerns are minimized or "too complex to correct in this release." In other words, insist on seeing the product in early development, so that you can tell whether the product is evolving in the way that you envisioned.

There is a relatively new framework, called "agile" software development, that emphasizes ITERATIVE software development. A core aspect of this is not rigid adherence to some previously agreed upon spec, but rather an emphasis in understanding and responding to customer need. You have to be careful, however. Many software developers claim to be using an agile development approach, using terminology borrowed from the approach, such as holding "SCRUM" meetings, but when problems arise they "run home to momma" and revert to their old defensive positions, such as holding firm to the initial specification as written when everyone acknowledges that the application as specified does not do what is required. There is even an extreme version of "agile" software development called "continuous delivery"[75]that pushes for a continuous development process with nightly builds in preproduction, so that the on-going release of modifications becomes a business decision rather than one driven by a release schedule sometimes developed a year or more prior.

A great friend of mine, Dr. James Kurien, is a senior software scientist at the Jet Propulsion Laboratory. He is now implementing this kind of approach to the development of software for the 2020 Mars Lander. He says that his software developers are "all on 2 week development sprints with customer demos after each." The point here is that software development shouldn't be a closed, secret shop until the software is deemed "ready for testing." The customer and customer representatives (the role data scientists often play) should see the product as it was being developed.

It goes further than that, as well. The Netflix development team runs a service called "Chaos Monkey"[76] (awesome name, I think) that attacks their own production system, forcing the developers and operators to always be ready…before naturally occurring problems arise.

Evidence-based practices

The term "evidence-based practice" is one of the most abused terms in use today. Some might argue that it would be great (however unlikely) if the government created a single body (the National Science Foundation, perhaps?) that determined whether a practice was evidence-based, and all other organizations agreed only to use this term when the governing body had applied it to the practice in question. Alas, this is not to be. Federal, state, and local agencies use this term at will, asking for only evidence based practices when they issue grant solicitations or requests for proposals (RFPs). Sometimes they name the specific practice, other times they don't. Sometimes they provide criteria for what constitutes an evidence-based practice; sometimes they don't. Sometimes organizations responding to grant solicitations or RFPs will assert the practice they are proposing is evidence-based,

---

[75]   See "Continuous Delivery, the ING story," Presentation at CA World 2014.

[76]   http://whatis.techtarget.com/definition/Chaos-Monkey

when this has not really been established in any formal sense. Sometimes, knowing they really don't yet have a practice that is truly evidence-based, they instead label the practice as a *promising practice*. This is a term that is truly meaningless, but one which is very handy when there are no data to support a claim that a program is evidence-based. To be fair, sometimes a practice does show promise…it may be innovative, clients may be engaged, and there may be anecdotal or preliminary evidence that the practice should be explored further…but, as happens sometimes with calls for evidence-based practices, there are no real criteria set forth to determine whether a practice is promising or not [and the claim that, "if it keeps getting funded it must be promising" really doesn't fly].

Usually, if a practice is truly evidence based, there has been actual, formal, scientific study of the practice (or even better, more than one)[77]. A formal program evaluation, using a random control trial or similar rigorous approach, has been undertaken, and the intervention has been shown to have a real, measurable, and substantial effect. Program practices have been documented, and the aspects of the program that are most directly related to the success of the practice have been identified and codified. Ideally, the practice has been attempted in different environments with different target populations, and any adjustments in practice required for the practice to be successful in those alternative environments and with those alternative target populations have been articulated and documented.

If all of these things are true of a practice that is claimed to be evidence-based, I would agree that it is. *If the practice has essential elements that must be followed to ensure the success of the practice, those essential elements should be measured on an on-going basis.* Using measures like "the percentage of essential elements in place," or "the percentage of customers receiving services fully consistent with the evidence based practice" are important process measures to insure fidelity to the program model. Sometimes these measures might be collected in a database, but more often a periodic, ad-hoc data and record review is necessary to compile, calculate, and report such measures.

---

[77] See Pawson, Ray (2006). <u>Evidence-based Policy: A Realist Perspective.</u> Sage Publications, Thousand Oaks, CA. Pawson argues that before we call something evidence-based there should be multiple studies conducted, and a meta-analytic approach used to synthesize this evidence.

15

THE PROMISE OF PLACE-BASED ANALYSIS

"**The land here is strong, strong beneath my feet…**"....*Peter Gabriel, The Rhythm and The Heat*

Geographic Information Systems (GIS) have been around for a while now, and we are all used to seeing maps of certain kinds of data (like census maps showing population distributions, or "hot spot" crime maps showing where crimes occur most frequently in a city or neighborhood. But there is so much more placed-based analysis can do. Big data sets are so much more accessible now, and so much easier to connect to mapping software, that we can see different types of data together on maps much more easily than we used to. And, new approaches to using maps as analytic tools for problem solving are constantly being developed.

If you are examining population level data, there are many on-line tools available that will allow you to map a lot of important data right there, on-line, on demand. Figure 66 is a population density map of those in poverty generated via the US Census website.

FIGURE 66 POVERTY IN NEW HAVEN, CT

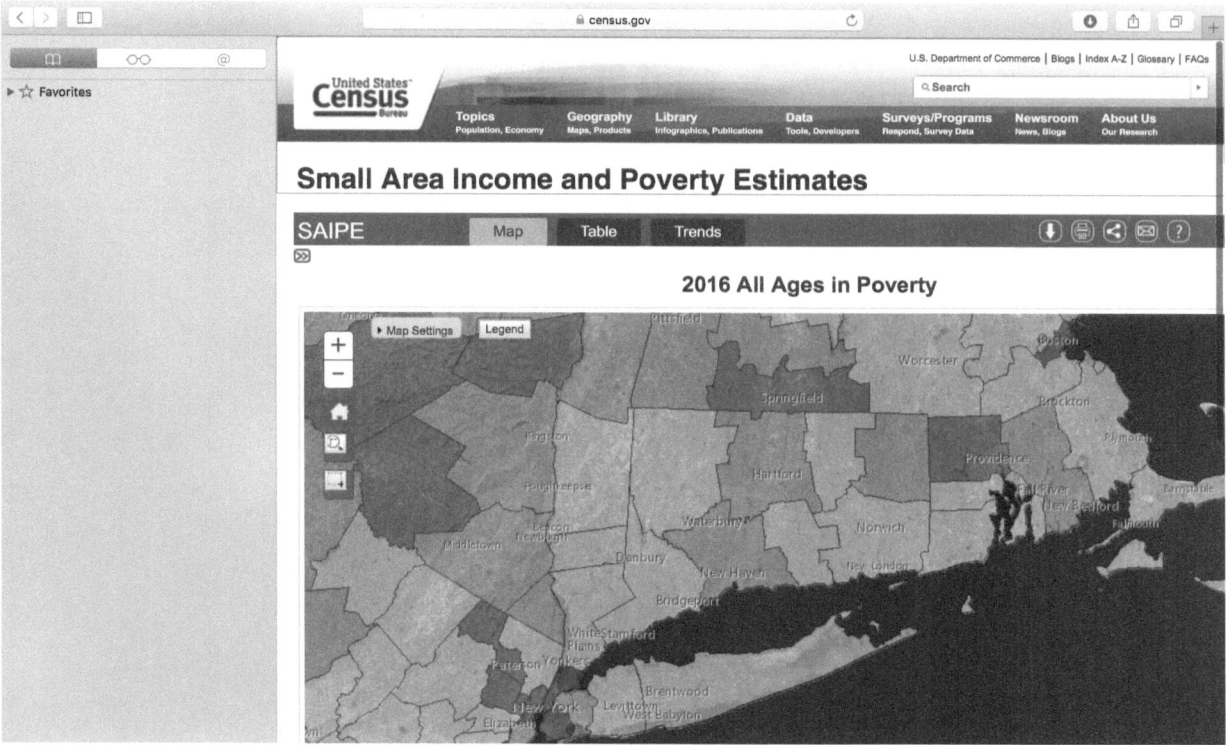

Sometimes, however, you want to map program data. Most on-line tools will not allow you to do that. Figure 67 is a map showing the distribution of participants in a juvenile justice program in New Haven, with borders for each "neighborhood." Simply plotting program participants on map can be very informative. First and foremost, it shows where the participants are coming from, and where they are *not*. This can be an incredible tool for targeting recruitment efforts, and can help trigger further investigation of assets and risks in the neighborhoods where the majority of program participants live. Note that these maps were produced using R, not a more elaborate GIS program like ArcGIS.

Figure 67 Map of a participants in a juvenile justice program in New Haven, CT

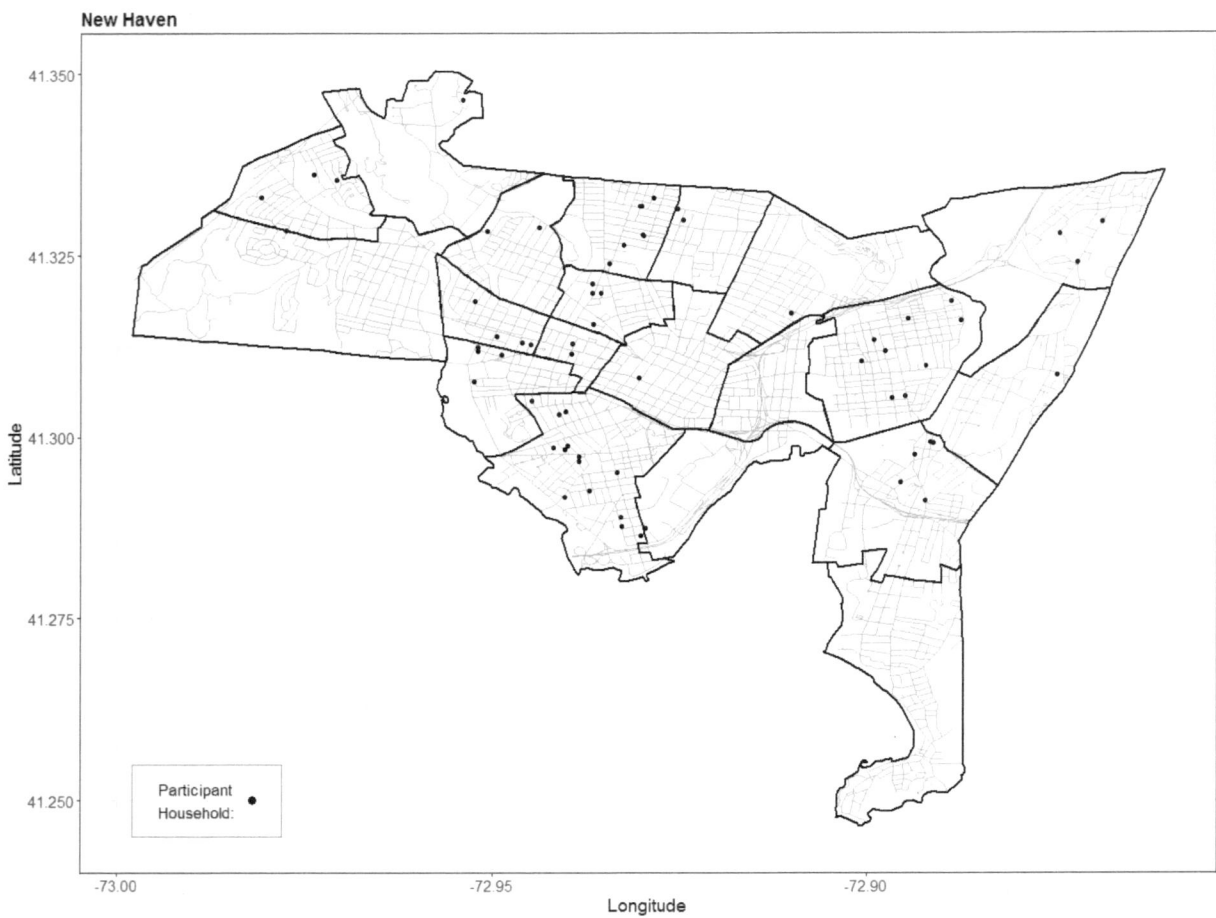

For example, participants in many programs, whether they be education programs, juvenile justice programs, employment programs or behavioral health programs find it difficult to get to the programming that is offered. Figure 68 shows participants in the same juvenile justice program, and the density of bus stops available to them. As you can see, most of them live in areas where the density of bus stops is closer to the "sparse" end of the continuum.

FIGURE 68 BUS STOP DENSITY IN RELATION TO PROGRAM PARTICIPANTS

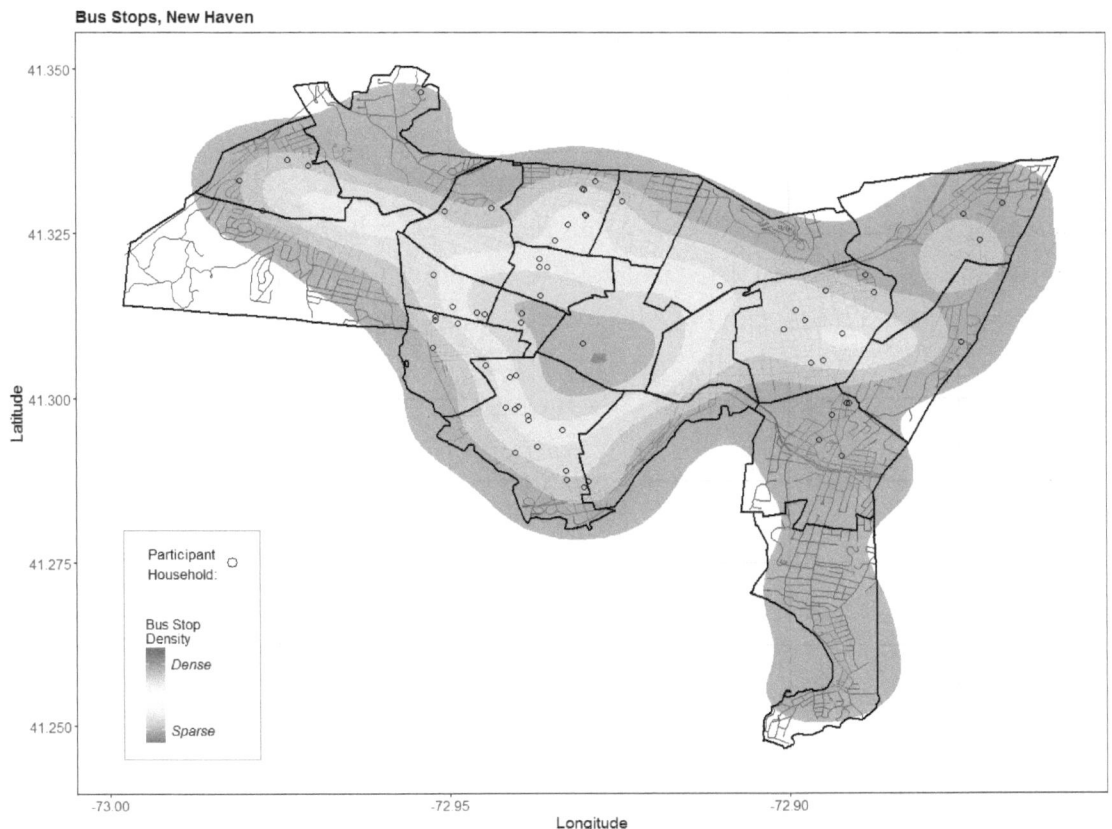

Not only can you plot a specific feature, like bus stops, and clients to see their proximity, you can use these data to calculate ***proximity measures,*** such as the average distance to the nearest bus stop. Such proximity measures at the individual record level can be used as an "environmental" variable in developing explanatory or predictive program models.

One new approach to analyzing crime and location data is called "risk terrain modeling." This approach, developed at Rutgers[78], examines the relationship between crime-instance data and different geographic features, like package stores, gas stations, bus-stops, clubs, bodegas, and bowling alleys. Using the number of instances of crime in proximity to these features, a predictive model is developed. This model can then be used to assess the risk of the terrain features around any location. This obviously could be very important for law enforcement officers, in real time...to have a "threat estimate" when responding to a crime, or to target locations for prevention efforts.

---

[78] Caplan, Joel M; Kennedy, Leslie W; Barnum, Jeremy D; Piza, Eric L. **Cityscape; Washington** Vol. 17, Iss. 1, (2015): 7-16.

Myself and a colleague of mine, Anne MacIntyer-Lahner, believe that this risk terrain modeling approach can be used to create "asset terrain" models as well, to show the proximity of community assets to program participants, or target populations for programs. While we are still developing the approach, the series of maps on the following pages are suggestive of what could be done. Figure 69 sets the stage showing the locations of crimes, by type of crime in one neighborhood in New Haven. Figure 70 shows the locations of assets and "risk locations" in the same neighborhood. Figure 71 plots the assets, risk locations, incidence of crime, and program participants. This information can now be used to develop a predictive model. The model would provide information on the likelihood of a crime occurring at any location, and the degree of "asset saturation" for the same location.

FIGURE 69 CRIME IN HILL NEIGHBORHOOD (NEW HAVEN, CT)

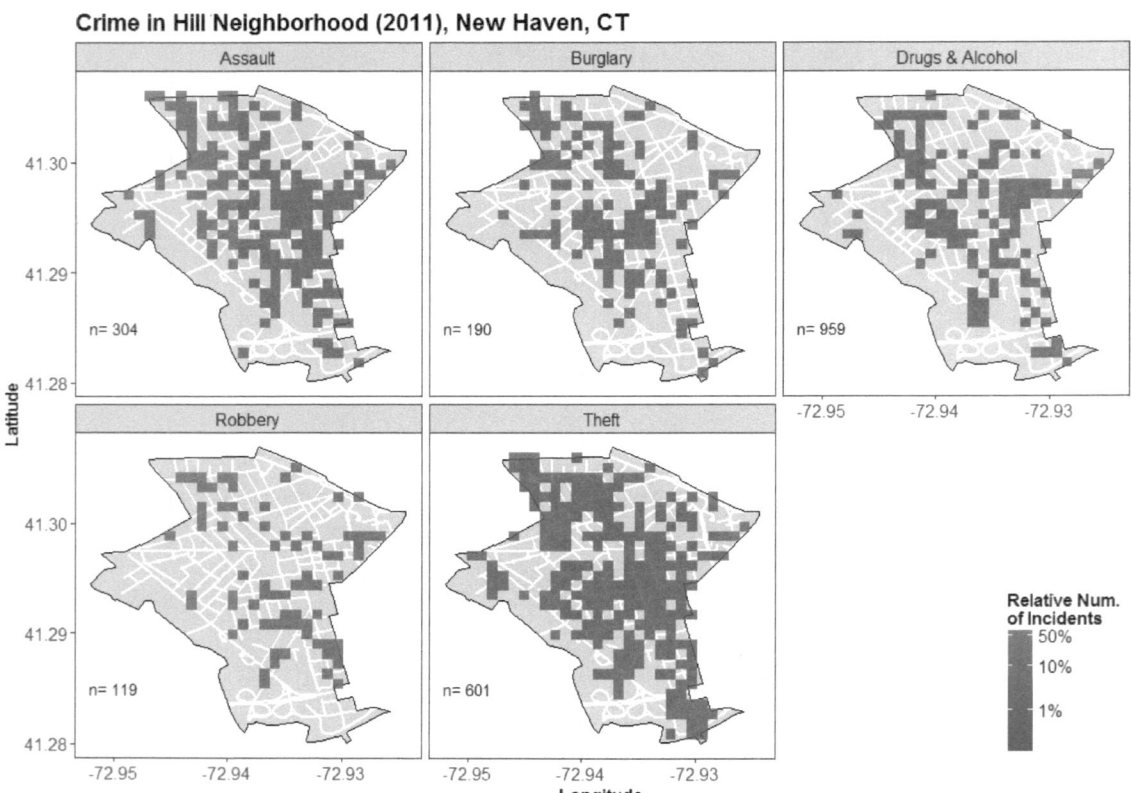

FIGURE 70 RISK/ASSET TERRAIN FEATURES (HILL NEIGHBORHOOD, NEW HAVEN, CT)

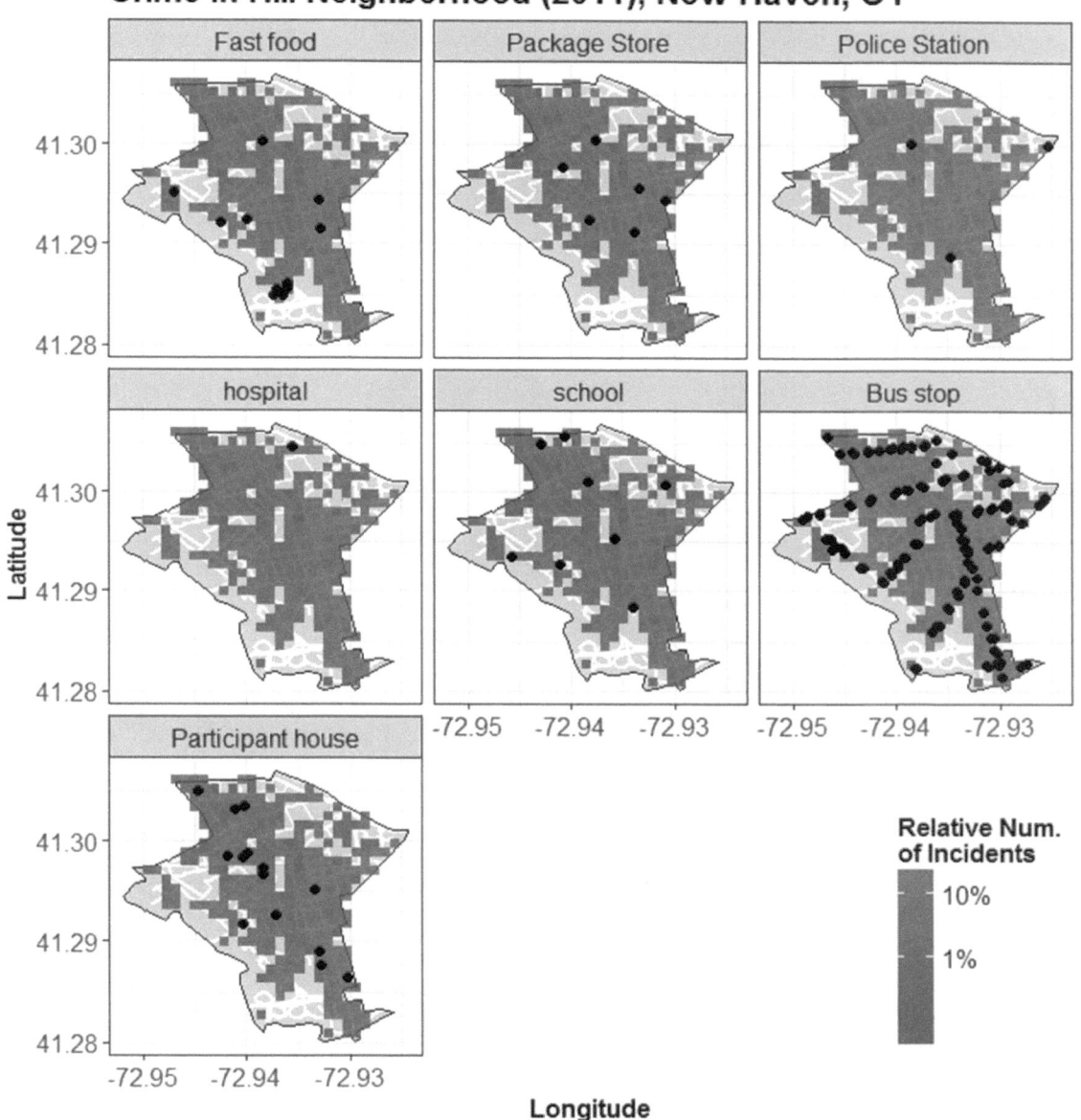

FIGURE 71 PARTICIPANT/CRIME/RISK/ASSET MAP OF HILL NEIGHBORHOOD, NEW HAVEN CT

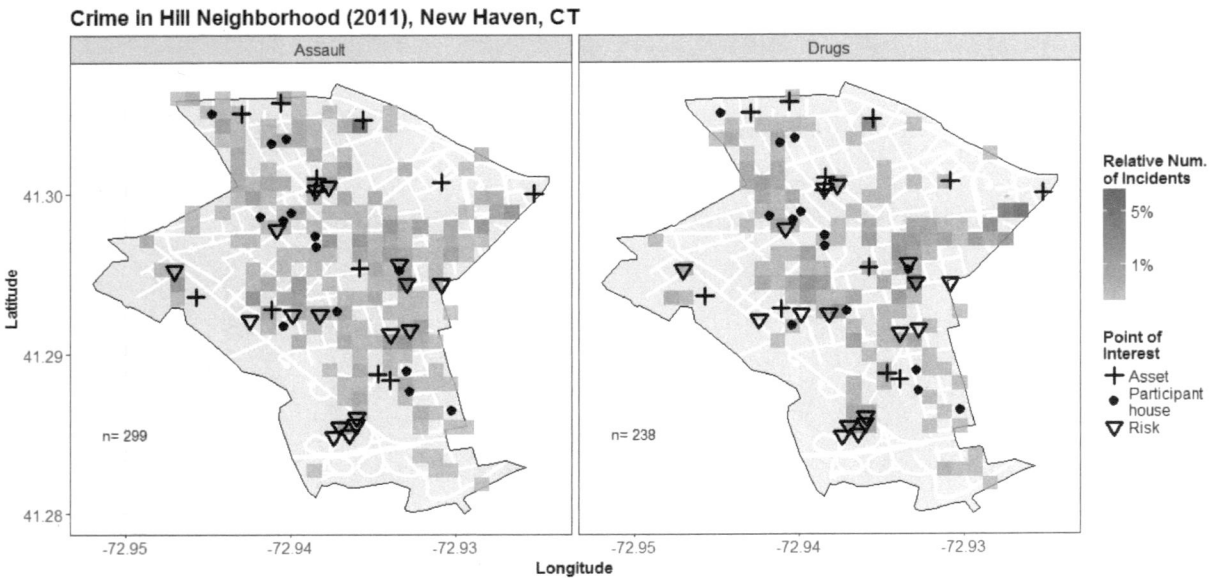

The above sequence of maps is just one example of how powerful GIS can be for social data analysis. I believe GIS is STILL a very under-utilized tool, especially in the areas of social public policy and performance analysis. One of the reasons for this, I think, is the natural sequence of data analysis (as described in Chapter 4) tends to leave such "ancillary" analysis approaches toward the end of whatever analysis is being done—and that leaves little time or energy for such approaches. We need to be more intentional about incorporating place-based analysis into our analysis protocols and project plans... and make sure stakeholders understand the potential value of such analyses.

16

THE ROLES OF THE DATA SCIENTIST

I have been successful as a data scientist both as a staff analyst as well as a consultant. While many of the skills required are the same, the roles can be substantially different. In this chapter I will share what I have learned about each of these roles, providing some important tips for success in each.

The Data Scientist As Staff Analyst

Being a "staff" data scientist is a great job. Normally, you work in a unit with other staff analysts, and can bounce ideas off your co-workers and get advice from them. You are in some ways "protected" by your unit or your organization, and usually have substantial organizational resources to draw from (although if you are a staff analyst in a smaller agency or non-profit this may not be the case).

If you have some interest in advancement, however, it can be difficult to move up the ladder. Usually, there are not that many analyst "tiers" above you, and if someone inhabits the next tier it may be difficult to advance. My advice is simple: do the best work you can, and be a resource to your fellow analysts. Also, try to get involved in projects outside of your analysis shop. Volunteer to work on an improvement initiative, or participate in the development of a new service, program, or product. Get involved in strategic and operational planning (where your data analysis skills will surely be appreciated). This will demonstrate

> **Schackziom Number 11:**
>
> **Learn about the organization you work for as a whole, not just where your analysis work fits in.**
>
> **Demonstrate that you "get it" and that you are not so narrowly focused on numbers and data. Be a multi-dimensional resource to your organization.**

your willingness to transcend your data analyst role, and "pitch in" any way you can. This is always appreciated and often recognized when promotion time rolls around.

The Data Scientist As Consultant

As I stated earlier, data scientists acting in a consulting role use the same tool box as those that are staff analysts. However, the environment can be very different. As a consultant, you are more often looked upon as an "expert" than you are when you serve as a staff analyst. You may also be seen as more of a threat by employees of the organization for which you are working. You are usually expected to have access to your own computer, printer, software, and supplies…and unless you are working for a large consulting firm, you often don't have the same level of resources available to you. I have found that if you communicate with your client, they will often cover costs such a printing when necessary, and may have a workspace that can be provided (sometimes with a computer and necessary software). In the public and non-profit sector, sometimes there are limits on what an agency can pay a consultant in terms of an hourly or daily rate, but they can assume some costs that otherwise would be passed on to the consultant. Of course, these days many consulting data scientists can do the work they do in a completely virtual way…never leaving their little home computer nest. The data can be accessed virtually, the analysis can be done with on-line products or with open source software, and the presentation of the results can be done via video conference or conference call. This happens all the time now, and is perfectly acceptable for certain kinds of data work.

> **Schackziom Number 12:**
>
> **Avoid the temptation to do *ALL* of your work virtually. Data scientists need to get out into the real world and get their "pristine little data hands" dirty once-in-a -while. Participate in in-person data collection efforts; *actually meet clients in person;* perhaps participate in, or even facilitate, workgroup sessions….these will give you real-world experience and demonstrate your flexibility.**

HOWEVER, and this is a BIG HOWEVER, I would caution against always operating in the above fashion. Data scientists need to get out into the real world and get their "pristine little data hands" dirty once-in-a-while. You should participate in in-person data collection efforts, you could *actually meet clients in person.* You could perhaps participate, or even facilitate, workgroup sessions once-in-a-while. This will give you real-world experience and demonstrate your flexibility.

Just like in the case of a staff analyst, it is important to be a multi-dimensional asset to your client. Many of my consulting engagements begin with the client asking me to do some performance measurement development or a specific data analysis. However, in the course of the project I make sure that the client understands that I can do other, related tasks as well. The clients are often surprised but pleased, and will extend my service engagement as a result. For me, these other functions include the development of budgets, managing projects, developing strategic and operational plans, writing proposals, even providing 'moral support" to the client during important meetings.

Non-Data Skills That Can Make A Difference In Your Career

Throughout the course of this chapter and book I have eluded to the fact that there are times when non-data skills are important to the success of a project, or your even your entire career as a data scientist. While one could argue that many of the following skills are needed by everyone, I think it is especially important to point out that data scientists need these skills, in addition to (and perhaps in spite of) their technical skills.

Verbal and Written Communication Skills

We data scientists, as "numbers people" get a bad rap as far as communication goes. We get lumped in with "computer guys" or worse, even economists or mathematicians ☺. We are seen as people who are better with numbers than people; people sometimes even hesitate to allow us to speak in certain situations... It is important that we show people that this is simply not the case...that we can communicate, verbally and in writing, with precision and without relying on technical jargon or getting too caught up in "technical matters" that may be beside the point to most listeners and observers.

Presentation Skills

Despite the fact that data scientists are viewed as poor communicators, we are still asked to present the results of our analysis to interested groups. Some groups can include high-powered stakeholders; others can be a mix of lay people and technical types; presenting to these diverse groups can be quite challenging. But, as with general communication skills above, we need to transcend these difficulties. We need to work to find ways to present data in easy to understand, non-technical, but accurate, ways. Some of the newer presentation tools, like Prezi and Tableau, can be helpful in this regard. However, presentations usually still come down to being prepared, being comfortable with the material, and imagining the VIPs in the room in their undergarments ☺ One technique that is particularly effective is the "single sheet of paper" presentation. Rather than a cumbersome powerpoint presentation, simply handing out a single sheet of paper with a couple of "key" data displays, casually talking through the results, can be much more focused, compelling and informative for the audience. But take care... while you might not be building an elaborate powerpoint presentation, these kind of informal dialogs can actually take *more* preparation and forethought to be truly effective.

Facilitation Skills

Many data projects are undertaken, or at least guided, by workgroups or committees. It is critical for data scientists to be able to take a lead role in facilitating these meetings. That means understanding how to run a meeting, create an agenda, control the meeting and not let one or a few voices dominate the meeting. When decisions are being made, it is important to have a systematic approach that can be understood before the discussion begins and that the group can buy into (see Chapter 7). Although there is a lot of literature out there regarding this topic, this is one of those things that you have to "learn by doing…" you should even practice tearing the flipchart paper from the easel…you know, "rip with confidence." There is such a thing as "facilitator" training (I attended such training as a wee lad) where they provide you with an overall approach, ground rules for use with groups, and even video you while you are facilitating to help you identify areas for improvement. This may seem like overkill, but good facilitators are hard to find, and if you are recognized as someone with these skills (especially if you also have analysis skills) your career will surely benefit.

Budgeting Skills

As the career of a data scientist progresses, the data scientist is sometimes asked to develop and manage the budget for a project, or even an entire analysis unit. Understanding basic principles of budgeting is a critical skill, and one that may not be obtained over the course of the development path of some data scientists. If you are involved in developing organizational performance measures, you should have some knowledge of budgeting and measures of financial condition. (see Chaper 8). In those instances, It is worth taking a budgeting course or training seminar either in person or on-line.

Project Management Skills

Data scientists are sometimes asked to be project managers for their data development projects. And like in the case of budgeting skills, sometimes data scientists have not had much exposure to the principles of project management. I would invest in the PMBOK (the "Project Management Body of Knowledge") which is a collection of up to date project management approaches and tools. If you have not yet developed these skills, this is another area where it is worth taking a course or a training seminar.

Negotiation Skills

This one, like communication skills, is surely one that "everyone needs," but I thought I should mention it. Especially as a consultant, it is important to have good negotiation skills when you define the scope of a project and the related payment structure. It is very easy to be out maneuvered, especially if you are not confident of your value or you are just trying to break into the consulting market. Even as a staff analyst, these skills come in handy. They can help to resolve conflicts within the organization or between partner organizations. They can be helpful when creating data sharing or resource sharing agreements. Conflict or potential conflict can arise anywhere. Having the skills to resolve, or anticipate and protect against these conflicts (without getting litigious) can make you very valuable indeed.

17

AFTERWARDS

"In the Bastille, there is no "afterwards".....Charlton Heston as Cardinal Richelieu

"D'Artagnan's cleverness made Richelieu smile".....The Three Musketeers, Alexander Dumas

Data science isn't going anywhere, ever. Like a lot of things, the character of the field will change, as tasks that used to take a lot of time are made simple through new technology. Data collection will become easier. Report generation will become easier. It will become easier to make comparisons on the fly using ad-hoc reporting tools. Open source analytic tools will proliferate while becoming more robust. This will allow the application of more sophisticated artificial intelligence, machine learning and predictive modeling approaches. More and more visual displays of data will be available at the push of a button. But those that support that this application infrastructure will still be needed.

And the essential questions will remain (these are just a select few):

- What are the preferences of our customers? How will they change? What are the key drivers of those changes?
- What will the demand for our services be in one, five or ten years?
- Are we achieving the results we want for our community? Are the strategies we are employing working? What indicators of success should we be examining?
- Is this program achieving the outcomes we are expecting? What parts of the program are driving this success?
- Are the services we are providing cost-effective? Are they providing an adequate return on investment?
- Where will our services be needed next? Can we see it on a map so we can start planning?
- What communities are at risk financially? How will our budget choices affect those communities?

Luckily for us, the list of questions for which we need to apply data science is never ending. For millennia, when humans asked questions we had limited ability to process information to develop the answer. This is rapidly changing, and data scientists are at the forefront of data driven policy-making and management.

We data scientists hold both power and responsibility. We have the power to provide the key information to inform important and complex questions. We have the responsibility to be ethical and conscientious as we collect data, conduct our analysis, and share our results. Our constituencies expect us to provide accurate data on a timely basis, and to help interpret those data and help facilitate the use of the data in a thorough and defensible way, so actual decisions can be made.

Sometimes decision makers look upon us like Richelieu looked upon D'Artagnan...they smile at our clever data analysis or performance report, knowing or believing that there is some other dynamic at work that renders our product imperfect or irrelevant. There will always be aspects of life that are not captured in our models. But, that does not mean that our models are not useful or that we should cease to fight the good data fight. Strive to demonstrate the utility of your work; be flexibly adaptive to new data needs, client expectations, and feedback. You will find this keeps you relevant and valuable, and our profession the better for it.

INDEX

APPENDIX A

COMPLETE LIST OF *SCHACKZIOMS*™

1. **Schackziom Number 1:** Always be ready to demonstrate the value of the data collection, compilation, or analysis task you are undertaking. You cannot expect others to intuitively understand the importance of your work.

2. **Schackziom Number 2:** Worry less about what performance framework an organization is using, and more about fully utilizing whichever framework is in use.

3. **Schackziom Number 3:** Information Density--- it is important to maintain a certain level of information density. Vast amounts of white space are a lost opportunity to include additional data that are relevant and allow the user to make different kinds of comparisons.

4. **Schackziom Number 4:** *Dr. Schack's Pantheon of Glorious Decision Therorists*: **Herbert Simon**: Satisficing; **Charles Lindlbom**: Successive Limited Comparisons; **Kahneman and Tversky and Slovic**: Decisions Under Uncertainty; **Egon Brunswik**: The Lens Model; **Cohen, March and Olsen**: Garbage Can Model; **Walter Shewart**: PDCA Cycle: **Col.John Boyd**: OODA Loop; **Sun Tzu**: The Art of War.

5. **Schackziom Number 5:** Cross-functional or multi-partner work teams often begin with what seems like a systematic decision process that gets abandoned as time goes on, relying instead on a loose *"preponderance of opinion"* that leads to resentment, an artificial reduction in the number of options considered, and an ultimate choice which may be somewhat workable but far from optimal or even satisfactory.

6. **Schackziom Number 6:** Fully diagnose a problem before rushing to implement a solution. Look carefully at solutions that involve information technology, training or marketing, particularly when they are proposed before a problem has been diagnosed.

7. **Schackziom Number 7:** When diagnosing performance problems, make sure you think of these three important domains: a) Policies and Process; b) Customer Characteristics and c) Environmental Factors.

8. **Schackziom Number 8:** Process mapping is a great way to 1) gain an understanding of the processes used in a program; 2) identify important decision/transition points which are good

opportunities or measurement, and 3) identify parts of the process that no longer make sense or could be made more efficient.

9. **Schackziom Number 9:** You can't report data that do not exist.

10. **Schackziom Number 10:** Never rely on statistical significance testing alone. Always look at the size of the effect as well as testing for significance. But, don't disregard statistical significance testing either…it can provide valuable insight when examined together with the size of the effect.

11. **Schackziom Number 11:** Learn about the organization you work for as a whole, not just where your analysis work fits in. Demonstrate that you "get it" and that you are a multi-dimensional resource to your organization.

12. **Schackziom Number 12:** Avoid the temptation to do *ALL* of your work virtually. Data scientists need to get out into the real world and get their "pristine little data hands" dirty once-in-a-while.

APPENDIX B

GENERALIZED ANALYSIS STEPS

Please see Chapters 3 and 4 for a full explanation of these steps.

1. **Frame The Question**
2. **Determine The Elements of the Analysis**
   a. Be aware of your level of analysis
   b. Be aware of your variable types
   c. Anticipate data integration issues
   d. Operationalization matters
   e. Anticipate different ways you might want to disaggregate the data; make sure collect/ obtain variables that will allow for this
   f. Anticipate the comparisons you want to make; select variables that will allow you to make those comparisons
   g. Consider threats to validity
3. **Import/Integrate the data; make sure there are no duplicates in individual record files**
4. **Once the data are integrated, be sure the data are clean and not corrupt**
5. **Disaggregate dependent variable(s) on basic characteristic or process variables**
6. **If appropriate, conduct factor analysis on attitude or behavior questions**
7. **If appropriate, create indices based on factors identified**
8. **TEST your hypotheses**
9. **Apply Cohen's Benchmarks to assess effect size**
10. **BUILD predictive models if needed**
11. **Re-check results; conduct sensitivity analysis; review threats to validity**
12. **Share Results—and have a well-deserved libation** ☺

APPENDIX C

SAMPLE FEDERAL AND STATE GRANT SUB-RECIPIENT MONITORING POLICY

It is our policy to conduct an annual monitoring of all sub-recipients of federal and state grant funds. The monitoring is intended to ensure that all funds are being spent in compliance with state and federal guidelines; all expenses charged to the grant are appropriate, adequately documented and conform to contract requirements; and expected deliverables and outcomes are being achieved.

The monitoring consists of three parts:

1. Fiscal compliance review
2. Service quality review
3. Performance review

Fiscal compliance review

A review of budget to actual expenditures will be conducted. This will consist of a comparison between the amount budgeted for the sub-recipient, expense category compared with the amount actually expended for each expense category, year to date. If there is a difference of more than 10% between the amount actually expended and the amount budgeted, the sub-recipient should be asked to explain/document why the differences occurred and how these differences can or will affect spending for the rest of the budget year in question.

For personnel expenditures, a review of timesheets should be conducted to ensure that the amount charged for personnel costs is consistent with the hours actually worked. Any fringe benefit charges should be documented through payroll statements, insurances statements, and other related information as appropriate.

For supply expenses, a review should be conducted to ensure that the supply costs charged to the grant are consistent with the number of program participants; sub recipients should not pre-order large amounts of supplies in anticipation of future use, unless it can be shown that such expenditures would result in significant cost savings, after accounting for the possibility of some of the supplies going unused.

For travel expenses, a review should be conducted to ensure that any mileage being charged to the grant is for grant purposes only, and that such mileage is tracked and reported on a per-trip basis, and charged at the appropriate current federal mileage reimbursement rate.

For consulting expenses, a review should be conducted including 1) name of contractor 2) role of contractor) 3) amount paid to each contractor 4) contractor expenses as percent of total sub recipient budget.

For overhead expenses, a review should be conducted including 1) components of overhead expenses (e.g., rent, utilities, telephone, internet, etc.) 2) overhead expenses as percent of total sub recipient budget.

Invoices submitted by the sub-recipient should be reviewed to ensure compliance with contract requirements, including detailing unit cost of services provided, number of services provided, number of participants served, and the time-period of the invoice.

Service Quality Review

A review of services provided by the sub-recipient under the grant should be conducted. This should include:

- ensuring there is documentation for each participant served
- ensuring that there is evidence that services noted on invoices were, in fact, provided
- ensuring that any work product associated with the delivery of the services conforms with contract requirements and expectations
- ensuring that any services requiring specific staff credentials are provided by staff with those credentials
- ensuring that any evidence-based services are provided consistent with evidence-based practice

Where practical, an observation of each standard service being delivered should be conducted, and an interview of participants receiving these services should be conducted. If sub recipients conduct customer surveys, they should provide the survey results as part of the monitoring process.

Performance Review

A review of performance reports should be conducted to ensure:

- Performance reports are being generated as required by the contract and the grant.
- Participant demographics, service, and outcome data are being collected in compliance with contract and grant requirements
- Expected service levels are being met, for
  - identification of participants in need of service
  - number of participants served
  - number of participants completing service
  - any required follow-up is being conducted
  - any task deliverables and work product are being produced on schedule
- any expected outcome measures (e.g., recidivism, credential attainment, school attendance, reduction in disciplinary incidents, graduation rate, enrollment in post-secondary programming) are being collected and reported, and meet expected targets (if any

APPENDIX D

SAMPLE RBA PROGRAM REPORT CARD

FIGURE 72 SAMPLE RBA PROGRAM REPORT CARD

2013 Program Report Card: Juvenile Probation – (Judicial Branch)

Quality of Life Result: Connecticut citizens live in safer communities. Connecticut children learn from their mistakes, and live in families that meet their needs and communities that support their success.

Contribution to the Result: The purpose of Juvenile Probation is to reduce the risk of recidivism by engaging juveniles and their families in meaningful services and ensuring compliance with court orders, all of which result in safer communities.

Program Expenditures	State Funding	Federal Funding	Other Funding	Total Funding
Actual FY 13	$15,455,669	$0	$0	$15,455,669
Estimated FY 14	$16,100,000	$0	$0	$16,100,000

Partners: Department of Children and Families, the Governor's Office, General Assembly, Office of Policy and Management, State Department of Education, DMHAS, Office of Workforce Competitiveness, Public Defenders, Prosecutors, parents, parent and juvenile justice advocates, treatment providers, Youth Service Bureaus, Department of Correction, and universities

---

How Much Did We Do?

Juvenile Court Intake, FY 2006-FY2012

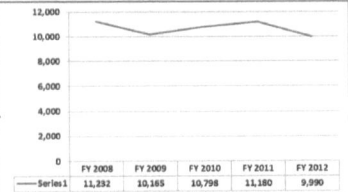

Story behind the baseline: Juvenile court intake fell 27% from 13,626 in FY2008 to 9,990 in FY2012. The decline erases slight increases in prior years and represents an intake level lower than FY2009 when 16 and 17 yr.-olds were not in the JJ system. This reduction is significant. Caseload sizes remain at levels allowing officers to focus on recidivism reduction strategies. Nationwide juvenile crime is down but some of the declines in CT are attributable to the Court's returned summons policy (361 police and school referrals in 2012) and greater use of Juvenile Review Boards in the state.
Trend: ▲

How Well Did We Do It?

Juveniles Engaged in Criminogenic Need-based Treatment, 2009-2012

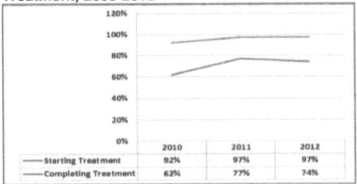

Story behind the baseline: Juvenile probation officers are required to refer to treatment and services to address criminogenic needs. This measure shows the extent to which juveniles start and complete treatment. Research shows that completion of targeted treatment is connected to lower recidivism rates. The positive trend in this area is a reflection of consistent identification and attention to the criminogenic needs of juveniles. The drop in completing treatment reflects a small number of juveniles moving to a higher level of care or away from the service area.
Trend: ▼

How Well Did We Do It?

Technical Violation Percentage, 2007-2012

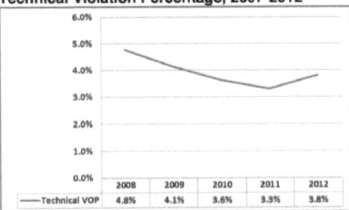

Story behind the baseline: Take Into Custody Orders or Warrants can be issued when is a technical violation of probation orders occurs. Having steadily declined the past four years to a low of 3.3% of court intake in 2011, the rise in TIC rates is due to older clients coming into the system. In July 2012, 17 yr.- olds entered the JJ system. Juvenile Probation Officers employ a system of graduated incentives and sanctions, including more contact, additional treatment, or electronic monitoring, prior to seeking a Take Into Custody Order.

Trend: ▼

Rev. 5 (1/18/13)   **Trend Going in Right Direction? ▲Yes; ▼ No; ◄► Flat/ No Trend**   Page 1 of 2

FIGURE 73 SAMPLE RBA PROGRAM REPORT CARD, CONTINUED

2013 Program Report Card: Juvenile Probation – (Judicial Branch)

Quality of Life Result: Connecticut citizens live in safer communities. Connecticut children learn from their mistakes, and live in families that meet their needs and communities that support their success.

Is Anyone Better Off?

24-Month Rearrest Rate, 2008-2012

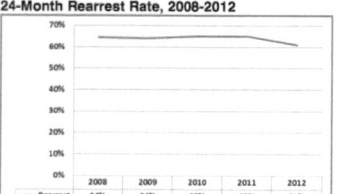

	2008	2009	2010	2011	2012
Rearrest	64%	64%	65%	65%	61%

Story behind the baseline: This performance measure examines the rate of re-arrest (recidivism) at 24-months after the start of a period of probation or supervision. For example, 64 percent of the juveniles placed on probation or supervision in 2006 were re-arrested by the time their 24-month follow up period ended in 2008. This trend has been fairly steady over prior years but showed a 4% decline in 2012 falling to 61%. It is important to note that the 2012 figure includes the first cohort of 16-year olds served in the juvenile justice system.

Trend: ▲

Is Anyone Better Off?

Juveniles Committed to DCF, 1999-2012

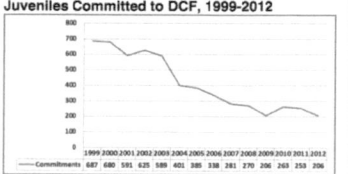

	1999	2000	2001	2002	2003	2004	2005	2006	2007	2008	2009	2010	2011	2012
Commitments	687	680	581	625	589	401	385	338	281	270	206	263	253	206

Story behind the baseline: Juveniles committed to either long-term residential placement or to incarceration at the Connecticut Juvenile Training School have decreased by 63 percent over the past 12 years and by 37 percent from 2004-2011. Even with the addition of 17-year olds to the juvenile justice system beginning in July of 2012, the number of commitments fell matching 2009 numbers. The continued reliance on the use of Case Review Teams over the past several years has contributed significantly to serving more high-risk juveniles in more cost-effective community settings.

Trend: ▲

Proposed Actions to Turn the Curve:

- Creation of a gang intervention strategy in the three major cities, Hartford, New Haven, and Bridgeport. The RESTORE initiative calls for longer periods of probation, more intensive treatment interventions and vocational training.
- Partner with DCF to create early intervention strategies for juveniles 12 yrs. and under identified with greater risk for further delinquency or Out-of-Home Placement. The focus is on the identification of the child's and families' challenges/strengths to employ interventions designed to prevent recidivism and the child's further penetration into the Juvenile Justice system.
- Ongoing participation with the Center for Juvenile Justice Reform at the Georgetown University on the Juvenile Justice System Improvement Project (JJSIP) and the Crossover Youth Project to employ evidence-based approaches to better client outcomes and reduced recidivism;
- Furthering collaborations with in-state partner to improve behavioral interventions and opportunities for reduced school-based arrests;
- In consultation with the Center for Children's Law and Policy, utilize working groups in Hartford and Bridgeport to develop strategies to reduce Disproportionate Minority Contact.

Data Development Agenda:

- Developing data collaboratives with education systems to track long-term education outcomes

APPENDIX E

CONNECTICUT RESULTS STATEMENTS

The following result statements, developed by myself and my partners at the Charter Oak Group, LLC together with The Connect General Assembly Appropriations Committee and The CT General Assembly's Office of Fiscal Analysis, were designed so that any state government program could be aligned to at least one of these results in developing a program's RBA framework or report. They could also be thought of as "system classifiers" which could inform the re-organization of the budget by result-area.

1. All CT residents live in safe families and communities
2. All CT residents are economically secure
3. All CT residents are developmentally, physically, and mentally healthy across the life span
4. All CT residents who are elderly or have disabilities live engaged lives in supportive environments of their choosing
5. ALL CT residents succeed in education and are prepared for careers, citizenship and life
6. All CT residents grow up in a stable environment, safe, healthy, and ready to succeed
7. All CT residents have a safe and efficient transportation system
8. All CT residents have a clean and healthy environment
9. All CT residents have a fair, ethical and efficient government
10. All CT residents and visitors enjoy the state's rich artistic and cultural life

ACKNOWLEDGEMENTS

This book was in the gestation stage for a long time. I have wanted to write a book about data science and performance measurement for many years. I have had several false starts, and it wasn't until I hit upon this format that the words began to flow with passion and precision. I want to thank several people for the encouragement and support they provided while I was writing this book (or making sure I didn't forget I wanted to write one). Special thanks to my wife, Lisa; my daughter, Carolann; my stepsons, Bryan and Liam Kilmurray: my parents, Ron and Irene Schack; my sisters, Laura McKay, Sandra Baranowski and Amy Schack, and my friends James Kurien, David Smith, Randall Dumas, Dan Mulligan, Jon Rogers, Chris LeBlanc, and Matt Straznitskas. *I especially want to thank Carolann for her help with the cover art and some of the data visualizations in this book (particularly the maps), and to Lisa for her assistance with some of the diagrams in the book.* The most important mentor of my life, my dad, passed away in 2018. I really don't have the words to use to convey my gratitude for all he did for me throughout my life.

I also want to again acknowledge my Charter Oak Group, LLC business partners and mentors, Barry Goff and Bennett Pudlin. Much of the experience I have drawn upon to write this book was "co-experienced" with them, and some of the approaches and solutions I present were co-developed with one or both of them. But the fundamental premises of the book, the specific articulation of the lessons and solutions, and the opinions expressed throughout, are my own.

I want to thank several other mentors I have had over my career: Rick Batt, Alice Carrier, Dr. Carmen Cirincione, Dr. David Kenny, Dr. Robert Kravchuk and Dr. Carol Lewis. Other business associates, too, have provided me with support, humor, and understanding…these include Jim Boucher, Bill Carbone, Joe Carbone, Laura Downs, Sarah Dudzik, Kelly Fitzgerald, Scott Gaul, Julie Geyer, Sherry Haller, Brian Hill, Alex Johnson, Alissa Johnston, Peter Kuckol, Anne MacIntyre-Lahner, Mary Lansing, Barbara Mazzonna, Kim Oliver, Adrienne Parkmond, Alice Pritchard, Julie Revaz, Brian Sperry, Tracy Stephenson, Pamela Tonello, Julie Watson and Laura Whitacre. I also want to remember the late Justice David Borden, who was such a great leader and a joy to work with while I was providing analytic support to the CT Eyewitness Identification Taskforce.

Some of the material in this book I developed for courses I recently taught at Trinity College in Hartford, Connecticut. I want to thank my students for being test subjects for this material. Three students provided especially good constructive feedback: SB Chatterjee, Jay Patel and Bartek Reska. Thanks also to Dr. William Barnett and Dr. Barry Feldman for providing the opportunity for me to teach these courses.

Unrelated to this book, but important to my sanity, is the comradeship I enjoy with the musicians that I work with on a regular basis ….my on-going thanks to Dave Brasefield, Sean Grant, Jon Rogers, Joe Scalara and Tony Villalba. I would also like to thank my "cigar circle" at Carolina Tobacco Emporium in Manchester, CT for great conversation and encouragement while I worked on the book.

If I have forgotten to thank anyone, I will catch you next time ☺

"all data and no music makes Ron insane"
Ron with his Hamer 12-String Bass

ABOUT THE AUTHOR

Ron Schack Ph.D., has been fighting the good data fight for the past 25 years. Ron holds a Ph.D. in Political Science from the University of Connecticut, where he also earned a Master of Public Affairs degree and studied Philosophy as an undergraduate. Since 2000, Dr. Schack has been a partner with **The Charter Oak Group, LLC,** a well-regarded public policy/performance management consulting firm based in Glastonbury, CT. Prior to joining The Charter Oak Group, Ron managed the Connecticut Department of Labor's performance measurement unit for five years, after holding several analyst and technician positions with the department.

Dr. Schack has consulted to federal, state, local, and non-profit agencies on performance measurement, performance management system development, program evaluation, and advanced statistical analysis. Dr. Schack's areas of expertise include decision support, public budgeting, research methods, performance management, strategic and operational planning, and statistical modeling, including structural equation modeling (SEM).

Dr. Schack recently created **Datagrotto**, a "command center for environmental and social data analysis," a think-tank emphasizing fresh perspectives on the use of data to solve social and environmental problems.

Ron also enjoys teaching, and has taught statistics, computer applications for public administration, public budgeting, research methods, and homeland security policy. When not consulting or teaching, Dr. Schack enjoys fine cigars and single malt scotch; composing music, playing bass, rifle and pistol shooting, practicing medieval longsword, and reading philosophy, cosmology, military history, and classic fantasy and science fiction literature. He lives in Manchester with his wife, Lisa, and their dog, Rocko.

Confessions of a Data Scientist...or Warrior-Priest?
Lessons from 25 Years of Data Science, Performance Measurement and Decision Support

Dr. Schack Onstage with "Minds of One"

Delve into the mind of a well-regarded, experienced (and perhaps slightly "twisted") data scientist...Let Dr. Schack share some of his analytic arsenal, while regaling you with stories of his data science journey-- challenging situations, abject failures, and rousing successes...Read how Kant's Ding un Sich, Sun-Tzu's Art of War, Col. Boyd's OODA Loop, and Egon Brunswik's Len's Model all inform our work as data scientists.

https://www.facebook.com/datascientistconfessions/

datagrotto.com